Family Environment and Intellectual Functioning: A Life-Span Perspective

Family Environment and Intellectual Functioning: A Life-Span Perspective

Edited by

Elena L. Grigorenko
Yale University
Moscow State University

Robert J. Sternberg
Yale University

Psychology Press
Taylor & Francis Group
NEW YORK AND LONDON

First published 2001 by Lawrence Erlbaum Associates, Inc.

Published 2014 by Psychology Press
711 Third Avenue, New York, NY, 10017, USA

and by Psychology Press
27 Church Road, Hove, East Sussex, BN3 2FA

First issued in paperback 2014

Psychology Press is an imprint of the Taylor & Francis Group, an informa business

Cover design by Kathryn Houghtaling Lacey

Library of Congress Cataloging-in-Publication Data

Family environment and intellectual functioning: a life-span perspective
/ edited by Elena L. Grigorenko, Robert J. Sternberg.
    p. cm.
    Includes bibliographical references and index.
    ISBN 0-8058-3184-3 (cloth : alk. paper) —
    1. Family—Psychological aspects. 2. Cognition. 3. Intellect. 4.
Developmental Psychology. I. Grigorenko, Elena, L. II. Sternberg,
Robert J.

HQ728 F3118 2001
306.2'6—dc21   00-053567
                                                    CIP

ISBN 13: 978-0-8058-3184-9 (hbk)
ISBN 13: 978-0-415-64774-8 (pbk)

Contents

Preface

Many of us spend a good part of our adult lives trying to either recapture or escape from the family structure and family processes we observed when we grew up. Even as we pass into middle age and then old age, these family structures and processes continue to enrich our lives—or to haunt them. What is the role of the family environment, particularly with regard to our intellectual functioning? Does the role of early family environment wear off, as some researchers have suggested, or does it maintain or possibly even become more important as we grow older?

This volume examines the interrelationship between family environment and intellectual functioning in a life-span perspective. Its 11 chapters cover a wide range of topics and provide what is perhaps the most comprehensive examination available of life-span family influences on various aspects of intellectual function. In addition the book can serve as a companion volume to *Environmental Influences on Intellectual Functioning,* also published by Lawrence Erlbaum Associates.

The present book is written for all students and professionals with an interest in family influences. Students will find it useful when learning about family effects. Researchers will find it useful to update themselves in this currently active area of investigation. Therapists will find the information useful for understanding problems of intellectual functioning in their clients and in treating these clients successfully. And educators may have a better grasp of how the students they teach are products, not only of their genes and environments, in general, but of their family environments, in particular.

ACKNOWLEDGMENTS

We are grateful to the National Science Foundation (Grant REC-9979843) and the U.S. Office of Educational Research and Improvement (Grant No.

R206R950001) of the U.S. Department of Education, which have funded much of our related research and our time in preparing this book. This book, of course, does not necessarily represent the position or policies of the National Science Foundation, Office of Educational Research, or the U.S. Department of Education, and no official endorsement should be inferred. We are also grateful to Sai Durvasula for help in the preparation of this manuscript, and to Judi Amsel for contracting the book.

—*Elena L. Grigorenko*
—*Robert J. Sternberg*

1

The Family as a Context of Psychological Functioning

Alice S. Carter
Karla Klein Murdock
University of Massachusetts, Boston

Men are like plants: the goodness and flavour of the fruit proceeds from the peculiar soil and exposition in which they grow.

—Michel Guillaume Jean de Crevecoeur (1782/1968, p. 50)

Few would question the notion that the family endows some qualities of the composition, cultivates the growth, and bears witness to the ripening of an individual's potential. Philosophical and poetic musings about the importance of the family are difficult to challenge. At the same time, exploring the role of the family in psychological development is a complex puzzle. This volume illuminates pieces of this puzzle that have received empirical attention. In this chapter, we address some of the complexities encountered when evaluating influences of "the family context" and describe a systemic foundation, or frame, for figuratively fitting the puzzle pieces together. We begin by offering working definitions of *the family context* and then consider theoretical frameworks for understanding the complex forces operating in family and social contexts. Using these theories as a guide, we discuss the multitude of constellations and practices that characterize families in our time. We explain general family processes that may affect development directly and in combination with other factors. We conclude with a discussion of the interplay between nature and nurture, emphasizing notions of reciprocity and responsivity within family relationships. We also emphasize goodness of fit with respect to the fit between an individual family member and systemic features of the family context.

The first step in exploring the family context is to define it. From a scientist's perspective, some aspects of families must be held constant in order to examine how variations in family contexts are associated with variations in child, adolescent, and adult development. However, families in our time are comprised of a multitude of constellations. The blessing and curse of this diversity in family forms and practices is that both between and within families, little is constant. Furthermore, "the family" is a moving target. It is a dynamic unit of social organization that changes across history, setting, circumstance, and stage of the life cycle. Thus, the family context can be defined and redefined according to multiple dimensions. Even the task of identifying the members who should be counted within a given family can be complicated. Family membership may be defined on the basis of biological relationships or perceptions of psychological relationship (i.e., a household of unrelated individuals who view themselves as "family").

Systems theories emphasize the interdependence of, and interactions between, the components of social systems. By focusing on this dynamic interplay between factors that influence individuals' development, systems theories promote an appreciation for multiple processes that foster and/or inhibit optimal development. One such issue is the goodness of fit between the individual and the environments in which development occurs. Goodness of fit refers to the concordance between an individual's capacities and the environmental demands, expectations, and supports (Chess & Thomas, 1991; Thomas, Chess, & Birch, 1968). Systems theories also allow a competence-focused, rather than deficit-focused, perspective of individuals and families. In other words, these perspectives emphasize factors that may promote as well as inhibit healthy intellectual development.

ECOLOGICAL SYSTEMS THEORY:
FAMILIES IN CONTEXT

Bronfenbrenner's ecological theory (Bronfenbrenner, 1986, 1995) provides a model for understanding the interactions between multiple levels of the environment that affect development. This theory was recently expanded to include biological influences on development (Bronfenbrenner, 1995; Bronfenbrenner & Ceci, 1994; Bronfenbrenner & Morris, 1997). However, its main emphasis remains on five environmental systems that range from unique, direct interactions between individuals to the global cultural and historical settings in which development takes place. The developing person is viewed as embedded in a series of environmental systems that directly and indirectly interact with one another and with the person to influence development.

The innermost layer of this set of nested systems is the *microsystem*, which consists of the immediate contexts that individuals actually experience. Throughout development, individuals typically operate within more and more microsystems. For instance, although an infant may exist primarily or solely in a microsystem that includes his parents and siblings, his microsystems are likely to expand to include relationships within day-care, preschool, and neighborhood play-group settings. An individual is not only influenced by others in his microsystems, but is viewed as an active agent within the system, influencing the systems and the individuals within those systems as well.

The next environmental layer in the ecological theory of development is the *mesosystem*, which refers to the links or interconnections among microsystems. Bronfenbrenner proposed that development is likely to be optimized when strong, supportive links exist between an individual's multiple microsystems. For example, a child's mastery of academic skills may stem from the academic support that she receives from her teachers as well as her parents. Parents who support teachers' efforts and teachers who build on preacademic skills learned in the family may introduce additive as well as nonlinear effects in children's acquisition of academic competence. Similarly, an adult's satisfaction with assuming dual roles of parent and employee may be largely dependent on the availability of high quality child care and other "family-friendly" policies in the workplace. The mesosystem reflects connections between multiple microsystems that interact with one another, as well as with the individual, to influence the course of development.

The third environmental level, the *exosystem*, consists of settings that are not directly experienced but that may still affect development. For example, a parent's workplace may exert an indirect influence on a child's development through a variety of forces. Demands for working late hours might reduce the time or resources the parent can devote to parenting, which could impact the child's functioning. In this example, the child does not have an active role in the workplace (i.e., an aspect of the exosystem), but is indirectly influenced.

Finally, Bronfenbrenner proposed two broad, overarching environmental systems that influence development. The *macrosystem* is the cultural context in which microsystems, mesosystems, and exosystems are embedded. It refers to the ideology that dictates (among other things) how children, adolescents, and adults, should be treated, what they should be taught, and what goals are important. Finally, the *chronosystem* involves the patterning of environmental events and transitions over the life course and sociohistorical circumstances. The chronosystem captures the concept of time at multiple levels, ranging from individual processes of adaptation to life events to sociohistorical trends.

The impact of poverty on children's intellectual functioning may be understood as having an impact at each of the levels of the ecosystem described thus far. Poverty is consistently associated with poorer intellectual outcomes and is viewed as a cumulative rather than an unitary risk factor in children's development (e.g., Huston, McLoyd, & Garcia-Coll, 1994; Roberts, Burchinal, & Durham, 1999; Sameroff, Seifer, Barocas, Zax, & Greenspan, 1987). Despite the known deleterious impact of poverty on children's healthy development, the number of children living in poverty in the United States has increased in recent years (Carnegie Task Force, 1994; National Center for Children in Poverty, 1996). This increase is due to a variety of factors, including an increase in single parent families and changes in welfare legislation (Duncan, 1991; Zaslow, Tout, Smith, & Moore, 1998).

Within the microsystem, families who live in poverty are less likely to be able to afford age-appropriate toys and books that can stimulate development (Klebanov, Brooks-Gunn, McCarton, & McCormick, 1998). Families may also be less emotionally available due to the psychological stress of economic hardship. Assessments of the early home environment using the Home Observation Measurement of the Environment (HOME) Inventory have yielded stronger predictions of children's academic and cognitive outcomes than maternal education (Bradley et al., 1989; Brooks-Gunn, Klebanov, & Liaw, 1995). Moreover, children who live in poverty are more likely to be born as small for gestational age or low birth weight due to limited access to prenatal care and inadequate nutrition (Starfield, 1991). At the level of the mesosystem, community resources within poor neighborhoods are often less adequate than those in wealthier neighborhoods and community problems such as exposure to violence may further compromise development (Garbarino, 1990; Gelles, 1992).

Although many programs such as Head Start specifically target children who live in poverty, these programs have not met the needs of poor children in our country in terms of the number of children served and have varied in quality and duration of services provided (Zigler & Gilman, 1997). Finally, at the level of the exosystem, programs aimed at reducing poverty in our country have often failed to consider the impact on children. A good example of this is the recent Welfare to Work policy in which mothers of young children are encouraged to return to work and/or enter job training programs without adequate provision for appropriate child care (cf. Zaslow et al., 1998).

SOCIOHISTORICAL CHANGES IN CONSTRUCTIONS OF THE FAMILY IN THE UNITED STATES

When exploring the family as a context for development, it is crucial to consider the chronosystem, as it reflects sociohistorical changes in constructions of the family. In this nation, typical images and ideas about the family still appear to revolve around a somewhat mythical, "traditional" family model in which married heterosexual parents raise children until they are launched into an independent lifestyle during late adolescence. However, the data about real families in the Unites States scarcely fits this model. Since the 1970s, family forms and practices have changed considerably in response to social changes such as increasing rates of divorce and remarriage, gender-based shifts in the labor force, and instabilities in the nation's economic well-being.

Perhaps the most significant departure from the *traditional family* concept is reflected in emergent patterns of caregiving for children. One of the most notable of these caregiving trends is the substantial decline in families with married and cohabiting parents. The U.S. Census Bureau reported that in 1960, 88% of all children under the age of 18 years resided with both of their parents. In 1998, just 68% of children resided with two parents. This pattern varied across racial and ethnic groups. In 1998, 76% of White, non-Hispanic children lived with two parents, compared to 36% of Black children and 64% of Hispanic children (U.S. Census Bureau, 1998a).

The overall decrease in two-parent households can be accounted for by a matched increase in single-parent households. In 1960, only 8% of children lived in mother-headed households, contrasted to 23% of children in 1998. Although only 1% of children lived with single fathers in 1960, 4.5% of children lived in single father households in 1998. Although single mothers still provide custodial care to the majority (84%) of children living in single-parent households, there is evidence for a relatively dramatic recent increase in father's custodial care. Between 1995 and 1998, the number of single fathers in the United

States grew 25%, whereas the number of single mothers remained constant (U.S. Bureau of the Census, 1998a).

The increasing diversity of family forms is also reflected in a rising number of gay and lesbian parents raising children. Estimating the prevalence of same-gender parenting is complicated by methodological inconsistencies in the assessment of homosexuality (e.g., operational definitions of homosexuality vary in their focus on dimensions of sexual desire, sexual behavior, and/or same-gender cohabitation). However, through recent analyses of three large datasets including 1990 U.S. Census data, Black, Gates, Sanders and Taylor (2000) estimated that approximately 21% to 28% of lesbians and 5% to 14% of gay men have children at home. The "baby boom" among lesbians and gay men during the 1990s (Johnson & Colucci, 1999) may be attributed in part to the emergence of public and private advocacy for their fertility and adoption rights and needs. Families headed by gay and lesbian parents may be vulnerable to stressors surrounding the lack of legal protection and social norms to protect family life (Slater, 1995). However, there do not appear to be significant group differences in the psychosocial development of children raised by heterosexual, versus homosexual, parents (Patterson, 1992).

Of course, parents are not the only agents of socialization and caregiving within the family. Psychosocial research has also begun to recognize the importance of extended kin networks in children's caregiving and in day-to-day family life. Studies have documented substantial and meaningful ways in which aunts, uncles, and cousins of children and their caregivers directly and indirectly provide crucial emotional, instrumental, and parenting support to families (e.g., Dressler, 1985; Wilson & Tolson, 1990). Census reports recently highlighted the increasing importance of grandparents in children's caregiving. Between 1970 and 1997, the proportion of children living in a grandparent-headed household rose from 3.2% to 5.6%, representing a 76% increase over a 27-year period. This increase was observed across all types of grandparent-headed households, regardless of the presence or absence of the children's parents. However, it is notable that since 1990, the most dramatic increase occurred in the number of children residing with their grandparents only, with neither parent present (Casper & Bryson, 1998).

Psychosocial research has also revealed the important ways in which development is influenced by siblings (e.g., McHale & Crouter, 1996). Although children's sibling relationships are a relatively understudied area of family functioning, older siblings may provide cognitive stimulation, modeling, and direct caregiving for younger siblings. Sibling relationships also have important implications for early social development (Dunn, 1996; Stocker & McHale, 1992).

For example, Dunn and her colleagues (e.g., Dunn, Slomkowski, & Beardall, 1994) reported that amicable sibling relationships are more likely to be associated with close peer relationships. In contrast, Patterson (1986) found that hostile and aggressive sibling relationships are more likely to be associated with antisocial behavior toward peers. With direct relevance to cognitive development, recent research indicated that birth order can be associated with children's language experience and language development (Hoff-Ginsberg, 1998). Given these varied influences of siblings on individual psychosocial development, it is notable that shifts in family composition over the past several decades have included a decline in family size. This trend translates into Americans growing up with fewer siblings, if any at all. In 1970, the average family in the United States included 3.58 persons, as opposed to just 3.18 persons in 1998. Family size also differs across racial and ethnic groups. Hispanic families are generally larger, with an average of 3.92 members, while African-American families average 3.42 members and non-Hispanic White families average 3.02 members (U.S. Census Bureau, 1998b).

A substantial number of children in the United States have one or more stepparents who serve in important caregiving roles. After a considerable increase in divorces between 1960 and 1980, the divorce rate has remained steady through 2000. At present, approximately 45% of first marriages in the United States end in divorce (Lamb, Sternberg, & Thompson, 1997). Approximately 75% of divorced mothers and 80% of divorced fathers remarry. Thus, it is not surprising that as many as one third of all children are expected to live in a remarried family for at least 1 year before reaching the age of 18 (Hetherington, Stanley-Hagen, & Anderson, 1989). Because approximately 54% of women and 61% of men go through a second divorce (Glick, 1989), many children experience a series of family and caregiving transitions.

Finally, as shifts have occurred in the employment patterns of parents in the United States, adults who are not related by blood or law have provided children's caregiving to a greater extent. In fact, parents' work outside the home, and the implications that it has for family management and child care, is arguably one of the most significant factors that contribute to changes in family practices during the past half-century. The traditional "breadwinner–homemaker model" that characterized three-fifths of American families in the 1950s, in which fathers earned income outside the home while mothers were primarily responsible for raising children and worked inside the home, bears little resemblance to contemporary family styles. In fact, 1997 to 1998 annual averages from the Bureau of Labor Statistics revealed that this model described only 22% of married-couple families with children between the ages of 6 and 17 years. Instead, both parents were employed outside the home in 70% of such families. Among single parents with children in this age group, 75% of single mothers were employed and 87% of single fathers were employed outside the home. These proportions were roughly paralleled in families with children under the age of 6. Approximately 58% of married couples with young children were dual-earner families, whereas 61% of single mothers and 85% of single fathers were employed outside of the home before their children began elementary school.

Because the majority of families include working parents, adults outside of the family and home commonly provide children's caregiving. In 1995, approximately 61% of children under the age of 6 were in child care, including 45% of children under the age of 1. Approximately half of all children under the age of 3 spend some part of each week in nonparental care (Hofferth, 1996; Scarr, 1997). Researchers remain divided on the consequences of infant child care. Some feel that early nonparental care has no impact on the development of children, rather the parent–child relationship determines the consequences of early child care (Howes, Rodning, Galluzzo, & Myers, 1988; NICHD, 1997; Scarr, 1998). Others argue that low quality child care can be detrimental to young children, but infant child care is not inherently bad (Field, 1991; Gamble & Zigler, 1986; Zigler & Gilman, 1997). Yet others have shown the positive value of child care, demonstrating that early child-care experiences increase a child's social interaction and play with peers (e.g., Andersson, 1989; 1992; Aureli & Procacci, 1992; Field, 1991). For example, studying the typically high quality day-care centers in Sweden, Andersson (1992) found that children who entered Swedish infant day-care centers and family child care before their first birthday were more independent, popular with other children, and socially confident at both 8 and 13 years of age than children who were in full-time parental care. Finally, it is also possible that the costs and benefits of day care vary with different characteristics of children and families. For instance, Caughy, DiPietro, and Strobino (1994) found that day-care participation functioned as a protective factor in the cognitive development of school age children from low socioeconomic backgrounds. Burchinal, Campbell, Bryant, Wasik, and Ramey (1997) reported similar findings in a longitudinal study of low-income children who participated in intensive early educational child care.

FAMILY SYSTEMS THEORIES: PROCESSES AS CONTEXT

Family systems theories view families as complex structures comprised of interdependent groups of individuals. Members of a family system devise strategies for meeting the needs of individual family members and the group as a whole. A central tenet of most family systems theories is that all family members are interdependent, such that the experiences of an individual member of the system impact other members as well as the system itself. A visual analogy for this belief is the dynamic movement of a mobile. In a mobile, a force on any single element transmits energy to every element in the mobile system and influences the movement of the mobile as a whole. This association is transactional in nature. In other words, the family context does not simply exert a unidirectional influence on an individual's development. Rather, each member of a family system, however it is defined, influences the other members and the system as a whole. Thus, in the family systems approach, the family context is defined in terms of transactions between individuals in a subjectively defined family system.

The family life-cycle perspective (Carter & McGoldrick, 1999) recognizes the dynamic nature of family systems across time. Family life is shaped by the constantly transforming set of tasks that occur throughout development. Families must respond to varying demands arising from metamorphoses in physical, social, cognitive, psychological, and emotional needs of family members. The changing demands brought on by developmental and situational transitions require families to exist in a relatively constant state of adaptation, generating new strategies and patterns of interaction.

For instance, it could be argued that across all developmental stages, families must achieve a balance between providing a safe and nurturing environment for all members while simultaneously encouraging exploration of the world and the self. Although the spirit of this task may remain the same throughout the family life cycle, its manifestations take different forms. The demands of raising a toddler arise from a level of cognitive development characterized by a burgeoning sense of curiosity and physical development that allows an explosion of freedom through mobility. Thus, the family's task is to achieve a balance in providing stimulation, guidance, and encouragement for exploration while also providing comfort and reassurance when the toddler's new territory begins to feel overwhelming. Furthermore, other family members (e.g., parents) must simultaneously negotiate their own as well as siblings' needs for safety and security with those for autonomy, exploration, and stimulation. The family tasks involved in raising an adolescent are similar in theory—encouraging the development of a sense of identity and independence—but the behaviors that comprise this task are completely different. The job of introducing a toddler to the world bears little resemblance to the job of launching an adolescent into adulthood. Thus, to optimize development over the life span, the same family goals, beliefs, and relational qualities may look, and should look, different across time.

Family systems researchers have identified a number of processes that illuminate a family context regardless of particular composition, organization, or
stage in the family life cycle. There are several dimensions of family process that
may set the stage for individual development, including: cohesion, adaptability,
expression and modulation of emotion, communication, structural processes,
affiliation and interdependence, achievement orientation, and family satisfaction (cf. Sparrow, Carter, Racusin, & Morris, 1995). These dimensions are typically assessed through self-reports and observational methods. They have been
associated with multiple individual outcomes, such as social competence and
psychopathology. The pathways of these associations are not always direct,
which reflects the complexity of the family context.

Family Cohesion

Family cohesion is a term that describes the extent to which family members report that they are close and share similar goals and values. One extreme of this
dimension is *enmeshment*, which refers to a family system in which members
must sacrifice their own autonomy, wishes, desires, or goals for the sake of preserving family unity. The other extreme is disengagement, in which commitment to family goals is so limited that members report feeling disconnected from
other members of the system. The healthy system is viewed as a balance of the
competing demands of individuation, individual expression, and
connectedness (Olson, Russell, & Sprenkle, 1983).

Communication

Aspects of communication that have been extensively studied include clarity,
consistency, and blaming, or scapegoating. Thus, clarity is jeopardized when
nonverbal cues are not consistent with verbal cues or when the tone or intona-
tion of the communication does not match the content of the communication.
Such ambiguous communications have been referred to as "double binds," because the recipient does not know which communicative channel to attend to
and will be noncompliant with a part of the communication no matter what op-
tion is pursued.

Affective Expression

Affective expression is one important component of communication within the
family. Families vary dramatically in the frequency, type, and intensity of emotion expression. In some families, a member who shouts in anger is a daily occur-

rence. In other families, the same event would indicate a major family crisis. The family environment is the first place that individuals learn about affective communication and social display rules. Malatesta and colleagues (Malatesta, Culver, Tesman, & Shepard, 1989; Malatesta & Haviland, 1982) demonstrated that in early infancy children begin to model facial emotions that are unique to the family. A considerable body of knowledge on expressed emotion has documented that negatively charged home environments are associated with poorer course of chronic mental illness across cultures. However, research also suggests that the manner and level of hostile expression of emotion, as well as the course of illness, is strongly associated with sociocultural factors (e.g., ethnicity, religiosity, developing status of a society; Weisman, 1997). Sequential analysis of affective displays among family members is a powerful tool for understanding synchrony of relationships as well as the function of specific displays within the family system. For example, the expression of depressive affect may at times serve to inhibit the expression of hostility or aggression in other family members (e.g., Hops et al., 1987; Nelson & Beach, 1990).

Adaptability

As a family undergoes developmental transitions and members encounter positive and negative life events, the homeostasis of the family may be threatened. In other words, the family's routine method of coping may no longer be adequate to face new developmental and/or external challenges. Extreme positions in this dimension are viewed as maladaptive. At one extreme, a family is so adaptable as to have no rules or permanent power structure, such that life is unpredictable and chaotic. At the other extreme, rules and boundary structures are rigidly employed to all situations despite negative consequences that may ensue. This represents a low level of adaptability, which can create high levels of stress in family systems as they are faced with changing demands produced by life events or transitions through different stages of development.

Structural Processes

Minuchin (1974) and others associated with the structural approach to family therapy, examined patterns or hierarchies of authority and power within the family system as well as the permeability of boundaries between subsystems in the family (e.g., parents and grandparents). Thus, a developmental approach is needed to determine the appropriateness of the locus of authority and power in the family system. For example, as children become older they are expected to have more authority and autonomy when decisions regarding educational placements and activities are made. Similarly, older adults who are marginalized within the family system by not being allowed to make independent decisions may show greater declines in functioning (chap. 10, this volume).

Achievement Orientation

All families have an investment in their children's success in the world. However, how families define success may vary dramatically. Achievement orientation reflects the extent to which families value and/or strive to achieve academic and occupational success. Assessment of this domain may be important in understanding "over-" and "underachievement" in school and occupational settings.

Family Satisfaction

Many family configurations and styles can lead to highly adaptive outcomes for family members. Therefore, knowledge regarding family composition, developmental life stage, and dimensions of family functioning are not adequate without a sense of how satisfied family members are with the patterns maintained within the family. For example, the family's orientation to achievement might be quite low, with little investment made in children's schooling or academic performance, but some individuals in the family might be dissatisfied with the family's orientation to achievement. In particular, the individual who is the target of investigation may hold a different set of values than the family that he or she belongs to. This may be due to extrafamilial experiences or to unique experiences in the family or personal talents that may have predisposed the individual to acquire aspirations that are not consistent with his or her family's shared values. For example, a young man who is extremely gifted in movement may choose to pursue a career in dance despite his family's concern that dancing is not an appropriate career for a man.

Dimensions of the family are believed to moderate other dimensions within the family, which have interactional effects on intellectual and/or academic achievement outcomes. Thus, to the extent that family life is characterized by warm, loving relationships as contrasted with conflictual or antagonistic relationships, children and adolescents may be more likely to adopt the achievement orientation that is presented in the family. Thus when achievement orientation is high in the family and family relations are warm and caring, children are likely to develop a positive orientation toward achievement. However, when achievement orientation is high and family relations are conflictual, children may develop a negative orientation toward achievement. Similarly, children living in family environments that optimize relational skills and social competence may be more compliant with school-related tasks, may show greater persistence in the face of challenge, and may form more positive relationships with peers and teachers that allow them to obtain both additional information and support within the classroom.

Transactions in Development

It is important to restate the idea that individuals within the system exert their own influence on the dynamics of the family system. Thus, when one takes a snapshot of a family's current level of functioning it is impossible to disentangle the history of the transaction of reciprocal influence between the individuals that comprise the system and the dynamics of the system that shape the individuals within it. The word *transaction* reflects the notion that the individual and systems with which they interact represent reciprocal influences on development. The transaction of the individual and context throughout development is highlighted in recent research on family functioning (Sameroff, 1995). This research showed that shared family environment appears to exert some influence on children's development. However, a child or adolescent's unique experience within the family appears to have a much greater impact on that individual child or adolescent's development (Plomin, 1986).

Family Narratives

When a group of urban school-aged children were asked to contemplate what would happen if there were no stories in the world, one child responded "There wouldn't be a world, because stories make the world" (cited in Sameroff & Fiese 1999, p. 122). Family researchers and therapists who consider stories, or narratives, to play powerful roles in family systems embrace this eloquent perspective. *Family narratives* refer to the meanings that family members jointly construct about the important events in their lives (Fiese et al., 1999). The process and content of such narratives provide a manner of regulating social interactions as a well as of communicating family held rules of social interaction, values, and beliefs across generations. It has been proposed that where family narratives are coherent, consistent, and congruent in meaning and emotion, the family context is most likely to foster adaptability and positive adjustment within individual members as well as relationships (Sameroff & Fiese, 1999). Similarly, family rituals provide predictability and structure within the family that can promote individual development while maintaining feelings of family identity. Family rituals may include practicing religious ceremonies at predetermined times during the week or year, eating special foods on certain secular or religious holidays, exchanging gifts, or having a family night when all family members are expected to participate in family activities. Thus, families that create and plan special predictable family events and are able to make sense of their experiences, both joyful and stressful, provide a meaning-making system that can better prepare members for coping with the numerous and unrelenting challenges of development.

When considering the impact of each of these family processes, it is important to note that some dimensions of family functioning are hypothesized to exert indirect influences on intellectual and/or academic achievement outcomes within the family. Family factors found to be associated with children's language development include distal measures of the family such as living in poverty and occupational status, as well as proximal measures such as the quality of the home environment and maternal interaction style (Roberts, Burchinal, & Durham, 1999). Even studies that examine families from a restricted socioeconomic and ethnic range demonstrate that the quality of stimulation and responsivity in the home environment strongly influences linguistic outcomes. For example, Roberts and colleagues (1999) reported that African-American children who grew up in more stimulating and responsive home environments had more advanced language when compared to African-American children in less stimulating and responsive homes. Similarly, a variety of early reading related activities that parents engage in with their young children (e.g., playing word games) have been shown to predict reading ability (e.g., Scarborough, 1998). Recent findings have indicated that not only the frequency of reading to children by parents (Lyytinen, Laasko, & Poikkeus, 1998), but also variations in adults' reading style (Reese & Cox, 1999) can influence children's emergent literacy among preschoolers. Taken together, these findings demonstrate the importance of qualitative, as well as quantitative, aspects of stimulation and responsivity of the home environment.

However, the nature of these associations is complex and the possible contribution of genetic factors and/or interactive environmental dimensions cannot be overlooked when observing associations between complexity of parental language use and children's linguistic competence. For example, to the extent that parents are more capable in verbal domains of cognitive functioning, they may be more likely to value success in school. Families who hold a traditional achievement orientation that values school competence and success are more likely to provide early stimulation such as reading books to young children and playing word games. Thus, achievement orientation may be mediated by early stimulation practices in the prediction of reading achievement.

NATURE PLUS NURTURE: RESPONSIVITY AND GOODNESS OF FIT

The age-old nature–nurture debate has evolved into a general consensus that heredity and environment interact to influence human development (e.g., Kendler, 1996; Plomin, 1996). This consensus has not eliminated the controversy that surrounds the relative influence of genes and environment on various traits. In fact, behavior geneticists have devoted particular attention to examining genetic contributions to intelligence. The heritability of intelligence is estimated to be approximately 50% (Plomin, DeFries, & McClearn, 1990), which makes it more heritable than most behavioral phenomena (Plomin, Chipuer, & Neiderhiser, 1994). That 50% of the variance in intelligence is not accounted for by heritability highlights the idea that direct and interactive environmental effects are critical to explain individual differences.

Thus, behavior genetics research has increasingly focused on two related issues. First, research has sought to illuminate the processes through which heredity–environment interactions influence development. In most cases, parents provide genes as well as furnish environments for their children, which means that these forces are intertwined, generally referred to as *gene–environment correlation*. Developmental behavior geneticists have proposed that these interactive influences become manifest in passive, evocative, and active ways. *Passive genotype–environment interactions* occur when a child's biological parents provide a caregiving environment that is influenced by the genetic makeup of the parents. For instance, a mother may be genetically predisposed toward high levels of physical activity. Because she has a high energy level and enjoys playing sports, the mother provides her child with frequent opportunities to exercise and develop motor coordination. In combination with the probable likelihood that children of athletic parents will be genetically predisposed to athletic competence, the environmental exposure increases the likelihood that the child will become a skilled athlete and enjoy participating in sports teams. *Evocative genotype–environment interactions* occur because an individual's genotype elicits certain types of physical and social environments. For example, an infant with an easy temperament who is quick to smile may receive more positive social stimulation than a more difficult, less engaging infant. A highly distractible child is likely to evoke more angry or frustrated responses from adult caregivers than a child with a high level of impulse control. *Active (niche-picking) genotype–environment interactions* occur when individuals seek out environments that are experienced as comfortable and stimulating. Throughout the course of development, individuals tend to select from their surrounding environment some aspects that they respond to, learn about, or ignore. This active selection process is related to an individual's genotype because he or she will tend to gravitate toward relationships and activities that are best suited to his or her natural talents and inclinations. It is likely that the relative importance of these three genotype–environment interactions changes throughout development (Scarr, 1993). Namely, passive genotype–environment interactions are more important early in development, because infants have a limited capacity for actively structuring their environments. Thus, the adults who care for them and the environments these adults have selected largely determine infant experiences. Niche picking becomes increasingly relevant as children individuate and extend their experiences beyond the family, thus creating their own environments to a larger degree.

The emphasis in behavior genetics research on heredity–environment interactions has been accompanied by the recognition that environmental influences appear to operate on an individual-to-individual basis, as opposed to a family-by-family basis. Thus, research has shifted to incorporate aspects of nonshared environmental experiences (e.g., differential caregiving, life events, and peer experiences) along with more traditional measures of shared environmental experiences in families (e.g., social class, place of residence, and parents' personalities). Increasingly, researchers are aware that the same event may have a different impact on individual members of the family system (Plomin & Daniels, 1987). For example, in the case of a loss or death within the family, individual members who share a common structural identity within the family (e.g., siblings) will have a different experience of this event based on their developmental level (i.e., a 4-year-old will understand and encode this event differently than a 14-year-old), as well as their emotional relationship with the person who died (e.g., close or conflictual). Moreover, systems issues such as triadic relations within the family and the stage in the family life cycle will also color the experience of family life events.

CONCLUSIONS AND DIRECTIONS
FOR FUTURE INQUIRY

The next frontier for this domain of inquiry is to expand the exploration of subtle and interactive relationships between factors that influence intellectual development. Instead of simply focusing on the relative influences of a multitude of factors, it is arguably more useful to examine how multiple factors influence one another as well as an individual's path of intellectual development. With an increased understanding of "active ingredients" that influence intellectual developmental trajectories, it may be more feasible to provide effective psychoeducational and behavioral supports to optimize intellectual development.

Vygotsky's (1962) theory of cognitive development addresses the interplay between nature and nurture by focusing on the sociocultural context of development. Advances in cognitive development are embedded in social and cultural activities. This theory highlights the role of social learning and direct instruction in children's development. The *zone of proximal development* (ZPD) is Vygotsky's term for the range of tasks that are too difficult for children to master alone but that can be mastered with the guidance and assistance of adults or more highly skilled children. With instruction and practice, the child gradually masters tasks in the ZPD and can accomplish them independently. This concept emphasizes that learning is an interpersonal, dynamic social event that involves at least two people, one more experienced and knowledgeable than the other. Once a task is mastered, it becomes the foundation for a new ZPD. In terms of language development, this concept is demonstrated by the phenomenon of *motherese*. Motherese refers to adults' tendency to talk to infants using a high-pitched voice, more extreme intonations, simpler, more repetitive vocabulary, and shorter utterances. This practice is aimed at capturing the baby's attention and maintaining communication. The ZPD changes when the baby learns to coo and his or her parents begin to babble in response. When the baby begins to babble, the parents respond with single words until the infant begins to say words, at which point the parents begin to connect two words in their interactions with their baby. Essentially, as a child builds new cognitive abilities into his or her repertoire, the "bar is raised" through successively more complex modeling and tapering off of direct instruction of new tasks.

Perhaps the most essential aspect of the concept of the ZPD is the notion that individuals within a child's multiple microsystems must respond to the child's unique needs and pace to optimize cognitive stimulation and instruction. In fact, the responsivity of individuals' multiple ecological systems is crucial across all stages of development. It could be argued that this responsiveness, or recognizing the changing profile of cognitive capacities within the individual family member, is actually the key in promoting optimal intellectual development throughout the life span.

To view individual cognitive development in terms of a subjective ZPD development acknowledges that our very notions of intelligence are actually social constructions. In fact, intelligence or giftedness is defined differently across cultural contexts (Grigorenko, this volume). For example, although one cultural setting may value speed of completing many activities, another cultural setting may value reflectivity and depths of cognitive products. Thus, a child's temperamental predisposition to overactivity (a dimension of behavior not typically associated with intelligence) may lead him or her to be viewed as highly intelligent in the former culture and impaired in the latter culture. On the basis of this initial appraisal, opportunities for intellectual development may or may not be made available, thus fulfilling a culturally determined prophecy. In this perspective, individual family members perform optimally when their settings are responsive to variations in natural inclinations such that multiple levels of the individual's system work in synchrony to facilitate enhancements of strengths and development of compensatory strategies for relative weaknesses. These enhancements and/or compensations can occur at the individual or system level.

Given the subjectivity of definitions and values surrounding cognitive abilities, as well as the variability in individual profiles of intellectual strengths, the concept of goodness of fit deserves further attention in research on intellectual development. Studies that address the family as a context for cognitive development should focus on identifying factors associated with the goodness of fit between an individual and his or her environment. Important areas of inquiry may include people as well as resources that facilitate or hinder actualization of a person's cognitive potential, given the unique characteristics and demands of that individual's social context. It is important to recognize that goodness of fit between individuals and their contexts is not an all-or-none phenomenon, but instead a dynamic process that may become relatively better or worse with the changing demands of development. For instance, the goodness of fit may be relatively poor between a parent who prizes independence and her 2-year old child because toddlers need a high level of attention, supervision, and guidance. However, this fit could substantially improve over time as the child's emerging competencies translate into increasing capacities to succeed when offered autonomy.

The ecological and family systems perspectives expand our too often constrained views of intelligence and the forces that may optimize intellectual functioning. By placing development in the sociohistorical context it becomes possible to expand traditional notions of intelligence to include more culturally sensitive perspectives (Sternberg et al., in press). The dramatic variations observed in adaptive family life within and across cultures highlight the need for multiple definitions of intelligence, competence, and success. We would also advocate the importance of evaluating competence within dynamic learning relationships and broader ecosystems to evaluate goodness of fit. The complexity of influences on intelligence make this an extremely challenging yet exciting area of further inquiry.

REFERENCES

Andersson, B-E. (1989). Effects of public day-care: A longitudinal study. *Child Development, 60*, 857–866.

Andersson, B-E. (1992). Effects of day-care on cognitive and socioemotional competence of thirteen-year-old Swedish schoolchildren. *Child Development, 63*, 20–36.

Aureli, T., & Procacci, M. A., (1992). Day-care experience and children's social development. *Early Child Development and Care, 83*, 45–54.

Black, D., Gates, G., Sanders, S., & Taylor, L. (2000). *Demographics of the gay and lesbian population in the United States: Evidence from available systematic data sources. Demography, 37*, 139–154.

Bradley, R. H., Caldwell, B. M., Rock, S. L., Ramey, C. T., Barnard, K. E., Gary, C., Hammond, M. A., Mitchell, S., Gottfried, A. W., Siegel, L., & Johnson, D. L. (1989). Home environment and cognitive development in the first three years of life. A collaborative study including six sites and three ethnic groups in North America. *Developmental Psychology, 25*, 217–235.

Bronfenbrenner, U. (1986). Ecology of the family as a context for human development: Research perspectives. *Developmental Psychology, 22*, 723–742.

Bronfenbrenner, U. (1995). The bioecological model from a life course perspective. In P. Moen, G. H. Elder, & K. Luscher (Eds.), *Examining lives in context*. Washington, DC: American Psychological Association.

Bronfenbrenner, U., & Ceci, S. (1994). Nature nurture reconceptualized in developmental perspective: A bioecological model. *Psychological Review, 101*, 568–586.

Bronfenbrenner, U., & Morris, P.A. (1997). The ecology of developmental processes. In R. M. Lerner (Ed.), *Handbook of child psychology (5th Ed., Vol. 1)*. New York: Wiley.

Brooks-Gunn, J., Klebanov, P. K., & Liaw, F. (1995). The learning, physical, and emotional environment of the home in the context of poverty: The infant health and development program. *Child and Youth Services Review, 17*, 251–276.

Bureau of Labor Statistics (1997–1998). Table 4. Families with own children: Employment status of parents by age of youngest child and family type, 1997–98 annual averages. *Labor force statistics from the current population survey*. Washington, DC: U.S. Bureau of the Census.

Burchinal, M., Campbell, F., Bryant, D., Wasik, B., & Ramey, C. (1997). Early intervention and mediating processes in cognitive performance of children of low-income African American families. *Child Development, 68*, 935–954.

Carnegie Task Force. (1994, April). *Starting points: Meeting the needs of our youngest children*. New York: Carnegie Corporation.

Carter, B., & McGoldrick, M. (Eds.). (1999). *The expanded family life cycle: Individual, family, and social perspectives (3rd ed.)*. Boston: Allyn & Bacon.

Casper, L., & Bryson, K. (1998). *Co-resident grandparents and their grandchildren: Grandparent maintained families* (Population Division Working Paper No. 26). Washington, DC: U.S. Bureau of the Census.

Caughy, M., DiPietro, J., & Strobino, D. (1994). Day-care participation as a protective factor in the cognitive development of low-income children. *Child Development, 65*, 457–471.

Chess, S., & Thomas, A. (1991). Temperament and the concept of goodness-of-fit. In J. Strelau & A. Angleitner (Eds.), *Explorations in temperament: International perspectives on theory and measurement. Perspectives on individual differences*. New York: Plenum Press.

Dressler, W. (1985). Extended family relationships, social support, and mental health in a southern Black community. *Journal of Health and Social Behavior, 26*, 39–48.

Duncan, G. J. (1991). The economic environment of childhood. In A. C. Huston (Ed.), *Children in poverty: Child development and public policy* (pp. 23–50). New York: Cambridge University Press.

Dunn, J. (1996). Brothers and sisters in middle childhood and early adolescence: Continuity and change in individual differences. In G. Brody (Ed.), *Sibling relationships: Their causes and consequences* (pp. 173–195). Norwood, NJ: Ablex.

Dunn, J., Slomkowski, C., & Beardsall, L. (1994). Sibling relationships from the preschool period through middle childhood and early adolescence. *Developmental Psychology, 30*, 315–324.

Field, T. (1991). Quality infant day-care and grade school behavior and performance. *Child Development, 62*, 863–870.

Fiese, B., Sameroff, A., Grotevant, F., Wamboldt, S., Dickstein, S., & Lewis Fravel, D. (Eds.). (1999). The stories that families tell: Narrative coherence, narrative interaction, and relationship beliefs. *Monographs of the Society for Research in Child Development, 64* (2, Serial No. 257).

Gamble, T. J., & Zigler, E. (1986). Effects of infant day care: Another look at the evidence. *American Journal of Orthopsychiatry, 56*, 26–42.

Garbarino, J. (1990). The human ecology of early risk. In S. M. Meisels & J. P. Shonkoff (Eds.), *Handbook of early intervention* (pp. 78–96). New York: Cambridge University Press.

Gelles, R. J. (1992). Poverty and violence toward children. *American Behavioral Scientist, 35*, 258–274.

Glick, P. (1989). Remarried families, stepfamilies, and stepchildren: A brief demographic profile. *Family Relations, 38*, 24–27.

Hetherington, E. M., Stanley-Hagan, M., & Anderson, E. R. (1989). Marital transitions: A child's perspective. *American Psychologist, 44*(2), 303–312.

Hoff-Ginsberg, E. (1998). The relation of birth order and socioeconomic status to children's language experience and language development. *Applied Psycholinguistics, 19*, 603–629.

Hofferth, S. L. (1996). Child care in the United States today. *The Future of Children, 6*, 41–61.

Hops, H., Biglan, A., Sherman, O., Arthur, J., Friedman, L., & Osteen, V. (1987). Home observation of family interactions of depressed women. *Journal of Consulting and Clinical Psychology, 55*, 341–346.

Howes, C., Rodning, C., Galluzzo, D., & Myers, L. (1988). Attachment and child care: Relationships with mother and caregiver. *Early Childhood Research Quarterly, 3*, 403–416.

Huston, A. C., McLoyd, V. C., & Garcia-Coll, C. (1994). Children and poverty: Issues in contemporary research. *Child Development, 65*, 275–282.

Johnson, T. & Colucci, P. (1999). Lesbians, gay men, and the family life cycle. In B. Carter & M. McGoldrick (Eds.), *The expanded family life cycle: Individual, family, and social perspectives* (3rd ed.). Boston: Allyn & Bacon.

Kendler, K. (1996). Parenting: A genetic–epidemiologic perspective. *American Journal of Psychiatry, 153*, 11–20.

Klebanov, P. K., Brooks-Gunn, J., McCarton, C., & McCormick, M. (1998). The contribution of neighborhood and family income to developmental test scores over the first three years of life. *Child Development, 69*, 1420–1436.

Lamb, M. E., Sternberg, K., & Thompson, R. (1997). The effects of divorce and custody arrangement on children's behavior, development, and adjustment. *Family and Conciliation Courts Review, 35*, 393–404.

Lyytinen, P., Laasko, M.-L., & Poikkeus, A-M. (1998). Parental contribution to child's early language and interest in books. *European Journal of Psychology of Education, 8*, 297–308.

Malatesta, C. Z., Culver, C., Tesman, J. R., & Shepard, B. (1989). The development of emotion expression during the first two years of life. *Monographs of the Society for Research in Child Development, 54* (1-2, Serial No. 219), pp. 1–104.

Malatesta, C. Z., & Haviland, J. M. (1982). Learning display rules: The socialization of emotion expression in infancy. *Child Development, 53*, 991–1003.

McHale, S., & Crouter, A. (1996). The family contexts of children's sibling relationships. In G. Brody (Ed.), *Sibling relationships: Their causes and consequences* (pp. 173–195). Norwood, NJ: Ablex.

Minuchin, S. (1974). *Families and family therapy*. Cambridge, MA: Harvard University Press.

National Center for Children in Poverty. (1996). *One in four: America's youngest poor*. New York: Columbia School of Public Health.

Nelson, G. M., & Beach, S. R. (1990). Sequential interaction in depression: Effects of depressive behavior on spousal aggression. *Behavior Therapy, 21*, 167–182.

NICHD Early Child Care Research Network. (1997). The effects of infant child care on infant–mother attachment security: Results of the NICHD study of early child care. *Child Development, 68*, 860–879.

Olson, D., Russell, C., & Sprenkle, D. (1983). Circumplex model of marital and family systems: VI. Theoretical update. *Family Process, 22*, 69–83.

Patterson, C. (1992). Children of lesbian and gay parents. *Child Development, 63*, 1025–1042.

Patterson, G. (1986). Performance models for antisocial boys. *American Psychologist, 41*, 432–444.

Plomin, R. (1996, August). *Nature and nurture together*. Paper presented at the meeting of the American Psychological Association, Toronto.

Plomin, R., Chipuer, H. M., & Neiderhiser, J. (1994). Behavioral genetic evidence for the importance of nonshared environment. In E. M. Heterington, D. Reiss, & R. Plomin (Eds.), *Separate social worlds of siblings: The impact of nonshared environment on development*. Hillsdale, NJ: Lawrence Erlbaum Associates.

Plomin, R., & Daniels, D. (1987). Why are children in the same family so different from one another? *Behavioral and Brain Sciences, 10*, 1–16.

Plomin, R., DeFries, J. C., & McClearn, G. E. (1990). *Behavioral genetics: A primer*. New York: W. H. Freeman.

Reese, E., & Cox, A. (1999). Quality of book reading affects preschoolers' emergent literacy. *Developmental Psychology, 35*, 20–28.

Roberts, J., Burchinal, M., & Durham, M. (1999). Parents' report of vocabulary and grammatical development of African American preschoolers: Child and environment associations. *Child Development, 70*, 92–106.

Sameroff, A. (1995). General systems theories and developmental psychopathology. In D. Cicchetti & D. Cohen (Eds.), *Developmental psychopathology, Vol. 1: Theory and methods* (pp. 659–695). New York: Wiley.

Sameroff, A., & Fiese, B. (1999). Narrative connections in the family context: Summary and conclusions. In B. Fiese, A. Sameroff, H. Grotevant, F. Wambolt, S. Dickstein, & D. Lewis Fravel (Eds.), The stories that families tell: Narrative coherence, narrative interaction, and relationship beliefs. *Monographs of the Society for Research in Child Development, 64* (2, Serial No. 257), pp. 105–123.

Sameroff, A., Seifer, R., Barocas, R., Zax, M., & Greenspan, S. (1987). Intelligence quotient scores of 4-year-old children: Social–environmental risk factors. *Pediatrics, 79*, 343–350.

Scarborough, H. S. (1998). Predicting the future achievement of second graders with reading disabilities: Contributions of phonemic awareness, verbal memory, rapid naming, and IQ. *Annals of Dyslexia, 48,* 115–136.

Scarr, S. (1993). Biological and cultural diversity: The legacy of Darwin for development. *Child Development, 64,* 1333–1353.

Scarr, S. (1997). Why child care has little impact on most children's development. *Current Directions in Psychological Science, 6,* 143–148.

Scarr, S. (1998). American child care today. *American Psychologist, 53,* 95–108.

Slater, S. (1995). *The lesbian family life cycle.* New York: The Free Press.

Sparrow, S. S., Carter, A. S., Racusin, G. R., & Morris, R. (1995). Comprehensive psychological assessment: A lifespan developmental approach. In D. Cicchetti & D. Cohen (Eds.), *The manual of developmental psychopathology, Vol. I: Theory and methods* (pp. 81–105). New York: Wiley.

Starfield, B. (1991). Child morbidity: Comparisons, clusters, and trends. *Pediatrics, 88,* 519–526.

Sternberg, R. J., Nokes, K., Geissler, P. W., Prince, R., Okatcha, F., Bundy, D. A., & Grigorenko, E. L. (in press). The relationship between academic and practical intelligence: A case study in Kenya. *Intelligence.*

Stocker, C., & McHale, S. (1992). The nature and family correlates of preadolescents' perceptions of their sibling relationships. *Journal of Personal and Social Relationships, 9,* 179–195.

Thomas, T., Chess, S., & Birch, H. G. (1968). *Temperament and behavior disorders in children.* New York: New York University Press.

U.S. Census Bureau (1998a). Current population reports, Series P20-514, *Marital status and living arrangements: March 1998 (Update).* Washington, DC: U.S. Government Printing Office.

U.S. Census Bureau (1998b). Current population reports, Series P20-514, *Household and family characteristics: March 1998 (Update).* Washington, DC: U.S. Government Printing Office.

Vygotsky, L. (1962). *Thought and language.* Cambridge, MA: MIT Press.

Weisman, A. (1997). Understanding cross-cultural prognostic variability for schizophrenia. *Cultural Diversity and Mental Health, 3,* 23–35.

Wilson, M., & Tolson, T. (1990). Familial support in the Black family. *Journal of Clinical Child Psychology, 19,* 347–355.

Zaslow, M., Tout, K., Smith, S., & Moore, K. (1998). Implications of the 1996 welfare legislation for children: A research perspective. *Social Policy Report: Society for Research in Child Development, XII*(3), 1–34.

Zigler, E. F., & Gilman, E. (1997). Not just any care: Shaping a coherent child care policy. In E. F. Zigler, S. L. Kagan, & N. W. Hall (Eds.), *Children, families and government: Preparing for the twenty-first century.* (pp. 94–116). Cambridge: Cambridge University Press.

2

Arguing for the Concept of Developmental Niche

Elena L. Grigorenko
Yale University
Moscow State University

The world has changed. The world is changing. The world will continue to change. Today the urban population is growing and globalization is leading to both a gradual merging of national experiences and a widening of the gap between the rich and the poor. Today people live longer, eat more, have more fun, get married later in life, listen to more music, spend more time on their cell phones, and worry about AIDS. Consider the following snapshots of today's world (Walch, 1999).

Yesterday versus today:

- By the late 1990s, known military spending decreased to about two thirds of its level during the previous decade, from 5.2% of the world's gross national product (GNP) in 1985 to 2.8% in 1995.

- Between 1990 and 1997 the amount of polluting fuels was reduced by more than two fifths. Yet every year there are nearly 3 million deaths traced to air pollution, and more than 5 million die from diseases caused by water contamination.
- The economic distance between the richest and poorest countries was about 3 to 1 in 1820, 11 to 1 in 1973, 35 to 1 in 1950, 44 to 1 in 1973, and 72 to 1 in 1992. In 1997 it was roughly 727 to 1.

Today:

- Of people who live in developing countries, 80% derive medicine from local flora and fauna as the basis of their primary health care.
- Nearly 1.3 billion people do not have access to clean water.
- The illegal trafficking of women and girls for sexual exploitation is an estimated $7 billion-a-year industry.
- Nearly 160 million of the world's children are undernourished.
- Teens in North America hang out for 2 to 3 hours a day. In East Asia they socialize for less than 1 hour.
- There are approximately 300,000 child soldiers globally.

Tomorrow versus today:

- During the mid-1970s, less than 40% of the global population lived in urban areas; in 2000 almost 50% live in cities; for 2025, the projection is 60%.
- AIDS has left 8.2 million children without a mother or both parents. The number is expected to reach 13 million by the end of 2000.
- A yearly contribution of 1% of the wealth of the 200 richest people ($7 billion to $8 billion) could provide universal access to primary education for children globally.

The world is diverse. Moreover, changes in the world at large have also shifted, in many ways, the way we raise our children. The children change, and our expectations and worries about them change also. As an often told story goes, during the 1940s, U.S. teachers asked to identify the major discipline problems in their schools listed gum chewing, talking out of turn, running in the halls, cutting into lines, violating the dress code, littering, and making noise. When surveyed in the 1990s, the story continues, teachers listed drug abuse, alcohol abuse, pregnancy, suicide, rape, robbery, and assault (*Current Events, 1993*).

Since the emergence of developmental psychology as an independent field of research within psychology, it has been believed that the family is the major regulatory agency of child development (e.g., Reiss, 1989). The function of family in the context of child development encompasses a variety of processes, ranging from providing physical shelter and means of survival to being a major transmitter of cultural and social values. Yet belief in the ultimate importance of family to human development has also been challenged (e.g., Harris, 1998). The essence of these challenges, however, is not dismissing the institution of family but pointing out the residual of the variance after accounting for the family factor. In other words, family is important, but not enough to overbalance the meaningful variability of environments.

The purpose of this chapter is to argue that the concept of *developmental niche* (DN), initially introduced to psychology by Super and Harkness (1986), offers an opportunity to develop a research perspective in which the inanimate world, human culture, and human development are envisioned as systems of increasing complexity that represent physical, biological, sociopolitical, and cultural realities (Herrmann, 1998). The main point of this argument is that, when viewed as complex system, DN offers an avenue to understanding the conceptual continuity of forces engaged in the development of a child. In short, the concept of DN is a higher order metaconcept that has the potential to enhance our understanding of the complexity of human development.

DEVELOPMENTAL NICHE: THE BASES FOR ARGUMENT

Why the developmental niche? Because, unlike analytical approaches that disassemble and dissect the complex reality of development into its factors and study these factors separately, which dominate developmental psychology today, the DN approach allows a different type of understanding. This type of understanding was referred to by Herrmann (1998) as the establishment of conceptual continuity.

Developmentalists' dissatisfaction with the scientific paradigm of looking for simplifying generalizations has been clearly expressed by a number of scientists. For example, Sameroff (1994) has argued against the simplistic main effect-based models in psychology and pointed out the necessity of considering the complexity both in terms of the number of developmental factors involved and in terms of the interactions between these factors. "Conceptual continuity" between two complex systems (or between two states of the same system) assumes a situation where an element can be recognized as shared by the two systems. These systems might be previously unrelated, empirically correlated, or formally (algorithmically) related.

There are three forms of conceptual continuity, depending on the nature and structure of the complexity of the systems. The first form is specific to ideal systems; in such fully defined systems, simplifying abstractions are highly relevant and conceptual continuity is established by general elements. For example, photons are intrinsic to both a beam of light and to atoms of light-absorbing material. The second and third forms of conceptual continuity are characteristic of nonideal (not fully defined) systems. The second form is established by general elements modified by specific conditions. For example, when the parents of children–friends intend to establish their own relationships, they introduce additional linking units into the establishment of conceptual continuity. The third form of conceptual continuity is established by specific elements. For example, the essence of developmental plasticity is a change in the phenotype (physical appearance and behavior) of the individual caused by a change in the environment (Stearns, 1992). A given phenotype's fitness varies dramatically across a range of environments. When phenotypes are fixed early in development (e.g., sexual maturation comes soon after weaning, as in rodents), major environmental changes tend to result in high mortality. The introduction of additional developmental periods (e.g., childhood and adolescence) permits a slower development of adult phenotypes and the establishment of conceptual continuity between specific elements of the phenotype and the environment. This process is carried out through making these phenotypes experience a wider range of environments, thus achieving a better "fit" between the individual and the environment.

The perception of the simplifying generalization and complex specificities and the role of conceptual continuity have changed at various stages of the existence of the science of development. In science, the relationships between the parts of a system are explored by observing and recording responses of the systems when they are challenged by a variety of well-defined conditions. Such systematic experimentation is not possible with systems of human development. Therefore, our understanding of the complexities of human development is dependent on simulating experimentation, both through interpreting societal changes and challenges throughout human history and through modeling complexity via computers.

The argument for the concept of DN as a representation of complex systems starts unfolding at the juncture of a number of developmental psychology assertions based on research evidence. These assertions, questioned and scrutinized in the past, are now considered axiomatic.

First, one of the most "amazing" discoveries of the 1990s is that culture, society, and biology are all important in shaping human development. The infamous debates nature versus nurture or biology versus culture has long been considered unproductive (Scarr, 1993). The field has accepted the belief that development is not dichotomous; human development is multifactorial and complex. The question now is not what determines the child's development, but how to represent, understand, and model the complexity of that development.

Second, development is considered dynamic (i.e., changing in time) and systematic (engaging systems of factors). According to this view, developmental outcomes are never a function of the individual taken alone or the experiential context taken alone, and human competencies are products of an individual's experiencing and living in and through his or her environment (Sameroff, 1994).

Third, the bulk of research that depicts peculiarities of child development and upbringing around the world has convincingly shown that no matter how different the conditions in which children are raised, the overwhelming majority of children grow up to become competent survivors and promoters of their cultures (communal, social, religious, moral, state, and so on). Anthropologists have cautioned against overreliance on large-scale cross-sectional surveys of children at the expense of detailed studies of the circumstances, environments, and causes of their specific developmental niches (Panter-Brick, 1999).

Fourth, variation across human populations in rearing practices, milestones, and characteristics of behavioral development of children is broad and unpredictable from knowledge of universal human abilities and developmental laws. Moreover, no experiences of various developmental stages (e.g., infancy, childhood, adolescence) can be regarded as universal across different cultures (James, 1999). Stephens (1995), for example, stressed the fact that children in the developing world are most often depicted in more adult-like roles: as contributors to family income through wage labor and agriculture, as domestic workers, as caregivers, as soldiers, as prostitutes, or as street vendors. The expectations of what, for example, a 7- to 8 year-old boy is able to achieve vary enormously across different cultures: Children around the world today are soldiers (Namibia), factory workers (Peru), primary caregivers (Tanzania), healers (Zimbabwe), and pupils (United States). According to Peruvian national census records, many 6- to 14-year-olds are heads of households and the principal wage earners (Johnson, Hill, & Ivan-Smith, 1995). Thus, to remove children from the labor force in these areas, means simply to exacerbate their poverty. For example, Cain (1977) observed that Bangladeshi children began performing useful productive tasks at age 6, worked as long or longer (9 hours a day) than adults by age 13, and, if male, were already net economic producers in their household when 12 years old. Nag, White, & Peet (1978) collected their data in Java and Nepal. They discovered that, in percentage terms, 7-year-olds completed close to one third, 10-year-olds, one half, and 13-year-olds, three quarters of the work of adults. Neiuwenhuys (1994) interviewed children in Kerala, India: Children aged 5 to 15 spent 7 hours a day working in domestic, waged, and unwaged work. Super and Harkness (1986), who studied children of rural Kipsigis in Kenya, showed that by the age of 6 or 7, Kipsigi children spent more time working on household chores than they did resting or playing.

Fifth, many researchers have concentrated their efforts on understanding the active role of a child in carving his or her DN. Recent sociological and anthropological studies have researched the concept of children's subjectivity—the ways in which children themselves contribute to their development. In this context, Qvortrup, Bardy, Saritta, and Wintersberger (1994) argued that the structural space for childhood is a constant in society—that is, there are always going to be children and adults—but that the concrete filling of this space differs significantly for each given child.

These axioms of modern developmental psychology, among others, have formed the basis of the so-called new social studies of childhood. Among various approaches that form this conglomerate of studies, analysts identify four distinctive (also overlapping) research traditions (James, 1999): (a) the so-called studies of "the social structural child"—within this framework, researchers explore the ways in which childhood is embedded the social structure of society and the implications this has for children's daily lives in different cultures and societies; (b) the so-called studies of "the socially constructed child"—within this framework, researchers explore the ways in which children are perceived, represented, and understood within particular societies as "children," rather than simply as persons; (c) the so-called "tribal child" studies—within this framework, research investigates the ways in which children create and inhabit their own separate social worlds of childhood; and (d) the so-called "minority group child model"—within this framework, researchers study children as people inhabiting an adult rather than a child's world.

Given the richness and variability of the field of developmental psychology today, researchers search for new concepts, new models, and new interpretations that can encompass the diversity of nature and human culture (Kirkland & Morgan, 1991). The conclusions I work toward here is that the concept of DN is one that (a) reflects the moderns axioms of developmental psychology; (b) enhances our understanding of our adaptation to the world and patterns of more efficient exploitation of the world; (c) captures the reality, forms a representation of a complex, interdependent, and adaptive universe of being; and (d) allows developmental psychologists to capitalize on the theories of complexity developed in other sciences.

THE CONCEPT AND STRUCTURE
OF DEVELOPMENTAL NICHE

The Concept

The word *niche* originates from the French word for nest. The implicit search for a concept that grasps aspects of both organism and environment has persisted on for as long as the inquiry into development has existed,[1] but the scientific concept of "niche" was introduced into ecological research during the mid-1950s and was defined as all those combinations of resource levels at which a species population can survive and reproduce (Hutchinson, 1957, 1978).

The concept of niche occupies a pivotal position in population biology (Roughgarden, 1979). The scientific concept is considered sixth of the 20 most important concepts in ecology (Cherrett, 1989). The essence of the scientific concept of niche is that each species has unique needs, and therefore each species has a unique effect on an ecosystem. Among the primary features of the scientific concept of niche are the following: (a) varying the population of an organism affects an entire ecosystem, (b) varying the population of an organism affects other organisms in an ecosystem to a range of degrees, (c) each species has unique needs it is trying to meet by effecting an ecosystem, (d) species in an ecosystem have a unique niche, but may interact in dynamic ways (Munson, 1994). Correspondingly, the theory of niche brings together under one framework many of the central concerns about how species live in their environments.

Dynamism and interactionism are inherent to the concept of the niche. Thus, Pianka (1978) delineated a typology for types of interaction within ecological niches based on whether there is no impact of one species on another (0), there is a positive effect of one species on another (+), or there is a negative impact of one species on another (–). The most common relationships that evolve from these three types of impact are: neutralism (0, 0), competition (–, –), mutualism (+, +), predation (+, –), commensalism (+, 0), and amensalism (–, 0). Neutralism implies that neither species affects the other. In competition,

---

[1]Thus, in talking about English men of science, Galton stated that such men inherit England along with their genes and that, without England, "English nature" could do little.

each of the two populations affects the other adversely. Mutualism occurs when the relationship within the niche benefits both populations without harming either. In predation, one species within the niche benefits to the detriment of the other. Commensalism means that one population benefits from the existence of the other, whereas the latter is completely unaffected. Finally, amensalism suggests that one species in the niche is affected negatively, whereas the other is not affected at all.

As living organisms always exist somewhere, in something, to describe the where of the organismal existence, the concept of habitat is used. A niche is an interactive characteristic descriptive of the way an organism exists in its habitat. In a broader, interdisciplinary sense, a niche refers to how a living organism gets along and functions with what's available from the environment in order to grow, live, regenerate, adapt, thrive, and reproduce. The biologist Von Uxekull (1864) proposed the concept of "*umwelt*." Umwelt captures the wholeness of life-space of an organism (both its objective and subjective worlds)—the biology and neurology of an organism in the ways it perceives and acts in its environment. Umwelt is a developmental niche in action.

Psychologists have attempted to adapt the concept of *ecological niche*. The adaptation is mostly metaphorical, which permits the introduction of insightful analogy, but does not extend into a distinct strain of studies. West and King (1987), for example, offered three metaphors of developmental niche: (a) the niche as a legacy (niche as a heritage)—the essence of this metaphor of developmental niche is that it accounts not for what is inside the genes one inherited, but for what the genes one inherited are inside (p. 552), (b) the niche as a link—the essence of this metaphor lies in its reflection of transgenerational social dynamics—here a niche is a "descriptor of the context in which development takes place" (p. 555), and (c) the niche as a way of life—the essence of this metaphor stresses the active role of the organism in its habitat, the process of ontogenetic adaptation.

One of the most distinct differences in the usage of the concept of niche by ecologists and psychologists is that ecologists, unlike psychologists, do not study individual organisms. Thus, in ecology, the concept of niche addresses groups of individuals, a species; whereas in psychology, the concept of DN addresses individuals and individual patterns of development.

The Structure

A DN is a system, a whole (like habitat and organism, body and cell), but has distinct functional (often hierarchical) subsystems that in turn interact with one another and with the whole aggregate.

Super and Harkness (1986) proposed the concept of DN as a basis of a single framework considering simultaneously the psychological and the cultural contributions to human development. They identified three subsystems of the DN that connect human developmental processes directly to the culture: (a) the physical and social settings of development, (b) the customs of child care, and (c) the psychology of caregiver. This structure of the developmental niche was further explored by Pachter and Harwood (1996).

Gauvain (1995) argued that the subsystems described by Super and Harkness are more suited to examining social than cognitive development and offered three other subsystems of the developmental niche: (a) activity goals and values of the culture and its members; (b) historical means provided by the culture, such as material and symbolic tools, for satisfying these goals and values; and (c) higher level structures, such as scripts, routines, and rituals, that instantiate cultural goals and values in socially organized ways and thereby connect individual members to each other and to cultural goals and values in the course of everyday practices.

Here the developmental niche is viewed as the most elementary unit that forms an indivisible contextual structure for child development. Super and Harkness' list of the niche components is extended by adding the biopsychological profiles (meaning the set of individual biological and psychological characteristics) of both child and caregiver. This component of the developmental niche reflects the fact that each child has a unique niche simply because the biopsychological individuality of the child, as much as the individuality of the caregiver, contributes to the niche. DN helps explain why children in the same family are so different: Most of them, due to their individuality, grow up in different niches.

Most attempts to assess the theoretical implications of the concept of DN tend to be descriptive in nature. There is not yet a single study that represents an attempt at a quantitative analysis of the DN. The lack of solid empirical word in the DN perspective results from a number of causes. First, given the list of structural variables necessary to define and describe a DN, the DN approach requires quite a bit more data than psychologists are generally prepared to collect. Second, developmental psychologists encounter the complexity they observe in everyday life and realize the limited availability of mathematical models that would allow them to advance the understanding of that observed complexity. Finally, the field of developmental psychology is still primarily dominated by the ideas of determinism. Unlike many of the natural sciences (e.g., Flake, 1998), psychology is characterized by a lack of appreciation of the impact of random processes and chance. It is curious that, despite multiple demonstrations of the fact that direct influences rarely account for significant portions of the variance related to child outcome (Bakeman & Gottman, 1986; Patterson, 1986; Sackett, 1979), researchers continue to look for the "ultimate" variable (or a set of variables) that might explain all the phenomena of human development—crime, talent, poverty, illness, wars, attachment, and betrayal.

DEVELOPMENTAL NICHE AS AN EXAMPLE OF COMPLEX SYSTEMS

Having stated that DN can (and must) be conceptualized as a realization of a complex system, I discuss some of the characteristics of complex systems (based on Cilliers, 1998; Flake, 1998; Herrmann, 1998) in order to show how descriptive these features are of the concept of DN.

1. Complex systems consist of so many elements that the description of each element separately becomes impractical and prevents (rather than helps) understanding of the system.

Consider the following example. Sameroff and colleagues conducted a study to examine the relation between early characteristics of the child and the environment, and later mental health (for a brief overview see Sameroff & Seifer, 1995). In this project—the Rochester Longitudinal Study (RLS)—the researchers investigated the development of a group of children from the prenatal period through adolescence who lived in a socially heterogeneous set of family circumstances. From the 4-year assessment of the children in the RLS, the researchers (Sameroff, Seifer, Barocas, Zax, & Greenspan, 1987) chose a set of 10 environmental variables known in the literature as developmental risk factors. Among those factors were the following:

1. A history of maternal mental illness.
2. High maternal anxiety.
3. A parental perspectives core derived from a combination of measures that reflected rigidity in the attitudes, beliefs, and values that mothers had in regard to their child's development.
4. Few positive maternal interactions with the child observed during infancy.
5. Head of household employed in unskilled occupations.
6. Minimal maternal education.
7. Disadvantaged minority status.
8. Reduced family support.
9. Stressful life events.

10. Large family size.

The main outcome of this study was the finding that, although there were significant effects for the individual risk factors, no single risk factor resulted in major developmental problems. Specifically, on an intelligence test, children with no environmental risks scored more than 30 points higher than children with eight or nine risk factors (on average, each risk factor reduced the child's IQ score by 4 points). For the socioemotional scores, the difference between the group with no risk factors and the group with high counts of risk factors was more than one standard deviation. In sum, no single variable determined the outcome. Only in families with multiple risk factors was the child's competence put at risk.

To reconceptualize this result, the DN as a complex system is not decomposable into a set of single factors. A DN becomes inadequate and jeopardizes the development of the child's competencies when a set of factors becomes misaligned, when risk builds up, and when such accumulation, in the absence or lack of opportunity factors, overwhelms the child. Children in malfunctioning developmental niches are at significantly higher risk to become developmentally disabled.

2. No one element in the system possesses information descriptive of the system as a whole. Each element responds only to information that is available locally. (Were each element "aware" of the system as a whole, all of the complexity would be associated with this element.) When the behavior of a system is studied as a whole, the focus shifts from the individual element in the system to the complex structure of the system.

Available evidence has convincingly documented that there are multiple influences on development; in other words, there is no isolated single factor whose influence may "doom" a child to developmental disability. Quite to the contrary, the predictive power of any given isolated element for developmental outcomes is low.

One analytic approach that allows modeling interrelationships between factors of a DN and identifying what grouping of interactive factors is particularly relevant to developmental outcomes, is that developed by Magnusson and colleagues (Magnusson, 1988, 1993; Magnusson & Bergman, 1990). These researchers used pattern approaches to group individuals with different environmental and biologically influenced individual risk characteristics into clusters; cluster membership was subsequently used to predict and classify developmental outcomes. Wachs (1996) analyzed the importance of this approach and stressed that it (a) permits highlighting on naturally occurring interactions (individuals, whose DN[s] are characterized by similar patterns of interactions are put into a different cluster than are individuals whose DN[s]'s patterns of interactions differ) and (b) allows specification of combinations of factors that are most relevant for specific developmental outcomes.

The DN's feature of not "charging" any of its elements as a descriptor of the whole permits an enormous amount of flexibility and plasticity within DN(s).

3. Elements of a complex system are interactive, and their interaction is dynamic. Interactions in complex systems do not have to be physical; they have to be informative (i.e., guarantee the exchange of information).

To appreciate this feature of DN as a complex system, consider the following example. Researchers (Riggins-Caspers et al., 1999) examined the presence of a gene–environment interaction between adoptive-parent knowledge about biological-parent characteristics and biological-parent psychopathology. Adoptive-parent knowledge was the specific environmental effect and comprised three categories: none, physical, and medical. Biological-parent alcoholism and antisocial personality were the specific genetic effects. Dependent variables were adoptees' symptom counts of childhood and adult problem behavior. The results revealed the presence of a genetic effect only in the presence of either physical or medical knowledge. Several explanations are possible, which link the finding to the effects of recall bias: (a) adoptive parents might be more likely to remember negative things about the biological parents if the adoptee presented problems later; (b) adoptive parents might be more likely to remember more "severe" information, such increased awareness about biological parents, which might increase monitoring of the adoptee, regardless of the nature of the information; and (c) giving adoptive parents negative social or psychological information about the biological parents of the adoptee could result in a negative halo effect (adoptive parents who perceived the biological parents negatively also perceived the adoptees more negatively; Berry, 1992).

Bluebond-Langner (1978) worked with children with leukemia treated in North America. In her detailed accounts of the lives of these children, she described various ways in which children learned their own and other children's prognoses. Children learned about their illnesses through tacit knowledge of both treatment schemes and adult behaviors toward them. Moreover, children learned how to shield adults from the knowledge of their awareness of their own prognoses, believing that the parents preferred them not to know.

4. Complex systems' interactions are multidimensional and redundant; every (or almost every) element can be influenced by many other elements

and, in turn, can influence many other elements. Potentially, parsimonious and strong interactions exist that single-handedly can perform a given function, but the same function can also be performed by a number of sparsely connected elements.

In a DN, the security and the development of a newborn can be most robustly and parsimoniously guaranteed by the infant's mother. However, there are numerous mechanisms built into the infant's DN that will trigger protective and caring behaviors in adults other than the infant's mother. One such mechanism is the physical peculiarities of a human baby. The human brain achieves adult size when body growth is only 40% complete, dental maturation is only 58% complete, and reproductive maturation is only 10% complete (Bogin, 1999). Such disproportion of growth is evident in the appearance of infants (large cranium, small face and body, little sexual development), which, in turn, stimulates caregiving and protecting behaviors in older individuals. In fact, a human child maintains an infantile appearance longest among all mammalian species. Thus, the infantile appearance of children stimulates nurturing behaviors in other older individuals, in case there is a need to substitute for the infant's mother. Another mechanism, which assures the redundancy of infant protection and care, is the availability of both adolescents (individuals who are psychologically mature but sexually immature and, therefore, unoccupied with their own reproductive cycle) and grandparents (postreproductive individuals who also can offer substantial care to an infant or child).

5. Complex systems' interactions are characterized by a number of important features, of which the most important one is nonlinearity. When a system's elements are connected linearly, their relations can usually be collapsed into an equivalent system whose dimensionality is significantly smaller. The dimensionality of a complex system is usually irreducible. Moreover, nonlinearity of complex systems guarantees that small causes can have large results, and vice versa.

One of many examples of nonlinearity of interactions within DNs is that describing gene—environment interaction. For example, Cadoret and colleagues (Cadoret, Yates, Toughton, Woodworth, & Stewart, 1995; Cadoret et al., 1996; Ge et al., 1996) reported the importance of taking into account the gene—environment interaction in predicting adolescent aggression, adolescent conduct disorder, and adult major depression. Specifically, the authors showed increases in adoptee child and adolescent aggression and conduct disorder symptoms when an antisocial biological background and adverse adoptive home factors were both present. On the other hand, no effects of an adverse home environment were found for adoptees low on the genetic propensity for antisocial personality (Cadoret et al., 1995; Ge et al., 1996). In studying adult major depression (Cadoret et al., 1996), the researchers discovered that female (but not male) adoptees who had an alcoholic biologic background and who were placed into an adverse adoptive home had a greater likelihood of experiencing major depression. Female adoptees without the alcoholic biological background, regardless of environmental conditions, were not at an increased risk for major depression.

Another example of nonlinear interactions of the developmental niche's components comes from studies on the effects of socioeconomic status (SES) on child development. It has been shown that correlations between measures of income or SES and basic child outcomes tend to be higher in the United States than in other countries (Bronfenbrenner, 1986). When these correlational differences were compared, it became evident that low income is a better predictor of childhood deficits in the United States than in other countries because the social policies of the United States tend to increase rather than minimize the impact of family income on access to preventive, rehabilitative, and development-stimulating services. In other words, it is not poverty (or wealth) that matters. What matters is the availability of social services in a given society in exchange for money.

6. Some (often many) interactions in complex systems are recurrent (i.e., contain loops). In other words, the effect of any activity in a complex system can turn back onto itself, sometimes directly, sometimes after a number of intervening stages. The nature of feedback can vary—it can be positive (enhancing, stimulating), negative (detracting, inhibiting), or mixed (suppressing certain characteristics of the activity and promoting others).

One of the best illustrations of this property of the DN as a complex system emerged from the work of Patterson and his colleagues, who carried out a series of studies on the origins of antisocial behavior in children (Patterson, 1986). In the Patterson model, children who engage in noncompliant behaviors (developmentally appropriate during early childhood), elicit incompetent disciplining from some parents. Such disciplining, instead of preventing, reinforces old noncompliant behaviors or results in other maladaptive responses (e.g., whining, teasing, yelling, and throwing temper tantrums). These reactive maladaptive behaviors, in turn, escalate parental negative coercive responses that promote further child noncompliance, which might develop into strong aggression (direct and indirect), verbal as well as physical. Such noncompliant children tend to engage in poor interactions with peers and to ignore social norms. Patterson and colleagues demonstrated this sequence originating from "normal" noncompliance and leading to antisocial behavior, school failure, and accumulation of aggression.

In a different study, researchers showed that social peculiarities of the DN influence the biological functioning of children developing in this niche. Flinn, England, and their colleagues (Flinn & England, 1995, 1997; Flinn, Quinlan, Decker, Turner, & England, 1996) studied hormonal stress in children in families of various configurations as expressed in levels of cortisol, one of the major hormones produced in response to physical and psychosocial stressors. The researchers reported a number of striking findings: (a) the average cortisol levels of stepchildren are significantly higher than are those of biological children who live in the same household, (b) children in households who experience marital conflict show abnormally higher cortisol profiles following events of discord, and (c) a parent's absence (both brief and prolonged) is associated with cortisol level (effects are differential for mothers and fathers and boys and girls). Specifically, in one of their studies, Flinn and England (1997) worked for 8 years with 264 children (age 2 months to 18 years) from 82 households in a rural village of the Caribbean island of Dominica (Flinn & England, 1997). The main objective of the study was to investigate family environment and childhood stress response. The researchers collected (a) detailed ethnographic data on the children's individual histories and characteristics of their personalities, (b) behavioral observations and clinical information on symptoms of ill health, and (c) data on hormonal stress using salivary assays of cortisol.

The results revealed that household composition had a strong association with cortisol profiles. Specifically, children who lived with either distant relatives, stepfathers, or single mothers without kin support had significantly higher cortisol profiles than children who lived with both parents, single parents with kin, or grandparents. One of the many interesting aspects of these data is that episodes of ill health seemed to follow changes in cortisol responses. For example, Panter-Brick (1999) cited data, according to which, morbidity (principally from upper respiratory tract infections) is elevated by 17% above baseline levels following a lifestyle stressor (e.g., family fight), by 31% following an increase in cortisol level, and by 82% where both these conditions occur. Yet these data are not easy to interpret. Specifically, Pollard (1995) stated that cortisol is not a simple "stress hormone;" it reflects general emotional arousal rather than just distress. Thus, low cortisol levels may indicate low external stress or a blunted response to stress. Panter-Brick, Worthman, Lunn, and Todd (1996) found that a mixed group of Nepali children (aged 10 to 14—homeless, slum, school, and village boys) exhibited a 1.3 to 2.4 times lower level of cortisol than is considered to be typical for children of their ages. It is also interesting that, although homeless boys demonstrated higher mean cortisol values than villagers, they showed low cortisol variance, which possibly indicated low reactivity to day-to-day events or blunted response to stress (despite the obvious instability of their everyday lives).

Thus, many interactions within developmental niches form loops that either suppress or reinforce initial relations.

7. Complex systems tend to be open (i.e., they interact with their environment), so that sometimes it is difficult to define their borders. Therefore, the scope of the system is usually determined by framing—the purpose/observer-dependent description of the system.

No DN is fixed. The essence of the DN is its openness to the environment. For example, when children in a community that has previously had no schools begin to attend school, their DNs change. Their lives become different from those of children who never went to school in more ways than in what they learn, and how. They become subject to an authority outside the family and are increasingly connected to a wider social world outside the community (LeVine, 1999).

Studying the DN is based on understanding and appreciating the outcome of a change that occurs in response to a modification in the environment. Such "sensitivity to change" is central to a number of fields in the human sciences. Thus, biological anthropology stresses the importance of a research perspective that examines human behavior (of men, women, and children) elicited in response to external challenges from physical or socioeconomic environments. This research seeks to document the relative costs and benefits of observed behaviors in terms of short-term and long-term consequences, particularly for health (Carey, 1990; Harrison, 1993; Ulijaszek & Strickland, 1993).

Two of the immediate indicators of the well-being of children are rates of mortality and growth. Both of these characteristics are sensitive to changes in environmental conditions. For example, in 1662, John Gaunt recorded an infant mortality in Great Britain on the order of 300 deaths per 1,000 live births; by 1901, this rate was only 151 deaths; and by 1985, only 9.4 deaths per 1,000 live births (Pollard et al., 1974). In Gambia, the growth rate was shown to be related to the timing of the rainy season or seasons, through the influence of these seasons on food availability, parasite burden, and infection (Cole, 1993). Similarly, mortality rates have been shown to vary seasonally in Gambia and Nepal (Nabarro, 1984; Ulijaszek, 1993).

Hobcraft, McDonald, and Rutstein (1983) used the data from the 1976 World Fertility Survey and demonstrated the negative impact of closely spaced births on the survival of both index and subsequent children. Where birth intervals were short (less than 2 years apart), the index child showed a greater risk of mortality in 9 of the 23 countries studied; this could be explained by premature weaning if the mother was newly pregnant. The subsequent child also showed an elevated risk of death (by 50%) in 13 of the 23 countries surveyed; this could be explained either by a maternal depletion syndrome or by sibling competition for household and maternal attention. Another critical predictor of the mortality rates in poor countries is the mother's education (Cleland & van Ginneken, 1988).

The sensitivity and openness of the DN to the environment and environmental forces are also evident from studies of diversity of developmental milestones and the time of their occurrence around the world. For example, it has been shown that the attainment of motor milestones in the first and second years of life (sitting, standing, walking) can be accelerated or slowed down according to cultural peculiarities, parental preferences, and physical settings. Specifically, Super (1976) found that East African infants who exhibited "precocious" motor skills had been trained by parents who sought to facilitate the early development of these skills, and that parents of the same ethnic group who lived in urban areas and who had obtained at least some school education were less likely to provide this facilitation or to have infants with as early a development of motor skills. In a study of the motor development of infants in the Yucatan peninsula of Mexico, Solomons and Solomons (1975) found that Yucatan infants showed earlier acquisition of fine motor skills but showed delayed gross motor coordination compared with their U.S. peers. Specifically, Mexican children's scores on the Bayley Infant Motor Scale were lower for the items evaluating children's skills in cruising. It became apparent that these differences could be explained by differences in the settings in which U.S. and Mexican children are brought up. Thus, the Yucatan household had less furniture, such as tables and chairs, which provided the infant with fewer objects to use for cruising. Moreover, many Mayan Yucatan families still used dirt floors, on which parents were reluctant to place their children. In other words, Mexican parents were not providing the opportunity for their children to begin cruising as early as U.S. parents.

A similar set of results was obtained from a study of neonatal behavior in urban Zambians and Americans (Brazelton, Koslowski, & Tronick, 1993). When a group of Zambian and American infants were assessed for the first time (Day 1), the results suggested that Zambian infants lagged behind U.S. infants on several indices, including following with eyes, motor ability, and irritability. But by the time of the second assessment (Day 10), the Zambian infants showed greatly improved muscle tone and scored higher than the U.S. infants on indices associated with social responsivity (consolability, social interest, and alertness). This outcome was shown to be related to the kind of social and motor stimulation received by the infants. Specifically, Zambian mothers tended to engage in frequent vigorous bouncing behaviors with their newborns, and they rode their newborns around wrapped in a long piece of cloth, so that the infant, in order to keep his head steady, had to maintain a strong shoulder girdle and muscle tone and was constantly stimulated tactilely.

8. Complex systems operate primarily under conditions of dynamic equilibrium or disequilibrium to guarantee a constant flow of energy.

A DN is always in dynamic equilibrium, going through stages of disequilibrium to a subsequent succession of states. A DN is always "out-of-balance;" its essence is change. DN is where environmental changes occur and where they get lost. Given that DNs are so individually tailored to their occupants, environmental changes being dramatic and huge for any given individual, they appear to be short-lived for groups of individuals or across a life span (Dickens & Flynn, 1999). Both the magnitude and the rate of changes in DN are amazing, but individual-specific—that is why it is difficult to register these changes in large-scale studies. There are a number of interesting stories regarding apes raised in human cultural environments. Savage-Rumbaugh et al. (1986, 1993) tried to teach a wild-born bonobo (pygmy chimpanzee), Matata, a graphic symbol system. Matata's son Kanzi spent his first 2½ years holding onto and observing his mother while she was interacting with humans around the keyboard. Matata was not successful in acquiring linguistic skills, but Kanzi was. The peculiarities of his DN permitted him to master certain linguistic skills. However, it was a unique and short-lived accomplishment, specific to Kanzi and not preservable for the bonobo as a group.

Characterizing this feature of DN as a complex system, it is important to mention two fundamental concepts: *adaptation* and *accommodation*. Adaptation describes a beneficial response to poor environments, whereas accommodation draws attention to both the costs and benefits of a coping behavior (Frisancho, 1993; Scrimshaw & Young, 1989). For example, acquiring points of IQ in each subsequent generation is regarded as adaptation to the growing complexity of the world (Flynn, 1998); growth retardation is regarded as accommo-dation (Panter-Brick, 1999).

9. Complex systems have histories, that is, they evolve through time and their past is coresponsible for their present. Therefore, complex systems can be studied only within the dimension of time; nondevelopmental research re-sults not in understanding complex systems, but rather in taking snapshots.

Bogin (1999), based on the work of Martin (1995) and Harvey, Martin, and Clutton-Brock (1987), analyzed patterns of brain and body growth in apes, hu-mans, and their ancestors. The pattern of brain growth in apes and humans dif-fers: Specifically, apes' pattern of brain growth is rapid before birth and relatively slow after birth. Humans have rapid brain growth both before and after birth. Prenatally, relative to body size the human neonatal brain size is 1.33 times larger than that of the great apes; in adulthood the difference is 3.5 times. Given the mean rate of postnatal brain growth for living apes, the ratio of 3.5 times can be achieved by all hominoids (including extinct ones) by lengthening the foetal stage of growth. That is how, Bogin argued (1999), the human pattern of early development appeared—namely, the pattern characterized by rapid postnatal brain growth and slow body growth. In both apes and humans, brain growth ends at the start of the juvenile stage. But apes complete their brain growth dur-ing infancy, whereas human beings, in order to provide the time and continua-tion of parental caring necessary to grow the larger human brain, have childhood between the infant and juvenile stages. According to modern esti-mates, in humans, brain growth in weight is complete at the mean age of 7 years (Cabana, Jolicouer, & Michaud, 1993).

To explain this pattern of human development, Bogin (1999), over and above the traditional brain—learning explanations (extended period for brain growth, time for acquisition of technical skills, time for socialization), enforced an evolutionary perspective on the emergence of childhood. In particular, he viewed childhood as a "feeding and reproductive adaptation for the parents of the child as a strategy to minimize the risks of starvation and predation for the child, and as a mechanism that allows for more precise "tracking" of ecological conditions via developmental plasticity during the growing years" (p. 30). In support of his hypothesis regarding the evolution of childhood, Bogin (1999), presented a work-in-progress summary of the evolution of the human pattern of growth and development from birth to age 20 years. Both chimpanzee and *Australopithecus afarensis* (a hominid who shares many anatomical features with nonhominid species) have an adult brain size of about 400 cc and share the typi-cal tripartite stages (infancy, juvenile, adult) of postnatal growth of social mammals. The achievement of the larger adult brain size of A. *africanus* (442 cc) required lengthening of infancy, suggested Bogin. The rapid expansion of adult brain size in *Homo habilis* (650 to 800 cc) was probably supported by both a lengthening the infancy and the addition of a brief childhood period. The brain of *Homo erectus* expanded in size even further (850 to 900 cc). Bogin suggested that, during this period, childhood increased while infancy decreased in length, giving hominoids time both to grow the brain and attain reproductive advantage. (Having longer nursing is consequential because it precludes more frequent reproduction. Thus, the female chimpanzee waits for 5.6 years between successful birth of offspring, the orangutan—7.7 years; whereas a female of the !Kung traditional society of hunters and gatherers produces births about every 3.6 years.) Later *H. erectus*, whose adult brain size reached up to 1,100 cc and who demonstrated increased complexity of social structure and technology, further expanded childhood and introduced a period of adolescence. Finally, modern *H. sapiens* expanded both childhood and adolescent periods even further, to its current dimension.

The addition of childhood and adolescent stages and the prolongation of the juvenile stage of human development, among other things: (a) guarantees the transition between the infant's dependency on the mother for food via nursing and the feeding independence of the juvenile, (b) delays the age of both menarche and first birth, and (c) decreases the birth spacing interval and increases the number of offspring a female can produce during her life. The entire process results in increased reproductive fitness if the additional offspring survive to maturity. Monkeys and apes rear between 12% and 36% of live-born offspring to adulthood. Humans in traditional societies (i.e., hunters, gatherers, horticulturalists) rear about 50% of their live-born offspring to adulthood.

Human parents help to ensure the survival of their offspring by sharing this responsibility and collectively provisioning all their children with food. Anthropological studies have revealed an amazing amount of variability in how this provisioning is accomplished. In a hunter–gatherer society of Hazga, a significant amount of food for children is provided by grandmothers and great-aunts (Blurton Jones, 1990). In the Philippine hunter–gatherer society of Agta, where women are also hunters, people live in extended family groups (siblings, their spouses, children, and parents; Goodman, Griffin, Estioko-Griffin, & Grove, 1986). The Aka Pygmies, a hunting–gathering people of central Africa, take their children with them on hunting trips (Hewlitt, 1991).

This example encompasses the history of the development of childhood as the human-species-specific DN. Moreover, each individual DN has a trajectory of development, developing and changing along with its occupant.

10. Complex systems behave as if goal-related. They show adaptation and purpose, even though they do not sense to have a conscious idea of goal and purpose.

This characteristic of DN as a complex system brings us back to one of the modern axioms of the developmental psychology—irrespective of the characteristics of environment in which they exist, various cultures manage to structure DN(s) of their children in such a way that they produce competent and skilled bearers and promoters of that culture. For example, most rural communities of the world experience chronic or acute shortages of manpower; to distribute the load of work and to free a senior man in a household for more profitable tasks, among the Andean Quechua, most of herding is done by children rather than adults (Leonard & Thomas, 1989; Thomas, 1976).

Cultures are extremely imaginative in terms of shaping and forming DN(s) of their children. Thus, even "similar" cultures (e.g., cultures of hunters and gatherers) differ in the ways they socialize their children. For example, Hadza children, at 7 years of age, routinely walk a 10 km round trip to berry groves. In contrast, !Kung children are seldom expected to help adults forage for food until the age of 10.

Cooper and colleagues (1994) studied the accommodation that parents make when they immigrate to a new culture. In particular, the researchers compared the aspirations and guidance of low-income Mexican immigrants to the United States and Euro-American parents of children and adolescents. The main differentiator of the two samples of parents was that of education obtained (Mexican-American parents, on average, completed only elementary grades, whereas Euro-American parents, on average, completed high school grades and some college). Most Mexican-American families reported that they moved to the United States because they wanted their children to get a better education and to learn English. Yet, despite their verbal commitment to education, support, and encouragement, Mexican-American families were unable to help or inspire their children after they graduated from elementary schools; the third grade appeared to be the threshold above which few Mexican-American parents were able to provide any school-rated scaffolding to their children. In fact, the domain of schooling became a responsibility of the children. Thus, by Grade 5, the most distinct differences between the average DN(s) of the low-income Mexican-American children whose parents immigrated to the United States and the low-income Euro-American children was in that the involvement of Mexican-American parents in their children's school affairs was minimal. To maintain conceptual continuity, to strengthen relationships with their children in the absence of their ability to contribute to their school experience, Mexican-American parents tended to pay much more attention to the social skills of their children.

In closing, until the 1950s, systematic studies of complexity were avoided. One of the major reasons for this scientific "inclination" was that simplifying generalizations of physics had generated an apparently adequate account of the universe as we knew it then. Since that time, researchers have learned a tremendous amount about the universe and, having exceeded the potential of simple generalizations, developed various types of theories of complexity (e.g., systems theory or chaos theory).

In this chapter, I presented a number of characteristics of complex systems and mapped them on the data available in developmental psychology. I argued that the concept of DN appears to be instrumental in representing the axioms of developmental psychology and providing an interpretive framework for developmental findings. I tried to demonstrate how the concept of DN (a) addresses the diversity of the world and the variability of the patterns of development, (b) encompasses the idea of change and evolution, and (c) admits the conceptual continuity of human development. I attempted to show that a closer look at the data accumulated in developmental psychology and specific characteristics of DN as a complex system shows the limitations of analytical methods when dealing with complexity of development.

The usefulness of analytical approaches is not in question, but the "analysis" of complex systems has been shown to impose serious distortions by "cutting out" parts of the system and ignoring complex interplays of the system's factors and components. Analytical approaches to complex systems have provided us with a meaningful insight—that complexity is incompressible. This suggests that in order to study complex systems we have to come up with ways of preserving the complexity itself. Because the purpose of models is to replicate the wholeness of the structure studied, the best available method of studying complex systems is via modeling. Computer technology has presented us with new possibilities of modeling complex systems.

REFERENCES

Bakeman, R., & Gottman, J. M. (1986). *Observing interaction: An introduction to sequential analysis*. New York: Cambridge University Press.

Berry, M. (1992). Contributions to adjustment problems of adoptees: A review of the longitudinal research. *Child & Adolescent Social Work Journal 9*(6), 525–540.

Bluebond-Langner, M. (1978). *The private world of dying children*. Princeton, NJ: Princeton University Press.

Blurton Jones, N. G. (1990). Three sensible paradigms for research on evolution and human behavior. *Ethology & Sociobiology, 11*(4–5), 353–359.

Bogin, B. (1999). Evolutionary and biological aspects of childhood. In C. Panter-Brick (Ed.), *Biological perspectives on children* (pp. 10–44). Cambridge, UK: Cambridge University Press.

Brazelton, T. B., Koslowski, B., & Tronick, E. (1993). Neonatal behavior among urban Zambians and Americans. In M. Gauvain & M. Cole (Eds.), *Readings on the development* (pp. 63–69). New York: Freeman.

Bronfenbrenner, U. (1986). Ecology of the family as a context for human development research perspectives. *Developmental Psychology, 22,* 723–742.

Cabana, T., Jolicoeur, P., & Michaud, J. (1993). Prenatal and postnatal growth and allometry of stature, head circumstance, and brain weight in Quebec children. *American Journal of Human Biology, 5,* 93–99.

Cadoret, R. J., Yates, W., Troughton, E., Woodworth, G., & Stewart, M. (1995). Genetic–environmental interaction in the genesis of aggressivity and conduct disorders. *Archives of General Psychiatry, 52,* 916–924.

Cadoret, R. J., Winokur, G., Langbehn, D., Troughton, E., Yates, W., & Stewart, M. A. (1996). Depressive spectrum disease, I: The role of gene–environment interaction. *American Journal of Psychiatry, 153,* 892–899.

Cain, M. (1977). The economic activities of children in a village in Bangladesh. *Population and Development Review, 3,* 201–227.

Carey, J. W. (1990). Social system effects on local level morbidity and adaptation in the rural Peruvian Andes. *Medical Anthropology Quarterly, 4,* 266–295.

Cherrett, J. M. (1989). Key concepts: The results of a survey of our members' opinions. In J. M. Cherrett (Ed.), *Ecological concepts* (pp. 1–16). Oxford, England: Blackwell Scientific Publications.

Cilliers, P. (1998). Complexity and postmodernism: Understanding complex systems. New York: Routledge.

Cleland, J., & van Ginneken, J. K. (1988). Maternal education and child survival in developing countries. The search for pathways of influence. *Social Science and Medicine, 27,* 1357–1368.

Cole, T. J. (1993). Seasonal effects on physical growth and development. In S. J. Ulijaszek & S. Strickland (Eds.), *Seasonality and Human Ecology* (pp. 89–106). Cambridge, UK: Cambridge University Press.

Cooper, C. R., Azmitia, M., Garcia, E. E., Ittel, A., Lopez, E., Rivera, L., & Martinez-Chavez, R. (1994). Aspirations of low-income Mexican American and European American parents for their children and adolescents. In F. A. Villarruel & R. M. Lerner (Eds.), *Promoting community-based programs for socialization and learning. New directions for child development* (Vol. 63, pp. 65–81) San Francisco, CA: Jossey-Bass.

Current Events. (1993). *School violence, 93,* 12.

Dickens, W. T., & Flynn, J. R. (1999). *Heritability estimates vs. large environmental effects: The IQ paradox resolved.* Unpublished manuscript.

Flake, G. H. (1998). The computational beauty of nature: Computer explorations of fractals, chaos, complex systems, and adaptation. Cambridge, MA: MIT Press.

Flinn, M. V., & England, B. G. (1995). Childhood stress and family environment. *Current Anthropology, 36,* 854–866.

Flinn, M. V., & England, B. G. (1997). Social economics of childhood glucocorticoid stress response and health. *American Journal of Physical Anthropology, 102,* 33–53.

Flinn, M. V., Quinlan, R. J., Decker, S. A., Turner, M. T., & England, B. G. (1996). Male–female differences in effects of parental absense on glucocorticoid stress response. *Human Nature, 7*(2), 125–162.

Flynn, J. R. (1998). IQ gains over time: toward finding the cause. In U. Neisser (Ed.), *The rising curve: Long term gains in IQ and related measure*. Washington, DC: American Psychological Association, 25–66.

Frisancho, A. R. (1993). *Human adaptation and accommodation* (enlarged edition). Ann Arbor: The University of Michigan.

Gauvain, M. (1995). Thinking in niches: Sociocultural influences on cognitive development. *Human Development, 38*, 25–45.

Ge, X., Conger, R. D., Cadoret, R. J., Neiderhiser, J. M., Yates, W., Toughton, E., & Stewart, M. A. (1996). The developmental interface between nature and nurture: A mutual influence model of child antisocial behavior and parent behaviors. *Developmental Psychology, 32*, 574–589.

Goodman, M. J., Griffin, P. B., Estioko-Griffin, A. A., Grove, J. S. (1986). The compatibility of hunting and mothering among the Agta hunter–gatherers of the Phillippines. *Sex Roles, 12*(11–12), 1199–1209.

Harris, J. R. (1998). *The nurture assumption: Why children turn out the way they do*. New York: The Free Press.

Harrison, G. A. (1993). *Human adaptation. Biosocial Society Series* (No. 6). Oxford, England: Oxford Science Publications.

Harvey, P. H., Martin, R. D., & Clutton-Brock, T. H. (1987). Life histories in comparative perspective. In B. B. Smuts, D. L. Cheney, R. M. Seyfarth, R. W. Wrangham, & T. T. Struhsaker (Eds.), *Primate societies* (pp. 181–196). Chicago: University of Chicago Press.

Herrmann, H. (1998). *From biology to sociopolitics: Conceptual continuity in complex systems*. New Haven, CT: Yale University Press.

Hewlitt, B. S. (1991). *Intimate fathers: The nature and context of Aka Pygmy paternal care*. Ann Arbor: University of Michigan Press.

Hobcraft, J. N., McDonald, J. W., & Rutstein, S. O. (1983). Child-spacing effects on infant and early child mortality. *Population Index, 49*, 585–618.

Hutchinson, G. E. (1957). Concluding remarks. *Cold Spring Harbor Symposium on Quantitative Biology, 22*, 415–427.

Hutchinson, G. E. (1978). *An introduction to population ecology*. New Haven, CT: Yale University Press.

James, A. (1999). From the child's point of view: Issues in the social construction of childhood. In C. Panter-Brick (Ed.), *Biological perspectives on children* (pp. 45–65). Cambridge, England: Cambridge University Press.

Johnson, V., Hill, J., & Ivan-Smith, E. (1995). *Listening to the smaller voices: Children in an environment of change*. London: Action Aid.

Kirkland, J., & Morgan, G. A. V. (1991). Radical ecology. *Early Child Development and Care, 72*, 93–98.

Leonard, W. R., & Thomas, R. B. (1989). Biosocial responses to seasonal food stress in highland Peru. *Human Biology, 61*, 65–85.

LeVine, R. (1999). Child psychology and anthropology: An environmental view. In C. Panter-Brick (Ed.), *Biological perspectives on children* (pp. 102–130). Cambridge, England: Cambridge University Press.

Magnusson, D. (1988). *Individual differences from an interactional perspective*. Hillsdale, NJ: Lawrence Erlbaum Associates.

Magnusson, D. (1993). Human ontogeny: A longitudinal perspective. In D. Magnusson & P. Casaer (Eds.), *Longitudinal research on individual development* (pp. 1–25). Cambridge, England: Cambridge University Press.

Magnusson, D., & Bergman, L. (1990). A pattern approach to the study of pathways from childhood to adulthood. In L. Robins & M. Rutter (Eds.), *Straight and devious pathways from childhood to adulthood* (pp. 101–115). Cambridge, England: Cambridge University Press. Martin, R. D. (1983). *Human brain evolution in an ecological context* (Fifty-second James Arthur Lecture). New York: American Museum of Natural History.

Martin, R. D. (1995). Phylogenetic aspects of primate reproduction: The context of advanced maternal care. In C. R. Pryce & R. D. Martib (Eds.), *Motherhood in human and nonhuman primates: Biosocial determinants* (pp. 16–26). Basel, Switzerland: S. Karger.

Munson, B. H. (1994). Ecological misconceptions. *Journal of Environmental Education, 25,* 30–34.

Nabarro, D. (1984). Social, economic, health and environmental determinants of nutritional status. *Food and Nutrition Bulletin, 6,* 18–32.

Nag, M., White, B., & Peet, R. C. (1978). An anthropological approach to the study of the economic value of children in Java and Nepal. *Current Anthropology, 19,* 292–306.

Neiuwenhuys, O. (1994). *Children's lifeworlds—gender, welfare, and labour in the developing world.* London: Routledge.

Pachter, L. M., & Hardwood, R. L. (1996). Culture and child behavior and psychosocial development. *Journal of Development & Behavioral Pediatrics, 17*(3), 191–198.

Panter-Brick, C., Worthman, C., Lunn, P., & Todd, A. (1996). Urban-rural and class differences in biological markers of stress among Nepali children. *American Journal of Human Biology, 8,* 126.

Panter-Brick, C. (1999). Biological anthropology and child health: Context, process and outcome. In C. Panter-Brick (Ed.), *Biological Perspectives on Children* (pp. 66–101). Cambridge, England: Cambridge University Press.

Patterson, G. R. (1986). Performance models for antisocial boys. *American Psychologist, 41,* 432–444.

Pianka, E. R. (1978). *Evolutionary ecology* (2nd ed.). New York: Harper & Row.

Pollard, A. H., Yusef, F., & Pollard, G. N. (1974). *Demographic techniques.* Australia: Pergamon Press.

Pollard, T. (1995). Use of cortisol as a stress marker: Practical and theoretical problems. *American Journal of Human Biology, 7,* 265–274.

Qvortrup, J., Bardy, M., Saritta, G., & Wintersberger, H. (Eds.). (1994). *Childhood matters: Social theory, practice and politics.* Aldershot Brookfield, VT: Averbury.

Reiss, D. (1989). The represented and practicing family: Contrasting visions of family continuity. In A. J. Sameroff & R. N. Emde (Eds.), *Relationship disturbance in early childhood* (pp. 191–220). New York: Basic Books.

Riggins-Caspers, K., Cadoret, R. J., Panak, W., Lempers, J. D., Troughton, E., Stewart, M. A. (1990). Gene environment interaction and the moderating effect of adoption agency disclosure on estimating genetic effects. *Personality and Individual Differences, 27*(2), 357–380.

Roughgarden, J. (1979). *Theory of population genetics and evolutionary ecology: An introduction.* New York: Macmillan.

Sackett, G. P. (1979). The lag sequential analysis of contingency and cyclicity in behavioral interaction research. In J. Osofsky (Ed.), *Handbook of infant development* (pp. 623–649). New York: Wiley.

Sameroff, A. (1994). Developmental systems and family functioning. In R. D. Parker & S. G. Kellam (Ed.), *Exploring family relationships with other social contexts.* Family research consortium: Advances in family research (pp. 199–214). Hillsdale, NJ: Lawrence Erlbaum Associates.

Sameroff, A. J., & Seifer, R. (1995). Accumulation of environmental risk and child mental health. In H. E. Fitzgerald & B. M. Lester (Ed.), *Children of poverty: Research, health, and policy issues*. Reference books on family issues, Vol. 23 and Garland reference library of social science, Vol. 968. (pp. 233–258). New York: Garland.

Sameroff, A. J., Seifer, R., Barocas, R., Zax, M., & Greenspan, S. (1987). Intelligence quotient scores of 4-year-old children: Social environmental risk factors. *Pediatrics, 79*, 343–350.

Savage-Rumbaugh, E. S. (1986). *Ape language: From conditioned response to symbol*. New York: Columbia University Press.

Savage-Rumbaugh, E. S., & Rumbaugh, D. M. (1993). In K. R. Gibson & T. Ingold (Eds.), *Tools, language, and cognition in human evolution* (pp. 876–108). Cambridge, England: Cambridge University Press.

Scarr, S. (1993). Biological and cultural diversity: The legacy of Darwin for development. *Child Development, 64*, 1333–1353.

Scrimshaw, N. S., & Young, V. R. (1989). Adaptation to low protein and energy intakes. *Human Organization, 48*, 20–30.

Solomons, G., & Solomons, H. C. (1975). Motor development in Yucatecan infants. *Developmental Medicine and Child Neurology, 17*, 41–46.

Super, C. (1976). Environmental influences on motor development: The case of 'African infant precocity.' *Developmental Medicine and Child Neurology, 18*, 561–567.

Super, C., & Harkness, S. (1986). The developmental niche: A conceptualization at the interface of child and culture. *International Journal of Behavioral Development, 9*, 545–569.

Stearns, S. C. (1992). *The evolution of life histories*. Oxford, England: Oxford University Press.

Stevens, S. (Ed.). (1995). *Children and the politics of culture*. Princeton, NJ: Princeton University Press.

Thomas, R. B. (1976). Energy flow at high altitude. In P. T. Baker & M. A. Little (Eds.), *Man in the Andes: A multi-disciplinary study of high altitude*. Qechua (pp. 379–404). Stroudsburg, PA: Dowden, Hutchinson, & Ross.

Ulijaszek, S. J. (1993). Seasonality of reproductive performance in rural land. In S. J. Ulijaszek & S. Strickland (Eds.), *Seasonality and human ecology* (pp. 76–88). Cambridge, England: Cambridge University Press.

Ulijaszek, S. J., & Strickland, S. S. (1993). *Nutritional anthropology—prospects and perspectives*. London: Smith-Gordon.

Von Uxekull, J. J. (1864). *Theoretical biology*. London: Kegan Paul.

Wachs, T. D. (1996). Known and potential processes underlying developmental trajectories in childhood and adolescence. *Developmental Psychology, 32*, 796–801.

Walch, A. (1999). War, wealth, and water … kids, condoms, and CDs. *Newsweek, December-Special Edition*, 72–75.

West, M. J., & King, A. P. (1987). Settling nature and nurture into an ontogenetic niche. *Developmental Psychology, 20*, 549–562.

3

Family Capital and Cognitive Performance

Kevin Marjoribanks
The Graduate School of Education
University of Adelaide, Australia

In the report of the Task Force established by the American Psychological Association to examine issues associated with the nature of intelligence and the meaning of intelligence test scores, Neisser et al. (1996) concluded that "the environmental contributions to those [individual] differences [in intelligence] are almost equally mysterious. We know that biological and social aspects of the environment are important for intelligence, but we are a long way from understanding how they exert their effects" (p. 96). This chapter develops a moderation–mediation model to examine relationships between family capital and children's cognitive performance. The model is generated from Bourdieu's theory of the social trajectory of individuals and from the bioecological model of human development proposed by Bronfenbrenner and Ceci (1994) and Ceci, Rosenblum, de Bruyn, and Lee (1997).

Bourdieu (1977, 1984, 1988) claimed that academic success in school is associated with two effects that may either reinforce or offset each other. First, there is an inculcation effect exerted directly by families or by the individual's initial social conditions. Second, there is a specific effect related to an individual's system of dispositions or habitus that acts as a mediation between family influences and eventual academic outcomes. Bourdieu (1984) indicated that "all positions of arrival are not equally probable from all starting points" (p. 110). Although individuals are subject to the forces that structure their social space, they may resist "the forces of the field with their specific inertia, that is, their properties, which may exist in embodied form, as dispositions, or in objectified form, in goods, qualifications, etc." (p. 110). Aschaffenburg and Maas (1997) observed that according to Bourdieu's field theory, "students from families with the skills and preferences of the dominant culture are better able to decode the implicit 'rules of the game,' are able to adapt and further develop the cultural skills and preferences rewarded in the schools, and hence are better able to negotiate their way through the highest educational levels" (p. 573).

In this chapter, I propose that for school academic performance, a cognitive habitus may develop, which mediates relationships between family influences and measures of achievement. Sternberg and Grigorenko (1997) suggested that "perhaps prediction of achievement could be improved by adding measures of [cognitive] styles to measures of abilities as predictors of performance" (p. 710). For this analysis, it was considered that prediction of achievement could be improved by adding a measure of cognitive attitudes to a measure of ability as predictors of performance and as dimensions of the children's cognitive habitus. Although the cognitive habitus was defined as consisting of cognitive ability and cognitive attitudes, it is considered that such a habitus is evolving and would incorporate successive cognitive performance and any attitude change, to provide a more comprehensive mediation between structures and practice throughout the life span. As Bourdieu (1977) indicated "it becomes necessary to study the laws that determine the tendency of structures to reproduce themselves by producing agents with the system of predispositions which is capable of engendering practices adapted to the structures and thereby contributing to the reproduction of the structures" (p. 487).

The definition of cognitive habitus adopted in this chapter is considered to have characteristics similar to Sternberg's (1998) developing-expertise model of abilities in which he claimed that "both abilities and achievement are forms of developing expertise. Neither is psychologically prior although one or the other may be temporarily prior in a protocol of assessment" (p. 16). Also, there are similarities with Vygotsky's zone of proximal development, which as Grigorenko and Kornilova (1997) indicated, is "a zone in which the actual level of intellectual development can be changed … in the zone of proximal development, children can change their levels of achievement with a teacher's help" (p. 416). In the context of the present chapter, associations between the developing cognitive habitus and academic performance are related to the help provided by parents. That is, the Bourdieu theory indicates that to understand differences in school academic success, it is necessary to examine to what extent measures of children's individual characteristics mediate relations between family social conditions and measures of academic performance.

In a further examination of relations among family social conditions, individual dispositions, and school-related outcomes, Bronfenbrenner and Ceci (1994) proposed that to explain variations in developmental outcomes it is necessary to understand relationships among distal environmental contexts, proximal settings, individual characteristics, and measures of those outcomes. They proposed:

> The form, power, content, and directions of the proximal processes affecting development vary systematically as a joint function of the characteristics of the developing person, of the environment- both immediate and more remote- in which the processes are taking place, and the nature of the developmental outcome under consideration. (p. 572)

In addition, Ceci et al. (1997) stated, "The efficacy of a proximal process is determined to a large degree by the distal environmental resources.… Proximal processes are the engines that actually drive the outcome but only if the distal resources can be imported into the process to make it effective" (p. 311). Also, the bioecological model infers that the relationships between individual characteristics and outcomes are moderated by distal contexts, whereas proximal settings mediate the influence of distal contexts on outcome measures. From the two theoretical frameworks, a moderation–mediation model of the relations between family influences and cognitive performance was developed for the present chapter.

A MODERATION–MEDIATION MODEL

Family Capital

Typically, in analyses of relationships between family background and students' school outcomes, distal family contexts are defined by global social categories such as socioeconomic status (SES). Rumberger (1995) observed, for example, that "Most empirical research on family background has focused on the structural characteristics of families, such as socioeconomic status and family structure" (p. 587). Bronfenbrenner (1994) indicated, however, the "necessity of going beyond the simple labels of class and culture to identify more specific social and psychological features at the macrosystem level that ultimately affect the particular conditions and processes occurring in the microsystems" (p. 1643). Similarly, Bottero (1998), Grusky and Sorensen (1998), Reay (1998), and Suzuki and Valencia (1997) proposed that conventional measures such as SES no longer capture the complexities of family social background. Reay (1998) claimed, for example, that "Class is a complicated mixture of the material, the discursive, psychological predispositions and sociological dispositions" (p. 272).

Distal Family Capital.   For this chapter, a refined definition of *distal family context* was developed from conceptual orientations proposed by Coleman (1988, 1990, 1997) and Darling and Steinberg (1993). Coleman examined the possible nature of the relationship between distal environmental contexts and proximal family settings and how that relationship might affect children's educational outcomes. He proposed that family influences are separable into components such as human and social capital. Human capital provides parents with the opportunity of creating supportive proximal learning settings, and it can be measured by indicators of family social status. As Wilson and Musick (1997) indicated, human capital refers to "those resources attached to individuals that make productive activities possible" (p. 698). Similarly, Caspi, Wright, Moffit, and Silva (1998) proposed that "Human capital refers to the resources, qualifications, skills, and knowledge that are available to and acquired by individuals" (p. 427). In contrast, social capital is generated from the strength of relationships between adults and children (Portes, 1998). It is the amount and quality of academic interaction between parents and children, for example, that provides access to parents' human capital. Coleman (1997) claimed "the education of a parent (or more generally, the parents' human capital) becomes available to the child if the relationship of the child to the parent is sufficiently strong that the human capital is transmitted" (p. 623).

In a further conceptual orientation relating to family capital, Darling and Steinberg (1993) proposed that family social capital is influenced by a context dimension in the form of parents' aspirations. They claimed that to understand relations among distal family contexts, family social capital, and children's outcomes, "one must disentangle three different aspects of parenting: the goal toward which socialization is directed, the parenting practices used by parents to help children reach those goals, and parenting style" (Darling & Steinberg, 1993, p. 488).

A combination of the conceptual orientations of Coleman and of Darling and Steinberg suggests that distal family capital might be defined by the dimensions of family human capital and parents' aspirations. There are differences, however, in the nature of the relationships among family social status measures and parents' aspirations for their children. Alexander, Entwisle, and Bedinger (1994) noted, for example, that in lower social status groups, parents often have particularly high aspirations for their children but they may be unable to put into practice those processes that might realize their aspirations. In contrast, many middle social status parents may express relatively moderate aspirations for their children because they consider that they can be realized (Hao & Bonstead-Bruns, 1998; Saha, 1997). Therefore, in the present chapter, distal family capital was defined conjointly by family human capital and by parents' aspirations for their children.

Family Social Capital. In the construction of a theory linking organizational and individual behavior, Coleman (1990) proposed:

> Social capital is defined by its function. It is not a single entity, but a variety of different entities having two characteristics in common: They all consist of some aspect of social structure, and they facilitate certain actions of individuals who are within the structure. Like other forms of capital, social capital is productive, making possible the achievement of certain ends that would not be attainable in its absence. A given form of social capital that is valuable in facilitating certain actions may be either useless or even harmful for others. Unlike other forms of capital, social capital inheres in the structure of relations between persons and among persons. (p. 302)

Darling and Steinberg (1993) claimed that children's academic performance is enhanced when parents' involvement in their children's learning is associated with certain parenting styles. They proposed that "Parenting practices are best understood as operating in fairly circumscribed socialization domains, such as academic achievement. Depending on the specific developmental outcome of interest, different parenting practices would be more or less important to investigate" (p. 493). As Hagan, MacMillan, and Wheaton (1996) indicated, "social capital theory's focus on parent–child relations places parental involvement and support at the center of its explanation of educational achievement" (p. 371). In contrast, parenting style conveys parents' attitudes to children across a wide range of situations, with differing styles altering "the parents' capacity to socialize their children by changing the effectiveness of their parenting practices"

(Darling & Steinberg, 1993, p. 493). Hofferth, Boisjoly, and Duncan (1998) noted that Coleman's "conceptualiztion of social capital also includes the style with which parents interact with their children" (p. 248). Investigations have shown, for example, that parental involvement is more likely to be related to children's academic achievement when the involvement is associated with an authoritative parenting style (Fletcher, Darling, Steinberg, & Dornbusch, 1995; Lord, Eccles, & McCarthy, 1994; Smetana, 1995; also see Scarr, 1997 for a reanalysis of data that examined relations among parenting style, parental involvement, and academic performance, after including measures of parental IQ and education).

One of the most significant socialization styles that differentiates between families relates to parents' individualistic–collectivistic orientations (Kim, Triandis, Kagitçibasi, Choi, & Yoon, 1994). Individualistic parents tend to socialize their children for self-reliance and independence, whereas collectivistic parents orientate children for dependence. Triandis (1996) observed that "Collectivists pay much attention to the needs of members of their in groups in determining their social behaviour. Individualists pay attention to advantages and costs of relationships" (p. 409). Parenting style in this study was defined by parents' individualistic–collectivistic orientations. That is, family social capital was defined by parents' involvement in their children's learning and parents' individualistic–collectivistic style.

Model for Analysis

The moderation–mediation model constructed to examine relationships among family capital and children's cognitive performance is shown in Fig. 3.1. In the model, the depiction of the relations is based on a presentation suggested by Keeves (1997). Distal family capital, family social capital, and the children's cognitive habitus have direct associations with academic achievement. The relationship between distal family capital and academic performance is also shown as operating indirectly through family social capital and the cognitive habitus. Family social capital has an indirect association with achievement through the cognitive habitus. These indirect relations suggest the potential mediating effects of the intervening variables. Furthermore, the model indicates the presence of joint effects in which distal family capital moderates the relations between family social capital, the children's cognitive habitus, and academic achievement. The moderated effects are carried by statistical interactions and they are represented by the new variables formed by the product (as

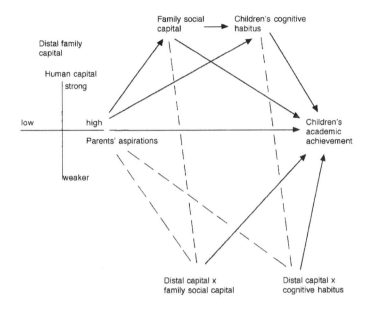

FIG. 3.1 Moderation–mediation model for relationships among distal family capital, proximal family capital, cognitive habitus, and children's academic achievement.

shown by broken lines) of distal family capital with family social capital and with cognitive habitus, respectively.

Although the moderation–mediation model is presented in a causal form, the present analysis is restricted by its correlational design. In addition, the model needs to be interpreted in relation to theoretical concerns about the direction of associations between the constructs being examined. Brody (1997) indicated, for example, that "the relationship between IQ test scores and educational achievement is reciprocal. IQ test scores change in response to the educational opportunities available to individuals" (p. 1047). Also, Sternberg (1996) concluded "IQ differences between groups may lead to differences in societal outcomes; differences in societal outcomes may lead to IQ differences; both may be dependent on some third factor" (p. 15). That is, the moderation–mediation model is limited to an examination of relations among refined family capital measures and children's academic performance, after taking into account the children's cognitive habitus. Also, in the analysis, the relationships in the model were investigated separately for boys and girls as previous research indicated moderate but significant gender-related differences in associations among measures of environmental influences, individual characteristics, and academic achievement (e.g., Halpern, 1997; Neisser et al., 1996).

In the present study, it was proposed that (a) family distal capital moderates the relationships between family social capital, cognitive habitus, and children's academic achievement; (b) family social capital and cognitive habitus dimensions mediate the associations between distal family capital and children's academic achievement; and (c) there are gender-related variations in the relations among the predictor and outcome measures.

AN EXAMINATION OF THE MODEL

Relationships in the moderation–mediation model were examined using data collected from 900 families. The families lived in Adelaide, a city with just over 1 million people and the capital of the state of South Australia. Families were selected to reflect the social status distribution of the city. Each selected family had an 11-year-old child and parents were interviewed in their homes to assess distal family capital and family social capital in relation to the 11-year-old. The final sample included 460 boys and 440 girls.

During the interviews, parents reported their levels of educational attainment, current occupations, and the educational attainment of their close friends. Coleman (1990) noted the potential importance of the human capital of adults, other than parents, on children's educational outcomes. Family human capital was defined by an equally weighted composite of parents' and close friends' educational attainment and fathers' occupation scores. A factor scale was formed to assess the parents' idealistic and realistic aspirations for their children. The correlations between family human capital and parents' aspirations were .08 and .13, for boys and girls, respectively, which provided support for considering the two measures as separate dimensions of distal family capital. Parents responded to questions that measured the extent to which they were involved in their children's learning and indicated whether they could be characterized as having an individualistic- or collectivistic-oriented parenting style.

The children's cognitive ability, cognitive attitudes, and academic achievement were measured in normal classroom settings to ensure that the students were able to understand the test instructions and to establish, as far as possible, uniform test-taking conditions. The Raven Progressive Matrices, normed to the Australian context, was used to measure children's cognitive ability (Raven, 1989). Standardized tests were used to assess the children's achievement in mathematics and word performance and a scale was developed to measure the 11-year-olds' cognitive attitudes toward school.

ANALYSIS

In the analysis, children were classified into four family distal contexts defined by the median split of scores on the measures of family human capital and parents' aspirations. The distal contexts were labeled as strong human capital/high parents' aspirations, strong human capital/low parents' aspirations, weaker human capital/high parents' aspirations, and weaker human capital/low parents' aspirations.

When the significance of family-context differences in the mean scores of the variables in the model were examined, the findings indicated that parents with strong human capital were more involved in their children's learning than parents with weaker human capital. In weaker human capital families, parents with low aspirations were more involved in their children's learning than parents with high aspirations. Within the human capital contexts, and when boys and girls are considered separately, parents with low aspirations had a more individualistic parenting style than parents with high aspirations. Children in strong human capital/high aspiration families had significantly higher ability scores than children in weaker human capital/low aspiration families. The cognitive attitudes of girls in strong human capital/high aspiration families were more positive than those of girls in strong human capital/low aspiration families and more favorable than boys' attitudes in any of the family contexts. Also, boys in high aspiration families had more positive cognitive attitudes than boys in weaker human capital/low aspiration families. Children in strong human capital/high aspiration families had significantly higher word achievement scores than the children in families defined by weaker human capital. In addition, the mathematics achievement of boys and girls in strong human capital/high aspiration families was significantly higher than that of boys and girls in the other family contexts. Within the weaker human capital/low aspiration family context: Parents had a more individualistic style for sons than for daughters, girls had more positive cognitive attitudes than boys, and boys had higher word achievement scores than girls. In strong human capital/high aspiration families, girls had more favorable cognitive attitudes than boys. These initial findings indicated the presence of distal family context variations and differences between boys and girls in the patterns of mean scores of the variables in the moderation–mediation model.

Moderation and Mediation

For moderation to occur in the current analysis, interactions between distal family capital categories and the measures of family social capital and the cognitive habitus would be related significantly to the academic achievement scores (Russell, 1997). If mediation occurred, then (a) distal family capital would be related to family social capital, cognitive habitus dimensions, and academic achievement; (b) family social capital and cognitive habitus measures would be associated with academic achievement; and (c) the relationship between distal family capital and academic achievement would be reduced when associations involving the proposed mediating variables and academic achievement were taken into account. As Baron and Kenny (1986) indicated, "a given variable may be said to function as a mediator to the extent that it accounts for the relations between the predictor and the criterion" (p. 1176). If full mediation occurred then the associations between distal family capital and academic achievement would become nonsignificant after taking into account the relations among family social capital, the cognitive habitus, and academic achievement. If the relationships were reduced but remained significant then partial mediation would be satisfied (Saks, 1995).

The findings revealed that distal family capital had significant associations with each of the other measures in the moderation–mediation model, which satisfied the first condition for mediation. Zero-order correlations between the proposed mediating variables and academic achievement indicated that in relation to effect sizes (Cohen, 1992), family social capital had small significant associations with cognitive ability, cognitive attitudes (except for the relations between involvement and attitudes), mathematics achievement, and medium associations with word achievement scores. In addition, cognitive ability had medium relations with word and mathematics test scores, while cognitive attitudes had small associations with academic achievement. That is, the results indicated that the second condition for mediation was, in general, satisfied.

Multistage Regression Analysis

Multistage regression analysis was used to test for moderation relationships and to examine the third condition for mediation in the moderation–mediation model. Variables were added to the regression equations in three stages. First, relations between distal family capital and academic achievement were investigated. In the second stage, the regression models included the family social capital measures and the interactions between distal family capital and family social capital. The cognitive habitus dimensions and the interactions between distal family capital and cognitive habitus were included in the full regression models. From the second and third regression equations it is possible to determine to what extent relations between distal family capital and children's academic achievement were attenuated by the intervening variables and whether distal family capital had a moderating affect on relationships in the model.

The regression models in Table 3.1, show the relationships for children's word achievement. In the regression equations, distal family capital was represented by a set of dummy variables with the omitted category being strong human capital/high parents' aspirations. The results in Model 1 indicated that distal family capital had small and medium associations with boys' ($R = .158$) and girls' ($R = .355$) word achievement scores, respectively. In addition, the unstandardized regression coefficients show that the word achievement scores for boys and girls were significantly higher in families defined by strong human capital and high parents' aspirations than in weaker human capital family contexts.

In the second-stage analysis, the family social capital and family interaction terms were added to the models. Aiken and West (1991) observed that "considerable multicollinearity can be introduced into a regression equation with an interaction when the variables are not centered. Centering variables will often help minimize these problems" (pp. 32–33). In the present analysis, therefore, deviation scores were used in the regression equations and only those interactions which were significant are shown. The results in Model 2 indicated that when variations in family social capital were taken into account, the differences between boys' word achievement scores in the two high parent aspiration family contexts became nonsignificant. In contrast, the difference in word scores for boys from the two strong human capital contexts was exacerbated ($b = -2.504$ in Model 1, $b = -5.93$ in Model 2) which, in part, reflected the more individualistic parenting style in strong human capital/low aspiration families. That is, when parents in strong human capital/low aspiration families were considered to have parenting styles only as individualistic as parents in strong human capital/high aspiration families, boys in the low aspiration families had lower word achievement scores. Also, the findings show the presence of a significant interaction term, which indicates that relative to boys in strong human capital/high aspiration families, boys' word achievement in strong human capital/low aspiration families was enhanced when their parents became increasingly involved in their learning.

For girls, the results in Model 2 show that after taking into account variations in family social capital, differences in word achievement scores between the two high aspiration groups became nonsignificant ($b = -8.774$ in Model 1, $b = -2.556$ in Model 2). In contrast, the difference in word scores for girls in strong human capital/high aspiration families and in weaker human capital/low aspiration families was reduced ($b = -10.835$ to $b = -6.154$) but remained significant.

TABLE 3.1

Unstandardized Regression Coefficients for Relations Among Distal Family Capital, Family Social Capital, Cognitive Habitus, and Word Achievement

Predictor variables	Boys			Girls		
	Model 1	Model 2	Model 3	Model 1	Model 2	Model 3
Weaker human capital/high aspirations (A)	-4.773**	-1.584	-1.094	-8.774***	-2.556	-1.263
Weaker human capital/low aspirations (B)	-5.296**	-4.138*	-1.779	-10.835***	-6.154***	-4.054*
Strong human capital/low aspirations (C)	-2.504	-5.930**	-5.224**	-1.699	-2.115	.202
Parents' involvement		.019	.010		.062***	.053***
Parenting style		.438***	.413***		.284**	.258**
(C) x parents' involvement		.087**	.088**			
Cognitive ability			.225***			.548***
Cognitive attitudes			.193**			.175**
(A) x ability						-.350**
(B) x ability			.190*			-.443***
(C) x ability						-.282*
Multiple R	.158**	.373***	.501***	.355***	.478***	.578***
R2	.025	.139	.250	.126	.228	.335

Note.   *p < .05, **p < .01, ***p < .001.

The regression coefficients in Model 3 show that when the cognitive habitus dimensions were added, the difference in word achievement scores for boys from strong human capital/high aspiration and weaker human capital/low aspiration families became nonsignificant. In contrast, the word score differences between boys from the two strong human family contexts remained significant. Furthermore, after controlling for differences in the cognitive habitus measures, family social capital continued to have significant and essentially unmediated associations with boys' word scores. The presence of a significant interaction relation indicated that distal family capital moderated the association between cognitive ability and word achievement, which suggested that increases in cognitive ability in weaker human capital/low aspiration family contexts is associated with relatively strong increments in boys' achievement. For girls, the difference in word scores between strong human capital/high parent aspiration and weaker human capital/low parent aspiration families was reduced but remained significant. Also, the significant interactions in the Model 3 regression equations indicated that relative to girls in strong human capital/high aspiration families, the relationship between cognitive ability and word performance was moderated by membership in the other family contexts. Overall, the full regression models revealed that the variables in the moderation–mediation model combined to have large associations with boys' ($R = .501$) and girls' ($R = .578$) word achievement.

In Table 3.2, the relationships for mathematics achievement are presented. The first regression models indicated that distal family capital had small to medium associations with boys' ($R = .244$) and girls' ($R = .281$) performance. In addition, the regression coefficients show that the mathematics achievement scores for boys and girls were significantly higher in strong human capital/high aspiration families than in other family contexts. In the second-stage analysis, when family social capital was taken into account, the distal family capital differences in mathematics achievement remained significant. Although parenting style was related to achievement, there was no independent significant association between parents' involvement and mathematics scores which, in part, reflects the multicollinearity of parenting style and parents' involvement. In Model 3, when variations in the cognitive habitus measures were controlled, the differences in mathematics achievement between children in the two strong human capital contexts became nonsignificant. The differences in relation to the other family contexts were attenuated but remained significant. Although cognitive attitudes were associated with boys' mathematics scores, they were not related to girls' scores. Also, the cognitive habitus dimensions mediated, in part, the relationship between parenting style and children's math-

TABLE 3.2

Unstandardized Regression Coefficients for Relations Among Distal Family Capital, Family Social Capital, Cognitive Habitus, and Mathematics Achievement

Predictor variables	Boys			Girls		
	Model 1	Model 2	Model 3	Model 1	Model 2	Model 3
Weaker human capital/high aspirations	-4.056***	-2.985**	-2.262*	-3.552***	-2.212***	-2.090*
Weaker human capital/low aspirations	-4.854***	-4.453***	-2.815**	-5.587***	-4.692***	-3.549***
Strong human capital/low aspirations	-2.111*	-2.467*	-1.706	-2.184*	-2.462**	-1.601
Parents' involvement		.007	.001		.005	.001
Parenting style		.142**	.105*		.150***	.098*
Cognitive ability			.244***			.223***
Cognitive attitudes			.074*			.038
Multiple R	.244***	.292***	.535***	.281***	.326***	.507***
R2	.059	.086	.287	.079	.106	.257

Note.   *p < .05, **p < .01, ***p < .001.

ematics achievement. There were no significant interaction relationships, which indicated that the associations between family social capital, cognitive habitus, and mathematics achievement were not moderated by distal family capital. Overall, the full regression models revealed that the variables in the moderation–mediation model combined to have large associations with boys' ($R = .535$) and girls' ($R = .507$) mathematics achievement.

In general, the findings in Tables 3.1 and 3.2 provided tentative support for the propositions of the study. Distal family capital moderated relations between parents' involvement, cognitive ability, and boys' word achievement, and the associations between girls' cognitive ability and their word performance. The family social capital and cognitive habitus dimensions mediated, in part, the relationships between distal family capital and children's academic achievement. In addition, the relations between family social capital and word performance were unmediated by the cognitive habitus dimensions, while the cognitive habitus measures mediated, in part, the associations between parenting style and children's mathematics achievement. There were, however, different patterns of relationships between the predictor and achievement measures, for boys and girls.

Regression Surface Analysis

Eckenrode, Rowe, Laird, and Brathwaite (1995) suggested that once there is evidence of moderation or mediation among a set of relations, then the nature of the associations among predictors and outcomes should be further explored. They indicated, for example, the need to examine possible curvilinear relationships. In this present analysis, therefore, linear and curvilinear relations among children's cognitive habitus dimensions, family social capital measures, and academic achievement scores were investigated further by plotting regression surfaces in each distal family capital context. Surfaces were generated from regression models that included product and squared terms to test for possible interaction and curvilinear relations. The models were of the form:

$$Z = aX + bY + cXY + dX^2 + eY^2 + \text{constant},$$

where Z, X, and Y represented measures of academic achievement, family social capital, and cognitive habitus. Because of space limitations it was not possible to present the tables of regression equations or to portray all the surfaces that were constructed from those regression models. Instead, surfaces that reflect the nature of the different associations between family social capital and children's academic achievement scores at varying levels of the cognitive habitus dimensions were chosen and presented. In Fig. 3.2, the surfaces show the regression-fitted relations among parenting style, cognitive ability, and word achievement scores in each distal family capital context. Scores for the surfaces were standardized with means of 50 and standard deviations of 10.

For children in the two strong human capital contexts, the surfaces show that parenting style and cognitive ability had significant linear associations with word performance. The possible complexity of the regression models is depicted in the surfaces for children in weaker human capital families. In weaker human capital/high aspiration families, for example, cognitive ability had significant curvilinear associations with boys' and girls' word-test scores. For boys, the nature of the curvilinear relationship indicated that cognitive ability acted as a threshold variable. That is, until mean cognitive ability levels were attained, ability was not related to word achievement. After reaching this threshold level, however, sizable increments in word scores were related to successive increases in cognitive ability. In contrast, for girls, the curvilinear relationship revealed that at each level of parenting style, cognitive ability had an association that negatively increased with word achievement. That is, cognitive ability had a significant association with word scores until about mean cognitive ability levels were achieved. After that mean level, further increments in cognitive ability were not related to significant increases in word performance.

The surfaces for weaker human capital/low aspiration families show the presence of significant interaction and curvilinear relations among the measures. In the boys' regression surface, for example, cognitive ability acted as a threshold variable such that until mean ability values were attained, cognitive ability and word performance were not related. After that threshold value was reached, changes in cognitive ability were associated with sizable increments in word achievement scores. The significant interaction effect is reflected in the relations between parenting style and word scores at differing levels of ability. At low ability levels, parenting style was not associated with word performance. In contrast, at high ability levels, changes from collectivistic to individualistic parenting style were related to substantial increases in word achievement. The regression surface for girls showed that parenting style and cognitive ability had curvilinear associations with word performance. As parenting style became more individualistic, the increments in word scores became more substantial while successive changes in cognitive ability were related to increasing changes in word achievement. That is, the regression surfaces, which are representative of other surfaces in the study, indicated that the nature of relationships among family social capital, cognitive habitus dimensions, and academic achievement varied among the distal family capital contexts and differed between boys and

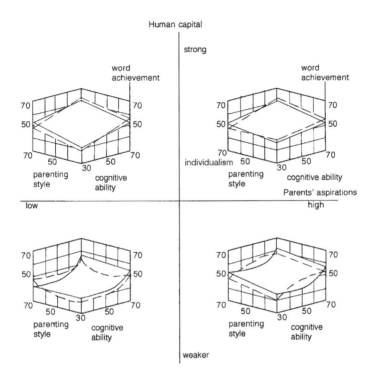

FIG. 3.2   Fitted-word achievement scores in relation to children's cognitive ability and parenting style, in each distal family capital context———boys, – – – –girls).

girls. Such findings support the claim that if moderation or mediation relationships are present in data analyses, then further investigations should be undertaken to explore the possible complexity of those relations.

DISCUSSION

The present study suggests the general propositions that when distal family capital is defined conjointly by family human capital and parents' aspirations: (a) Distal family capital moderates relations between family social capital, cognitive ability, and children's academic achievement; (b) The associations between distal family capital and children's academic achievement are mediated, in part, by family social capital and the children's cognitive habitus; (c) There are different patterns of significant relationships among distal family capital, family social capital, cognitive habitus, and academic achievement, for boys and girls; and (d) There are distal family capital differences in the linear and curvilinear nature of the relations among family social capital, cognitive habitus dimensions and academic achievement, that also vary between boys and girls in those distal family contexts. That is, the investigation provided initial support for the moderation–mediation model that was generated for the present study.

It needs to be stated, however, that when distal family capital and family social capital were combined, they were associated only with moderate amounts of variance in boys' (13.88%) and girls' (22.83%) word achievement scores, and more modest amounts of variance in boys' (8.55%) and girls' (10.62%) mathematics achievement scores. If more encompassing social capital measures had been included in testing the moderation–mediation model, it is possible that the relationship between the environment and achievement measures might have been more substantial. Wong (1998) suggested, for example, that family social capital should "include social relationships that are embedded in the larger community and through which parents can mobilize their organizational resources to aid socialization" (p. 4). Similarly, Stanton-Salazar (1997) argued that family social capital needs to be considered in relation to the wider social networks available to children. He proposed that children from different family contexts have networks of relationships that are differentially "converted into socially valued resources and opportunities" (p. 8). That is, in an elaborated model, social capital might be expanded to include children's interactions with a network of institutional agents such as community leaders, counselors, social workers, and teachers as well as family members. In such an elaborated model it would be valuable to examine children's perceptions of social capital. Grolnick and Slowiaczek (1994) observed that in environmental research, phenomenological experiences need to be stressed "as the child must experience the resources for them to have their influence. Such a viewpoint represents the child as an active processor of information rather than a passive recipient of inputs" (p. 248). Similarly, Wentzel (1994) concluded that children's outcomes "may be more highly related to their own perceptions of parenting than to what parents think they are doing in the home" (p. 264). Also, in an elaborated model, other cognitive habitus dimensions should be included. Neisser et al. (1996) concluded, for example, that "Successful school learning depends on many personal characteristics other than intelligence, such as persistence, interest in school, and willingness to study" (p. 81). Similarly, Sternberg and Grigorenko (1997) indicated in their theory of mental self-government, that cognitive styles "predict school performance significantly and add to the prediction provided by ability tests ... they can truly tell something about environments as well as interactions with these environments" (p. 710).

The enduring relationship between the refined distal family capital measure and children's academic achievement, and the distal family capital differences in the complexity of the associations among the predictor and achievement measures, suggests that future family environment investigations might consider family background as being defined by family human capital and parents' aspirations. If the findings from the present study, which was restricted by its correlational design, were replicated in longitudinal investigations, then the research would highlight the potential difficulties confronting parents as they attempt to enhance children's academic achievement by enriching family social capital. In the present study, the curvilinear nature of relationships between family social capital and academic achievement scores, for children in differing distal family capital contexts, suggests that children's social capital in certain situations might have to be enhanced substantially if there are to be meaningful changes in achievement outcomes.

This chapter demonstrates that associations between family capital and academic achievement are particularly complex because of the moderation and mediation relationships that involve children's cognitive ability. As Sternberg (1997) proposed:

> Intelligence is not just reactive to the environment but also active in forming it. It offers people an opportunity to respond flexibly to challenging situations. Because the landscape of an environmental context changes over time, adequate adaptation, shaping, and selection involve a process of lifelong learning, one that starts in infancy and continues throughout the life span. (p. 1030)

What is required now are longitudinal studies of the moderation–mediation that examine the possible complexity of relations among more elegant measures of social capital, the cognitive habitus, and children's school outcomes. Only after such investigations are completed, will we have a more complete understanding of the relations between family capital and cognitive performance, and of the challenges that confront family members and teachers as they attempt to influence school outcomes by altering children's social capital.

REFERENCES

Aiken, L. S., & West, S. G. (1991). *Multiple regression: Testing and interpreting interactions.* Newbury Park, CA: Sage.

Alexander, K. L., Entwisle, D. R., & Bedinger, S. D. (1994). When expectancies work: Race and socioeconomic differences in school performance. *Social Psychological Quarterly, 57,* 283–299.

Aschaffenburg, K., & Maas, I. (1997). Cultural and educational careers: The dynamics of social production. *American Sociological Review, 62,* 573–587.

Baron, R. M., & Kenny, D. A. (1986). The moderator–mediator variable distinction in social psychological research: Conceptual, strategic, and statistical considerations. *Journal of Personality and Social Psychology, 51,* 1173–1182.

Bottero, W. (1998). Clinging to the wreckage? Gender and the legacy of class. *Sociology, 32,* 469–490.

Bourdieu, P. (1977). Cultural reproduction and social reproduction. In J. Karabel & A. H. Halsey (Eds.), *Power and ideology in education* (pp. 487–511). New York: Oxford University Press.

Bourdieu, P. (1984). *Distinction: A social critique of the judgement of taste.* London: Routledge & Kegan Paul.

Bourdieu, P. (1988). *Homo academicus.* Cambridge, England: Polity Press.

Brody, N. (1997). Intelligence, schooling, and society. *American Psychologist, 52,* 1046–1050.

Bronfenbrenner, U. (1994). Ecological models of human development. In T. Husen & T. N. Postlethwaite (Eds.), *The international encyclopedia of education* (Vol. 3, pp. 1643–1647). Oxford, England: Pergamon.

Bronfenbrenner, U., & Ceci, S. J. (1994). Nature–nurture reconceptualization in development perspective: A bioecological model. *Psychological Review, 101,* 568–586.

Caspi, A., Wright, B. R., Entner, Moffitt, T. E., & Silva, P. A. (1998). Childhood predictors of unemployment in early adulthood. *American Sociological Review, 63,* 424–451.

Ceci, S. J., Rosenblum, T., de Bruyn, E., & Lee, D. Y. (1997). A bio-ecological model of intellectual development: Moving beyond h^2. In R. J. Sternberg & E. L. Grigorenko (Eds.), *Intelligence, heredity, and environment* (pp. 303–322). Cambridge, England: Cambridge University Press.

Cohen, J. (1992). A power primer. *Psychological Bulletin, 112,* 155–159.

Coleman, J. S. (1988). Social capital in the creation of human capital. *American Journal of Sociology, 94,* S95–S120.

Coleman, J. S. (1990). *Foundations of social theory.* Cambridge, MA: Harvard University Press.

Coleman, J. S. (1997). Family, school, and social capital. In L. J. Saha (Ed.), *International encyclopedia of the sociology of education* (pp. 623–625). Oxford, England: Pergamon.

Darling, N., & Steinberg, L. (1993). Parenting style as context: An integrative model. *Psychological Bulletin, 113,* 487–496.

Eckenrode, J., Rowe, E., Laird, M., & Brathwaite, J. (1995). Mobility as a mediator of the effects of child maltreatment on academic performance. *Child Development, 66,* 1130–1142.

Fletcher, A. C., Darling, N. E., Steinberg, L., & Dornbusch, S. M. (1995). The company they keep: Relation of adolescents' adjustment and behavior to their friends' perceptions of authoritative parenting in the social network. *Developmental Psychology, 31,* 300–310.

Grigorenko, E. L., & Kornilova, T. V. (1997). The resolution of the nature–nurture controversy by Russian psychology: Culturally biased or culturally specific. In R. J. Sternberg & E. L. Grigorenko (Eds.), *Intelligence, heredity, and environment* (pp. 393–439). Cambridge, England: Cambridge University Press.

Grolnick, W. S., & Slowiaczek, M. L. (1994). Parents' involvement in children's learning: A multidimensional conceptualization and motivational model. *Child Development, 65,* 237–252.

Grusky, D. B., & Sorensen, J. B. (1998). Can class analysis be salvaged? *American Journal of Sociology, 103,* 1187–1234.

Hagan, J., MacMillan, R., & Wheaton, B. (1996). New kid in town: Social capital and the life course effects of family migration on children. *American Sociological Review, 61,* 368–385.

Halpern, D. F. (1997). Sex differences in intelligence. *American Psychologist, 52,* 1091–1102.

Hao, L., & Bonstead-Bruns, M. (1998). Parent–child differences in educational expectations and the academic achievement of immigrant and native students. *Sociology of Education, 71,* 175–198.

Hofferth, S. L., Boisjoly, J., & Duncan, G. J. (1998). Parents' extrafamilial resources and children's school attainment. *Sociology of Education, 71,* 246–268.

Keeves, J. P. (1997). Trends in quantitative research methods. In L. J. Saha (Ed.), *International encyclopedia of the sociology of education* (pp. 263–275). Oxford, England: Pergamon.

Kim, U., Triandis, H. C., Kagitçibasi, C., Choi, S-C., & Yoon, G. (1994). *Individualism and collectivism: Theory, method and applications.* Newbury Park, CA: Sage.

Lord, S. E., Eccles, J. S., & McCarthy, K. A. (1994). Surviving the junior high school transition: Family processes and self-perceptions as protective and risk factors. *Journal of Early Adolescence, 14,* 162–199.

Neisser, U., Boodoo, G., Bouchard, T. J., Jr., Boykin, A. W., Brody, N., Ceci, S. J., Halpern, D. F., Loehlin, J. C., Perloff, R., Sternberg, R. J., & Urbina, S. (1996). Intelligence: Knowns and unknowns. *American Psychologist, 51,* 77–101.

Portes, A. (1998). Social capital: Its origins and applications in modern sociology. In J. Hagan & K. S. Cook (Eds.), *Annual review of sociology* (Vol. 24, pp. 1–24). Palo Alto, CA: Annual Reviews.

Raven, J. (1989). The raven progressive matrices: A review of national norming studies and ethnic and socioeconomic variation in the United States. *Journal of Educational Measurement, 26,* 1–16.

Reay, D. (1998). Rethinking social class: Qualitative perspectives on class and gender. *Sociology, 32,* 259–275.

Rumberger, R. W. (1995). Dropping out of middle school: A multilevel analysis of students and schools. *American Educational Research Journal, 32,* 583–625.

Russell, A. (1997). Effects: Moderating, mediating, and reciprocal. In J. P. Keeves (Ed.), *Educational research, methodology, and measurement: An international handbook* (2nd ed., pp. 508–513). Oxford, England: Pergamon.

Saha, L. J. (1997). Aspirations and expectations of students. In L. J. Saha (Ed.), *International encyclopedia of the sociology of education* (pp. 512–517). Oxford, England: Pergamon.

Saks, A. (1995). Longitudinal field investigation of the moderating and mediating effects of self-efficacy on the relationship between training and newcomer adjustment. *Journal of Applied Psychology, 80,* 211–225.

Scarr, S. (1997). Behavior-genetic and socialization theories of intelligence: Truce and reconciliation. In R. J. Sternberg & E. L. Grigorenko (Eds.), *Intelligence, heredity, and environment* (pp. 1–41). Cambridge, England: Cambridge University Press.

Smetana, J. G. (1995). Parenting styles and conceptions of parental authority during adolescence. *Child Development, 66,* 299–316.

Stanton-Salazar, R. D. (1997). A social capital framework for understanding the socialization of racial minority children and youths. *Harvard Educational Review, 67,* 1–40.

Sternberg, R. J. (1996). Myths, countermyths, and truths about intelligence. *Educational Researcher, 25,* 11–16.

Sternberg, R. J. (1997). The concept of intelligence and its role in lifelong learning and success. *American Psychologist, 52,* 1030–1037.

Sternberg, R. J. (1998). Abilities are forms of developing expertise. *Educational Researcher, 27,* 11–20.

Sternberg, R. J., & Grigorenko, E. L. (1997). Are cognitive styles still in style? *American Psychologist, 52,* 700–712.

Suzuki, L. A., & Valencia, R. R. (1997). Race-ethnicity and measured intelligence. *American Psychologist, 52,* 1103–1114.

Triandis, H. C. (1996). The psychological measurement of cultural syndromes. *American Psychologist, 51,* 407–415.

Wentzel, K. R. (1994). Family functioning and academic achievement in middle school: A socio-emotional perspective. *Journal of Early Adolescence, 14,* 268–291.

Wilson, J., & Musick, M. (1997). Who cares? Toward an integrated theory of volunteer work. *American Sociological Review, 62,* 694–713.

4

The Confluence Model: An Academic "Tragedy of the Commons?"

Joseph Lee Rodgers
University of Oklahoma

This chapter develops a meta-theory, in that it theorizes about theorizing. A popular theory of how the family environment influences the intellectual development of a child in that environment—the confluence model—has engendered controversy since its proposal in the mid-1970s. I am a consistent and vocal critic of the model, and that position is maintained and further developed in the current chapter. The confluence model is creative, complex, and intriguing. It also has critical weaknesses, both theoretical and empirical. Its major theoretical weakness is that it was built to match apparent patterns that weren't really there. It's empirical weakness is that when its predictions are compared to patterns that are really there, they simply don't match.

There has been too much written about the confluence model, and not enough written about what the confluence model is about. This chapter discusses both topics, the confluence model and the subject of the confluence model—the relationship between family structure and intellectual development. My starting point is that the confluence model, along with other models that explain systematic variance in intelligence that appears to relate to family structure, are in fact explaining mostly "phantom variance." My conclusion encourages intelligence researchers to move away from building their models from purely structural characteristics of the family environment and instead to use explanatory mechanisms as the building blocks for such models.

When we engage in JOOTSing ("Jumping Out of the System" to a meta level; Hofstadter, 1985), we may have a chance of bringing health back to an important and slightly unhealthy research arena. But only by being conscious of what we are doing, as well as doing it carefully and correctly, will we succeed. We have been trapped in a "tragedy of the commons" from which we can, with some effort, escape. This chapter begins with a metalevel description of the problem. The broad goals of this chapter are to provide some direction and tools to stimulate the healthy development of research on how the family environment affects intellectual development.

AN ACADEMIC TRAGEDY OF THE COMMONS

Hardin's Tragedy of the Commons

My "meta-theorizing" begins with reference to Hardin's (1968) "Tragedy of the Commons," and applies Hardin's ideas to the research domain. At a simplified level, Hardin suggested that what is good for an individual can in fact be bad for the collective group of which the individual is a part. The tragedy of the commons situation is analogous to a classic Prisoner's Dilemma, in which individuals must sacrifice some of their personal best outcome to achieve a positive (or even tolerable) outcome at a group level (this analogy was suggested by Kahan, 1974). Setting aside land for a park that some individual might have profitably farmed or legislating air standards to prevent profitable industrial activity leading to air pollution are examples of public efforts to protect the "commons" (land and air) from tragedy caused by individual or corporate largesse. The Prisoner's Dilemma situation occurs when the individuals who act to protect the public interest are exactly those who might benefit immediately from private exploitation of the commons. The difficult question—the dilemma—is whether an individual should act to promote their personal good or the public good. Some individuals would act altruistically in such situation, and others would not.

In the research domain, we might view the "commons" as the collection of all ideas—both good and bad, and everything in between—about how the world works in some particular domain. Hofstadter (1985) referred to this type of collection of ideas as "thought space." If science is concerned with building models of reality that both simplify reality and also match it in certain fundamental aspects, then ideas about how to define models of the world are the intellectual capital that push science forward. The positive and productive portion of thought space are those ideas that stimulate health, knowledge, and other good ideas.

Scientific Mistakes in Theorizing About the Structure of the Universe

All models are wrong in the particulars. Einstein's theory of relativity showed Newton's law of gravitation to be incorrect in some details (although the theory underlying Newtonian mechanics works remarkably well in a broad range of settings). Similarly, Quantum mechanics developed by Feynman and others showed relativity to be incorrect in some of its particulars. But no one doubts the value and success of each theoretical structure.

The most egregious scientific mistakes occur when a theory is wrong at a much higher level than the particulars, when the big picture is wrong. The geocentric view that the universe revolves around the earth is an example of such a mistake. There is little physical sense in which this theoretical structure is correct, and only by reference to philosophy and religion can the history of this popular belief be understood. There were important historical reasons for nonscientists to market the geocentric theory, and many stories abound to illustrate the fervor of this marketing effort. Such mistakes can be viewed as a scientific "tragedy of the commons." They may bring temporary fame to an individual scientist or religious satisfaction to nonscientists. But, they also waste the intellectual resources and creative scientific efforts of the research community in at least two different ways.

The least bothersome influence of incorrect theories is that they can lead to scientific effort devoted to testing and replication, which ultimately can help distinguish the good theories from the bad. That part of the process is natural and represents a form of scientific self-correction. The other sense in which incorrect theories waste intellectual resources occurs when scientists must spend extraordinary time attempting to dissuade the public (or even other scientists) of the incorrectness of a theoretical structure. When scientific theories are promoted or marketed for reasons other than their scientific quality, then the usual scientific approaches to self-correction will not necessarily work. The Catholic Church was motivated by a strong religious agenda in promoting the geocentric theory of the structure of the universe. The church's successful effort to force Galileo to recant his belief in a heliocentric universe is one spectacular example of abuse of scientific time and talent in defense of an incorrect theory.

In fact, the history of science is full of false starts and incorrect theories, some of which were elegant and exciting. An example is the idea of building "circles on circles," or epicycles, proposed by Ptolemiac theorists, and developed further by Copernicus even after he proposed the heliocentric theory. Epicycles were used to explain deviations from circular orbit and retrograde planetary movement, and their proposal was both scientifically creative and empirically successful. Then, Kepler's demonstration that a single ellipse could explain the data as well—and much more simply—than many epicycles was a substantial scientific step forward. Although false starts are an integral part of the advancement of science, the health of a research arena is at least partially defined by how quickly it can recover from false starts like the epicycle theory and supplant those with better fitting and/or simpler theoretical statements.

A Tragedy of the Scientific Commons

This chapter is not about astronomical theorizing, although some of the historical references just given excellent analogies to delineate what the chapter is about. It is about psychological and sociological theorizing, and, more specifically, about theories of how the family environment can influence the intellectual development of the children who are growing up within that environment. We are caught, I argue, in the throes of a social scientific "tragedy," one that is analogous to a number of previous scientific tragedies. Whether the analogy is closer to the geocentric theory of the universe (which was fundamentally incorrect) or to the epicycle theory (which was nearly correct in its mathematical predictions but much more complicated than necessary) is debatable; I argue that the former is a closer match.

I argue in this chapter that the confluence model is fundamentally invalid. In fact, a whole class of theories—of which the confluence model is only the best-known and most controversial example—are fundamentally incorrect. There are those who doubted the validity of the confluence model almost from its proposal (e.g, Galbraith, 1982; Page & Grandon, 1979), and it has engendered extraordinary levels of controversy. Zajonc and his colleagues argued that the model is empirically and theoretically valid. That position has been forceful and unwavering for over two decades (Zajonc & Markus, 1975; Zajonc & Mullally, 1997).

In fact, several overlapping and competing theories were proposed to explain the same empirical patterns that the confluence model originally attempted to explain. Blake's (1981) dilution model is an overlapping theory that explains the same empirical patterns in a similar but simpler manner (and therefore, in the spirit of replacing epicycles with an ellipse, might be preferable to some). Page and Granden (1979; also see Valendia, Granden, & Page, 1978) proposed a competitor model, the admixture hypothesis, that took a completely different approach to explaining the empirical patterns. They suggested that the within-family birth order patterns that the confluence and dilution models attributed to within-family processes were actually caused by sources outside the family. The Page and Granden theory was competing and inconsistent with both the confluence model and the dilution model. Either Zajonc and Blake were fundamentally correct, or Page and Granden were; there is little room for conciliation. I argue that Page and Granden were closer to being broadly and generally correct, although the admixture hypothesis has received little attention and generated minimal research effort.

The tragedy of the scientific commons is that, while defending the confluence model, the confluence theorists have distracted the research community from productive effort. The family structure enterprise itself has taken a two-decade hiatus from productive and creative theorizing on its own part to argue the merits of this particular model (Sulloway, 1996, provides an important and interesting exception). If the argument were, at this point, leading toward consensus that the confluence model is a useful scientific statement, the effort would be well spent. Originally, of course, the confluence model was built to match empirical patterns in family structure data, and to shed light on the processes that generated those data. But, in fact, the opposite occurred.

In the body of this chapter, I do four different things. First, I present and review the reasons that I believe that the confluence model is fundamentally incorrect. This part of the chapter engages the "meta-controversy," as it argues the validity of the confluence model itself. Next, I review the early literature that supports the assertion that the confluence model is fundamentally flawed. Following, I review three modern studies that combine to suggest an entirely different direction for family structure researchers to take. Finally, I conclude with suggestions for how to move in that direction, and how to disengage the meta-controversy in which we are currently mired. If successful, a whole new line of theorizing can emerge that must necessarily be wrong in some of the particulars. But, unlike the confluence model and related theories, it will be much closer to correct in a broad and general sense (like Page & Granden's admixture hypothesis was in 1979).

HOW DOES THE CONFLUENCE MODEL WORK, AND WHAT IS WRONG WITH IT?

A Description of the Confluence Model

Zajonc, Blake, and a number of other family scholars believe that birth order and family size play an important role in the development of intelligence. The confluence model is based on the belief that the other members of a child's family environment provide intellectual influences that lead to differences between children within a family. The confluence model is a specific statement of how that influence is spread, and how it differentially impacts children depending on their birth order, spacing, and family size at a particular point in time. The more intellectually mature the family environment is, the more intellectually facilitating it is for a child. Thus, a child in a family environment with only adults has better intellectual influence from which to draw than a child in a family environment with many children and relatively few adults. An additional component contained in the confluence model is the tutoring effect, which suggests that there is additional intellectual facilitation that a child obtains from having one or more younger siblings to tutor. A last-born child does not accrue this advantage, whereas all non last-born children do.

The confluence model has a number of attractions, including the following: (a) Whether one agrees with the specific statements of the model or not, it is plausible and has face validity. (b) Anyone can reflect on personal experiences to make sense of the model. (c) It is operationalized in a formal mathematical system that makes the assumptions of the model very clear and makes the model testable. (d) The statements in the model combine to account for empirical patterns in family structure-IQ data from many sources. Among its empirical successes include model predictions that match the patterns in many different national cross-sectional datasets, predictions that help explain depressed IQ averages among twin pairs, and predictions that match longitudinal trends in national achievement scores.

Invalidity Arising from Cross-sectional Data

Unfortunately, however, the confluence model was built to match data of questionable validity in support of within-family theorizing. The type of cross-sectional data that provide consistent patterns that the confluence model so successfully can predict, do not necessarily reflect the within-family processes on which the model is based. Literally thousands of articles on birth order and family size have appeared in the social science literature since the late 1800s. According to that corpus of literature, birth order and/or family size can account for the behavior of presidents, dentists, soldiers, strippers, artists, assassins, athletes, authors, and assorted others. The birth order of birth order researchers was even studied (see Rodgers & Thompson, 1985–1986 for a review). The most intensely studied area in the birth-order literature is the influence of family structure on the achievement and intellectual development of children. But for all the interest and research effort devoted to this study, the majority of previous studies are potentially invalid because of a critical flaw.

There are a number of methodological pitfalls into which birth-order researchers have fallen, and these are well documented (e.g., Adams, 1972; Kammeyer, 1967; McCall, 1980; Rodgers & Thompson, 1985–1986; Schooler, 1972; Schvaneveldt & Ihinger, 1979). The primary source of invalidity in this massive literature has been the use of cross-sectional data to build and test theories of within-family processes. Such data inherently confound within-family and between-family processes. As a result, researchers simply cannot determine whether a particular pattern was caused by processes operating within a family (e.g., parental influence or sibling interaction effects) or processes operating outside the family (e.g., peer influences, school influences, or larger societal influences like religion or television). To assume that one of these causal arenas is correct, as most birth order researchers have done, is to engage in risky inference. A simple example is presented that illustrates how these previous studies may have arrived at incorrect conclusions.

Suppose an idealized family structure research team collected IQ data of perfect reliability and validity from every 16-year-old in an imaginary country on one day in 1998. Now suppose that this team cross-classified these IQ scores by birth order and family size. If these data were plotted, the patterns would probably show declining IQ averages for increasing birth order and family size, a typical finding. The research team simply would be following previous family structure researchers if they concluded that later-born children and those born into larger families were at an intellectual disadvantage. But, it is critically important to notice that no siblings were compared in this assessment. With the exception of 16-year-old twin pairs (and a few sibling pairs who were born around 10 or 11 months apart and were both 16 at the same time), all 16-year-olds in the United States at a fixed point in time come from different families. Suppose a different research team of idealized family-income researchers next analyzed the same dataset previously described. Finding exactly the same patterns, and combining that information with previous research showing negative correlations between parental characteristics like income, socioeconomic status (SES), and IQ and their achieved fertility (a typical finding in most modern societies; see Retherford & Sewell, 1988, among others), they would arrive at a different conclusion. They might conclude that differences between families caused the IQ patterns, that higher income and higher educated parents had smaller families, and that income and education were translated into IQ scores.

Either research team may be correct (or both may be correct). But, a cross-sectional design simply cannot determine the degree to which each conclusion is correct because within-family differences and between-family differences are inherently confounded in such a design. Yet, hundreds of family structure articles were based on such data and have concluded that within-family processes are implicated as the cause of the observed patterns.

The confluence model, the dilution model, and many other less formalized theoretical statements about the role that the family environment plays in the intellectual development of children, have taken cross-sectional findings as their starting point. Zajonc and Markus (1975), for example, motivated the development of their theoretical structure with the use of the Belmont and Marolla (1973) data, which came from an entire population of almost 400,000 Dutch males in military service. Zajonc (1976, among others) used a number of other national cross-sectional datasets to suggest further support for the confluence model.

Suppose that the causes of the consistent IQ patterns in these data sources came primarily from between-family processes and not within-family processes. In this case, models positing within-family explanations are fundamentally incorrect. In fact, there is developing evidence that this is exactly the case. Later, I review three recent studies that provide strong support for this interpretation. These more recent studies give even more credence to the considerable body of criticism generated by the confluence model in the decade after its proposal (e.g., Galbraith, 1982, 1983; Page & Grandon, 1979; Price, Walsh, & Vilburg, 1984; Rodgers, 1984; Steelman, 1985; Velandia, Grandon, & Page, 1978). Page and Grandon (1979) provided a lucid statement of the between-family explanation in their admixture hypothesis.

It should be emphasized that virtually the whole body of birth-order literature is on the same shaky ground as the confluence model, because it derives from the information provided from cross-sectional studies. It may be time to move forward and to re-cast our thinking about the relationship between family structure and intellectual development. In fact, it is difficult to find supporters of the confluence model other than Zajonc and his co-authors. McCall (1984) is the only independent study of which I am aware that used data to reflect within-family processes that appeared to support the confluence model. His finding of IQ fluctuations in relation to the birth of a sibling is one of the few examples in the literature in which within-family patterns were used to demonstrate a within-family effect. That result supports the existence of a within-family effect in general (i.e., his findings support the dilution model and other within-family models as well as the confluence model). Even after he observed this empirical finding, however, his general evaluation of the confluence model (McCall, 1985) appeared much more neutral than supportive. On the other hand, there are many different independent scholars who have found theoretical, methodological, and, especially, empirical reasons to criticize the confluence model (and a number of these are reviewed later in this chapter). Why is it so hard to find empirical support for the confluence model? Why do so many scholars object to theoretical and methodological features of the model? Why haven't some subset of those studying the model rallied around Zajonc and his co-authors? Perhaps it is time to reframe our questions. Why are we still writing about the confluence model in the first place?

Emerging From Confluence and Cross-Sectional Research

The heat of the confluence battle has consistently obscured the basic scientific issues that are argued, which is unfortunate. In 1988, I suggested that "all confluence researchers should attempt to enlarge our view of the enterprise from its introspective fascination with a single model. Whether a child's birth order is related to intellectual development is a much more important question than whether the confluence model gets due credit for predicting aggregate relationships" (Rodgers, 1988, p. 477). A dozen years after I wrote those words, I feel even more strongly the importance of that statement. The battle itself may have generated methodological insights and some high correlations with empirical phenomena—the model is certainly predictive, even if not explanatory. But the tragedy of the academic commons referred to previously is that little advancement in either theoretical or empirical domain has occurred.

I argue that a major theoretical shift needs to take place. The empirical evidence has convincingly emerged, and our theories should respond in kind. The many family structure theorists during the 1900s, who observed cross-sectional results and built their theories around the importance of strong and consistent within-family processes, made the wrong call. Of the two possible causes of patterns in cross-sectional IQ data, the one that is seldom invoked is the one that appears to be the strong and abiding domain of influence. Between-family processes are the primary ones on which we should rely to explain patterns in cross-sectional IQ-family structure data. Reliable within-family variance probably exists, but it is small, relatively weak compared to the between-family sources of variance, and nowhere near the magnitude or consistency to justify theoretical propositions like those contained in Zajonc's confluence model or Blake's dilution model.

In the next two sections, I present evidence in support of the previously mentioned position, and ultimately focus on three studies that combine to provide support for this strong position. Taken together, these three studies provide a better understanding of the relationship between family structure and IQ than the hundreds of previous studies based on cross-sectional data published in the 125 years since Galton's (1874) original study, which showed a relation between birth order and scientific eminence. But before reviewing those studies, I draw on earlier research that set the stage for these three studies.

PAST RESEARCH THAT RAISED SUSPICIONS ABOUT THE CONFLUENCE MODEL

The three studies reviewed in the next section are recent and modern demonstrations of the invalidity that can result from the use of cross-sectional data. But, although the methods are modern, the position emerging from these articles—and the one being strongly asserted in the current article—is not new. To motivate the value of the three studies to be carefully inspected in the next section, I refer to earlier work.

Steelman's Review

Steelman (1985) conducted a careful review of the research literature that addressed the confluence model up to that point in time. Among her conclusions were the following: "Zajonc (1983) perhaps places too much faith in his theoretical model without proper regard to empirical evidence" (p. 378). Further, she commented:

> Zajonc contends that longitudinal data on whole families are required to test the model adequately. Because such data are impractical if not impossible to collect, the confluence theory may ultimately prove to be untestable.... In the history of the confluence model, the debate over data deficiencies has taken an ironic twist. The theory was deduced originally from patterns appearing in aggregate data. The methods and the data used to generate the original confluence theory by no means match

the stringent standards Zajonc now sets forth. Because these types of data are beyond the grasp of nearly every researcher, the theory comes perilously close to being
untestable. (p. 378)

In fact, Steelman and I are only two of many researchers who have recognized the inherent confounds and biases present in cross-sectional data (e.g.,
Anastasi, 1956; Bongaarts, 1983; Ernst & Angst, 1983; also see Berbaum &
Moreland, 1980; Zajonc, Markus, & Markus, 1979, who demonstrated a clear
understanding and appreciation of the importance of using within-family data).

Other Early Confluence Critics

In fact, Steelman's (1985) suggestion that longitudinal data from whole families
"are beyond the grasp of nearly every researcher" may overestimate the difficulty of obtaining these data, although only slightly. Such data are difficult and
costly to obtain, although not impossible. Close approximations have been used
for nearly two decades, some of which were collected many years earlier. In fact,
several studies conducted in the early 1980s used within-family data to evaluate
the confluence model. In Rodgers (1984), longitudinal within-family data were
analyzed from the Fels study, many of the families from which were complete
families. The empirical results suggested that simple regression models fit the
data better than the more complex mathematical formulation of the confluence
model. Berbaum and Moreland (1980) used within-family (but not longitudinal) data that Outhit (1933) collected many years earlier, and interpreted support for the model. However, a number of researchers subsequently criticized
their methods and suggested that their empirical patterns were negative rather
than positive (e.g., Galbraith, 1982; Price, Walsh, & Vilberg, 1984; Rodgers,
1984; Steelman, 1985). Olneck and Bills (1979) used a sample of brothers to investigate birth order effects and used a method to control for between-family
differences in their assessment of within-family differences. [They found neither birth order nor spacing relationships with a standard IQ measure of intellectual performance.] Galbraith (1982) used ACT scores and found virtually no
sibling differences among college bound high school students. Further,
Mascie-Taylor (1980) found no birth-order or family size differences in verbal
and spatial IQ scores in a family sample. If there are no birth-order differences
within families, there is nothing for a within-family theory like the confluence
model to explain. (Note that for a period from around age 5 until around age 11,
the confluence model can make positive or zero IQ birth-order predictions, depending on family spacing. See Zajonc and Mullollay, 1997. Only for children
beyond age 11 or so does the confluence model necessarily predict a negative

IQ-birth order relationship. The studies previously reviewed account for many ages from childhood into adulthood, all of which indicate approximately flat birth order-IQ patterns.) To summarize, I could not find an example that used within-family data that appeared to support the existence of meaningful and systematic within-family IQ patterns related to birth order. If there are no such patterns, then the development of models to explain those kinds of patterns is a moot issue.

Zajonc and his colleagues published many different refutations of confluence model criticisms. Given the substantial body of writing from dispassionate and independent scholars expressing doubts, objective evaluation of the strengths and weaknesses of the model from its developers is notable by its absence. In Rodgers (1988), I commented that Zajonc (1986) "incorrectly enhanced the status of the confluence model by failing to note the existence of a substantial body of criticism" (p. 477). This is only one of many such selective omissions of theory and empirical evidence. The most recent defense (Zajonc & Mullallay, 1997) is exemplary: While a legitimate and reasoned argument is presented accounting for the difference between using aggregate and individual-level data, no treatment is given of the much more important issue of cross-sectional versus within-family data. Furthermore, the several studies that have used within-family data—the only ones that shed light on the critical issue of selection bias and unobserved heterogeneity—were virtually ignored in that review.

THREE STUDIES SHOWING IMPORTANCE OF BETWEEN-FAMILY IQ VARIANCE

Three studies were chosen to build a strong case for the necessity of reorienting our thinking about how the family structure affects intellectual development. The studies reviewed are Guo and VanWey (1999); Retherford and Sewell (1991); and Rodgers, Cleveland, vanOrd, and Rowe (2000). All represent relatively recent research (conducted during the 1990s). All use innovative or sophisticated methods. All are based on nationally representative samples. And, of course, each one uses within-family data. The characteristics of each study are compared in the next paragraph, and then each study is treated individually.

Summary of the Three Studies

In terms of methodological and design innovation, Retherford and Sewell (1991) used a nonlinear mathematical representation of the confluence model and fit the model to their data. Rodgers et al. (2000) used a design and graphical methodology that demonstrated how results changed between analysis of cross-sectional and longitudinal data (the goals and orientation of that paper, not surprisingly, overlap substantially with those of the current chapter). Guo and VanWey (1999) used within-individual and sibling designs and analytic models to control for the unobserved heterogeneity that confounds cross-sectional data. In terms of external validity, two of the studies (Guo & VanWey & Rodgers et al.) used different subsets of the same datasource: the National Longitudinal Survey of Youth (NLSY) Children data. The NLSY-Children sample includes children born to women from a nationally representative household sample, whose respondents were 14 to 21 years old in 1979. Retherford and Sewell used the Wisconsin Longitudinal Study (WLS), a probability sample of Wisconsin high school graduates in 1957. Each datasource contained extensive within-family information because of the sampling procedure used in each case. The NLSY-Children data are completely intact-family data (except for attrition, nonresponse, and incomplete childbearing), because this source represents a survey of all children born to the original NLSY mothers. The WLS files contain extensive information about the high school graduates sampled in 1957. In addition, they also contain educational and family information about siblings of the sampled graduates. The within-family IQ data in this data source were obtained from a random sample of siblings in a subset of the overall WLS sample.

Retherford and Sewell's Wisconsin Study

Retherford and Sewell (1991) directed their study toward an evaluation of the confluence model. The mathematical representation of the confluence model (see Zajonc & Markus, 1975; Zajonc, Markus, & Markus, 1979) required from each child, information about parental IQ, birth timing of all siblings, and measures that were transformed into mental ability scores (e.g., IQ measures). To estimate the parameters in the confluence model required that a nonlinear model fitting routine be used to optimize the fit between the model predictions and the data values. Retherford and Sewell used the SAS procedure PROC NLIN to fit the confluence model's predictions to the within-family data in the WLS. This random subset of the WLS data contained 507 sibling pairs. They concluded that "the fit of the confluence model to the data is very poor" (p. 151).

For the purposes of this chapter, however, a different set of analyses is of more critical import than the direct test of the confluence model. Retherford and Sewell (1991) concluded that the confluence model did not generate predictions that matched the WLS data. A larger issue also existed: whether there were within-family birth-order patterns in general. To address this issue, they defined 1,131 sibling pairs who had complete IQ information and who lived together with both parents in 1957, and defined a ΔIQ value between the older and younger sibling. A birth-order relation to IQ would have resulted in a mean ΔIQ value different from zero. However, across several different comparison categories they failed to find a single significant ΔIQ, and concluded that "birth order has no discernible effect on measured intelligence in this sample of sibling pairs" (p. 156). The consistency of this type of finding when within-family data are used is of critical importance. Retherford and Sewell noted the similarity between their procedure and that used by Galbraith (1982), who also failed to find a birth-order relation using within-family information.

Rodgers et al.'s NLSY Study

In a study conducted by the author of this chapter and his colleagues (Rodgers et al., 2000), the NLSY children were used to study IQ patterns in within-family data. Using three subsets of the NLSY data, the largest including 443 one-child families, 565 two-child families, 233 three-child families, 56 four-child families, and 14 five-child families (N = 2,566 children in 1,311 families), they measured IQ using an average of three subscales of the Peabody Individual Achievement Test (PIAT) across 2 years of administration. They found statistically flat IQ–birth-order relationships within each family size category. In addition, results from several previous analyses of within-family and cross-sectional data sources were presented and reviewed.

The primary theme of that article is summarized in the following logic. If the typical attribution from cross-sectional research is correct—that cross-sectional IQ–birth-order patterns are caused by within-family processes—then results should approximately converge when between-family and within-family patterns are studied. Even if within-family processes provide only part of the explanation for the findings in cross-sectional data, patterns should be similar (although not identical) when results from the two are compared. But, in fact, completely different conclusions emerged when within-family and cross-sectional data results were compared—cross-sectional patterns typically appeared fairly systematic, within-family patterns appeared approximately random. Several other previous within-family analyses were also presented that showed similar relationships between cross-sectional and within-family results. The logical conclusion is that cross-sectional patterns are not caused by processes operating within families. Rather, their causal source appears to lie in between-family processes. The issue that Rodgers et al. (2000) identified, in particular, was the tendency for low IQ parents to make larger families, which is a pattern that was supported by additional analyses of the NLSY data.

Guo and VanWey's NLSY Study

The third article reviewed, Guo and VanWey (1999), is in many ways the most compelling and important of the three reviewed in this section. The potential fallacy in using cross-sectional data is long appreciated, and efforts have often been made to account for explicit biases. For example, Belmont and Marolla (1973) reanalyzed their data within SES levels in attempt to account for the causal directionality problem. But SES is only one of hundreds of such potential biases, and it would be impossible to think of, measure, and model every single such potential confound or bias. Guo and VanWey's methodology used a technique that controlled for unobserved heterogeneity, that is, it accounted for both known and unknown biases and confounds. The logic that supports their method ideally involves using control or comparison samples that differ from the sample of interest only in the specific independent variable (IV) that is being evaluated. Then, causal attributions can be made to the independent variable rather than to other confounding variables that the IV may be inadvertently measuring. In experimental studies, this equating is achieved by random assignment. But when random assignment is impossible, as it is in most family structure studies, then difference models (or change models) can be used to achieve at least some of the same effects.

Guo and VanWey (1999) used two types of difference or change models, one a within-individual model and one a sibling model (which requires within-family data). The specific relationship they investigated was the effect of family size on children's intellectual development. They noted in their abstract that "change models provide an opportunity ... to control for such unmeasured effects as family intellectual climate, family value system, and family genetic heritage." The data source they used was the NLSY-children data (data obtained from children who were not living with their mothers in both 1986 and 1992 were deleted during analysis), and they used the Peabody Picture Vocabulary Test (PPVT) as their dependent measure (a different outcome measure than that used in the Rodgers et al. study).

In a preliminary analysis, they fit regression models to cross-sectional versions of the data and entered a number of different controls for explicit confounders like gender, age, race, parental income and education, and region of the country. The findings from this analysis were consistent with previous cross-sectional literature, which supported a negative relation between family size and IQ and stronger patterns for verbal subscales than for the math subscale.

Two types of difference models were fit. When sibling models were fit, in which siblings were used to control for unobserved confounds and biases, weaker versions of the cross-sectional results were obtained. Results consistently showed a negative IQ–family size relation, but one smaller in size than found for the cross-sectional analyses (which were also based on larger sample sizes). When the sibling pairs were also entered into a difference model that used individuals as their own controls (and that, hence, required the type of longitudinal data available in the NLSY), the "typical pattern" completely disappeared. None of the coefficients were significant, and in fact, some of the coefficients became positive. They concluded that "While the conventional analysis has basically replicated the longstanding result of a negative family size effect, the sibling analyses and the analyses of repeated measures have failed to yield such an effect" (p. 182).

The logic of their pattern of analyses supports the interpretation that previous family size–IQ relationships were most likely caused by unobserved factors that the family size variable measured indirectly. They surmised that these unobserved factors were related to family environment, family genetic heritage, or a mixture of these elements. In the conclusion to their article, they reviewed both the strengths and weaknesses of change models. They noted that there was a fairly limited time span of 6 years in the longitudinal structure of their data. Furthermore, they noted the overrepresentation of young mothers in the NLSY-Children data. Finally, they expressed concerns about time-varying confounds that were not properly "differenced out" by their change models. These are certainly concerns, but it should be emphasized that they pale next to the overarching concern that has consistently been ignored in the family structure literature, that of controlling for such confounds in the first place.

Summary

In summary, these three articles build an extensive case for the relative lack of systematic within-family variance relative to between-family variance; identical conclusions have emerged from treatment of both birth order and family size, both children and young adults, and with the use of rather different methodological approaches. In particular, each study demonstrated that the type of cross-sectional data used in the past to support the existence of within-family processes are in fact misinterpreted; the processes that cause the systematic patterns in past cross-sectional family structure data sources are primarily between-family processes. In combination, the three articles make an even more compelling package than each does in isolation. Finally, when these are combined with the much larger body of literature that includes both methodological treatment of birth-order studies and careful evaluation of the confluence model, the case that emerges appears unambiguous. Models like the confluence model, the dilution model, and other within-family models, have simply placed their explanatory equipment in the wrong part of the process.

MOVING FORWARD

If within-family models of IQ–family structure like the confluence model are fundamentally incorrect in their orientation, then a legitimate question emerges as to where we should be directing research. A large body of literature is developing that provides answers to that question. In this section, I briefly outline some literature that can help guide future studies of how the family environment impacts intellectual development. The orientation provided by this literature points in completely different directions than most researchers have utilized. This point cannot be made quietly or it will continue to be ignored (as it has been a number of times in the past). What is needed is not adjustments or revisions in the confluence model, the dilution model, or similar models that focus on explaining substantial systematic IQ–family structure variance occurring within the family. Substantial systematic variance is simply not there to be explained. The small within-family variance that may be explainable by family structure variables—and in which psychologists and other social scientists will naturally have a great deal of interest—can only be understood and modeled in the context of other sources of influence on developing children.

A Reasonableness Criterion

I begin my "moving forward" commentary with the statement of a "reasonableness criterion." Since the early 1900s, psychologists and other social scientists have expected and/or hoped that simple measures of the family structure—birth order, family size, and birth spacing—would account for significant and important variance. But such an expectation is unreasonable. To understand a child's development, which would a reasonable psychologist rather observe, birth order or a parental treatment variable? Which should tell us more, birth spacing or parental intelligence? It is an entirely legitimate question to ask whether birth order and family size have any relation to intelligence net of other research variables. But to expect these factors to be major players appears, to me and many others, to be unreasonable.

Sulloway (1996), for all of his elegant theorizing about how birth order relates to personality and rebelliousness, provided cogent orientation for this position in two of his footnotes. One (p. 373) suggested that the birth order variable measures other important processes, however, birth order per se doesn't mean a great deal (the exact point of the cross-sectional fallacy on which this chapter is based). The second (p. 23, 373, among others) noted that birth-order effects are relatively small in individual-level data (especially for intellectual development). Zajonc and Mullally (1997) also made this point. The effect sizes are typically small or zero when the effect of family structure on individual-level intelligence is measured.

Emerging Theoretical Perspectives

Two relatively recent findings seem to provide direction for future research on the relation between the family environment and intellectual development. The first is that a great deal of environmental variance is contained in nonshared rather than shared environmental influences. The second is an emerging theoretical perspective that emphasizes the influence of the nonfamily environment in accounting for differences between siblings and between children. Each is discussed in turn.

Nonshared influences were recently identified as being extremely important in accounting for individual differences between children (e.g., Daniels & Plomin, 1985; Dunn & Plomin, 1990). They are, in many domains, apparently more important than shared environmental influences—intelligence is one of those domains. Birth order is a nonshared influence (or at least measures nonshared influence because most birth-order theorists point to differential treatments of various types across birth order as being critical family structure information). Family size can also be a nonshared influence as long as the family size is changing across children (i.e., it can be nonshared in relation to a fixed age of siblings, but is a shared environmental influence at any point in time). So the nonshared environmental literature would support the possibility that both birth order and family size would contribute to this explanatory package. But there are many potential nonshared environmental influences, and status as one of these does not necessarily mean that a measure is important. As the rest of this chapter documents, it does not appear that either birth order or family size are major players to account for the nonshared environmental variance.

Where are the nonshared environmental influences that account for the considerable (and still yet mostly unspecified) differences between siblings' environments? One possibility is that parental treatment creates sibling differences (although not in relation to birth order and family size). Another is that sibling influence contributes to sibling differences, although, again, this process must be unrelated to birth order and family size. Harris (1995) proposed the intriguing theory that families actually contribute little to sibling differences. Rather, she suggested that the peer environment in the neighborhood, the school, and the playground account for many of the nonshared environmental influences that act to make siblings substantially different from one another. These new perspectives, combined with some methodological rigor, can help the necessary reorienting that needs to occur among family structure researchers.

In the following treatment, several lines of research that converge within the two important developments previously outlined are discussed and integrated. Generally, this package of research takes a multiperspective view of the family environment, accounting for genetic influences, environmental influences, and the interaction between them. Furthermore, they emphasize the importance of defining mechanisms of influence, rather than correlates and superficial structural relationships.

Daniels and Plomin (1985), Dunn and Plomin (1990), and Plomin and Daniels (1987) convincingly documented that siblings within the same family were extremely different from one another. They motivated the recent interest in the behavioral genetic and psychological literature on nonshared environmental influences previously discussed. Rodgers, Rowe, and May (1994) provided a methodology that simultaneously accounted for shared and nonshared genetic influences, and shared and nonshared environmental influences. They used their methodology to demonstrate that owning books related to reading scores and going to the museum related to mathematical reasoning scores, even after shared genetic and environmental influences were already accounted for. Scarr and McCartney (1983) developed a theory of how environmental influences act on individuals in the context of their existing genetic structure. Their theory, called *niche-picking*, provides a straightforward and easily understood statement of how genes and the environment interact. Finally, Rowe (1994) and Harris (1995) suggested that parents and family environment simply don't make as much difference in intellectual and personality outcomes as most researchers (and, for that matter, most parents) believe. Harris attributed a great deal of important explanatory variance to the friendship and peer social network. She suggested that "children would develop into the same sort of adults if we left them in their homes, their schools, their neighborhoods, and their cultural or subcultural groups, but switched all the parents around" (p. 461). Finally, Wachs (1983) called for a blending of the two schools that separately study the environment, the so-called environmentalist school and the behavioral-genetic school. In later writing (Wachs, 1993), he called for research to identify the specific mechanisms that cause environmental influences, a particularly important suggestion in the context of the present chapter.

It is important to note that Harris and Rowe's suggestions did not necessarily imply that parents are unimportant. Rather, they suggested that there are not enough differences in typical parents to result in critical differences in developmental outcomes. Thus, if parents have substantial social influence on their children's intellectual outcomes, but all parents contribute approximately the same type and amount of influence, then this influence will not manifest as variance to be explained. I further develop this idea in relationship to birth order and family size.

In some cultures, there are definitional birth order differences that make tremendous differences in certain types of child outcomes. For example, in cultures where all family wealth passes to the first-born son, income outcomes are obviously highly dependent on birth order. In cultures with tremendous variation in family size, the amount of family wealth to be distributed between a few children would be much greater for a 2-child family than for a 10-child family. But in most modern posttransition societies, there is little or no legal status tied to birth order, nor is there tremendous variance in family size. Furthermore, intelligence is an entirely different child outcome than inherited wealth. According to genetic theory, whatever portion of intelligence is genetically defined should be assorted randomly across birth order, and should not be related to family size. Current estimates support that about half of the variance in intelligence is related to additive genetic variance (e.g., Bouchard & McGue, 1981; Rodgers, Rowe, & May, 1994). In this sense, parents have substantial prima facia influence on the intelligence of their children. But do parents act—actively or passively—in such a way as to suppress the intellectual development of a later-born child in relation to an earlier-born child (or vice versa)? In fact, many parents would find it abhorrent to imagine that they favored certain of their children in this way. Scarr and McCartney's niche-picking theory seems to be a much healthier parental model. It suggests that parents should actively seek to promote the individual talents and interests of their children so that those talents and interests can fill the appropriate and optimal niches. It also implies that children play an active role in the process. Those who believe that parents can discourage intellectual development—actively or passively—may be forgetting the persistence that a bright child can have in seeking out intellectual stimulation and growth.

The confluence model's notion of a passive family intellectual environment from which each child draws nurture is at the surface an interesting idea.

But, it falls far short of specifying mechanisms of influence. Furthermore, some features of the model become rather implausible immediately below the surface (e.g., Why does sibling tutoring exert such a powerful influence on intellectual development while learning from other siblings plays no role?). Finally, and most importantly, the processes on which the model is based are not consistent with empirical data when researchers look within families in an attempt to find them. Theoretical argumentation—which abounds in the literature generated by the confluence model—becomes moot when there is nothing to be explained (e.g., Guo & VanWey, 1999; Retherford & Sewell, 1991; Rodgers et al., 2000).

Moving Beyond Structural Models

The corpus of literature represented by the articles previously mentioned provides motivation for why our modeling of the relation between family environment and intellectual development must become more complex. Simple explanatory variables like birth order and family size consistently explain simple and minor amounts of variance, if any. Schooler (1972) noted that the simplicity of the birth-order index may account for much of its appeal. But, as Sulloway (1996) suggested, birth order per se is not an explanatory variable. Rather, we assume that birth order is measuring other variables, which are the actual mechanisms of influence in which we are really interested. It is in those mechanisms that we should naturally place our scientific interest.

I expand this point with reference to my own research. Rodgers and Rowe (1988) demonstrated a birth-order effect in age at first intercourse among adolescents. We found that early born siblings reported an average age at first intercourse that was reliably older than that reported by later-born adolescents. Like most family structure researchers, we attributed that difference to a within-family social process, sibling influence (and even placed that attribution in our title). But further inspection suggested that we were wrong. Rodgers, Rowe, and Harris (1992) tested for sibling influence and sibling opportunity processes using a national data source and found little evidence of sibling influence. But a pubertal development explanation was identified. In addition to an age-at-first-intercourse difference, we also found that younger siblings reported a reliably younger age at puberty. The original birth-order effect that we had identified was, apparently, a misattribution. Birth order acted as a proxy for pubertal development, which itself was a much more plausible mechanism to explain onset of sexual behavior than birth order per se.

Developing Theory Based on Mechanisms of Influence

Our theoretical future lies in the identification of mechanisms of influence. One of the most important findings from my research group was the identification of the link between owning books and reading scores and the link between going to the museum and mathematical reasoning scores (Rodgers et al., 1994). Those are obvious and plausible links, but that does not mean that they are measurable and statistically detectable. The unusual nature of this finding is that within-family variance in books and museum trips accounted for differences between siblings within the same family. The amount of variance explained was relatively small, so we expect many other factors to relate to verbal and mathematical reasoning as well. Birth order and family size may even be among the many different influences that should be included in the ultimate explanatory model. But they cannot justify their own elaborate and mathematically complex explanatory process and the "reasonableness criterion" does not suggest that they should.

The search for birth order, or family size, or birth spacing influences on intellectual development has been relatively unsuccessful. The value of the past 120 years of birth-order research may lie primarily in alerting us to the existence of variables for which birth order has been consistently acting as a proxy. Of more importance are answers to questions like the following: What are the actual environmental mechanisms that influence intelligence? How do those interact with genetic processes? If many of those processes create differences between families (instead of within families), how are those differences created? If many of those processes create differences between siblings (rather than similarities among siblings), how are those differences created? How can nonfamily sources of influence act on the intellectual development of children? How can parents, teachers, schools, or society at large create environments that best extract the genetic and biological bases of intelligence from children? In general, how can environments, genes, and the interaction between them broadly account for the substantial individual differences in intellectual ability that we know to exist among our children?

CONCLUSION

When those types of questions are considered, the question of whether the confluence model fits well becomes irrelevant and uninteresting. The meta-controversy needs to move back down to the level at which the science occurs, and the level at which policymakers can act. Policymakers have little use for statements about birth order (although they, like many others, will have interest in such statements). They have even less use for the kind of rhetoric that has been generated over the confluence model controversy. But educational policy can be strongly shaped by even crude and basic answers to questions like those posed in the previous paragraph. Books matter, museums matter, and siblings differ in intellectual performance for millions of reasons beyond their birth order and family size differences. We should identify and build models to account for those reasons.

REFERENCES

Adams, B. (1972). Birth order: A critical review. *Sociometry, 35,* 411–439.

Anastasi, A. (1956). Intelligence and family size. *Psychological Bulletin, 53,* 187–209.

Belmont L., & Marolla, F. A. (1973). Birth order, family size, and intelligence. *Science, 182,* 1096–1101.

Berbaum, M. L., & Moreland, R. L. (1980). Intellectual development within the family: A new application of the confluence model. *Developmental Psychology, 16,* 500–515.

Blake, J. (1981). Family size and the quality of children. *Demography, 18,* 421–442.

Bongaarts, J. (1983). The formal demography of families and households: An overview. *IUSSP Newsletter, 17,* 27–42.

Bouchard, T. J., & McGue, M. (1981). Familial studies of intelligence: A review. *Science, 250,* 223–238.

Daniels, D., & Plomin, R. (1985). Differential experience of siblings in the same family. *Developmental Psychology, 21,* 747–760.

Dunn, J., & Plomin, R. (1990). *Separate lives: Why siblings are so different.* New York: Basic Books.

Ernst, C., & Angst, J. (1983). *Birth order: Its influence on personality.* New York: Springer-Verlag.

Galbraith, R. C. (1982). Sibling spacing and intellectual development: A closer look at the confluence models. *Developmental Psychology, 18,* 151–173.

Galbraith, R. C. (1983). Individual differences in intelligence: A reappraisal of the confluence model. *Intelligence, 7,* 185–194.

Galton, F. (1874). *English men of science.* London: MacMillan.

Guo, G., & VanWey, L. K. (1999). Sibship size and intellectual development: Is the relationship causal? *American Sociological Review,* in press.

Hardin, G. (1968). The tragedy of the commons. *Science, 162,* 1243–1248.

Harris, J. R. (1995). Where is the child's environment? A group socialization theory of development. *Psychological Review, 102,* 458–489.

Hofstadter, D. R. (1985). *Metamagical themas: Questing for the essence of mind and pattern.* New York: Basic Books.

Kahan, J. (1974). Rationality, the prisoner's dilemma, and population. *Journal of Social Issues, 30,* 189–210.

Kammeyer, K. (1967). Birth order as a research variable. *Social Forces, 46,* 71–80.

Mascie-Taylor, C. G. N. (1980). Family size, birth order, and IQ components: A survey of a Cambridge suburb. *Journal of Biosocial Science, 10,* 309–312.

McCall, J. N. (1980). Limitations of the single-age sample for research on birth order. *Perceptual and Motor Skills, 51,* 831–837.

McCall, R. B. (1984). Developmental changes in mental performance: The effect of a birth of a sibling. *Child Development, 55,* 1317–1321.

McCall, R. B. (1984). The confluence model and theory. *Child Development, 56,* 217–218.

Olneck, M. R., & Bills, D. (1979). Family configuration and achievement: Effects of birth order and family size in a sample of brothers. *Social Psychology Quarterly, 42,* 135–148.

Outhit, M. C. (1933). A study of the resemblance of parents and children in general intelligence. *Archives of Psychology, 149,* 1–60.

Page E. B., & Grandon, G. (1979). Family configuration and mental ability: Two theories contrasted with U.S. data. *American Educational Research Journal, 16,* 257–272.

Plomin, R., & Daniels, D. (1987). Why are children in the same family so different from one another? *Behavioral and Brain Science, 10,* 1–60.

Price, G. G., Walsh, D. J., & Vilburg, W. R. (1984). The confluence model's good predictions of mental age beg the question. *Psychological Bulletin, 96,* 195–200.

Retherford, R. D., & Sewell, W. H. (1988). Intelligence and family size reconsidered. *Social Biology, 35,* 1–40.

Retherford, R. D., & Sewell, W. H. (1991). Birth order and intelligence: Further tests of the confluence model. *American Sociological Review, 56,* 141–158.

Rodgers, J. L. (1984). Confluence effects: Not here, not now! *Developmental Psychology, 20,* 321–331.

Rodgers, J. L (1988). Birth order, SAT, and confluence: Spurious correlations and no causality. *American Psychologist, 43,* 476–477.

Rodgers, J. L., Cleveland, H. H., van den Oord, E., & Rowe, D. C. (2000). Resolving the debate over birth order, family size, and intelligence. *American Psychologist, 55,* 599–612.

Rodgers, J. L., & Rowe, D. C. (1988). The influence of siblings on adolescent sexual behavior. *Developmental Psychology, 24,* 722–728.

Rodgers, J. L., Rowe, D. C., & Harris, D. (1992). Sibling differences in adolescent sexual behavior: Inferring process models from family composition patterns. *Journal of Marriage and the Family, 54,* 142–152.

Rodgers, J. L., Rowe, D. C., & May, K. (1994). DF analysis of NLSY IQ/achievement data: Nonshared environmental influences. *Intelligence, 19,* 157–177.

Rodgers, J. L., & Thompson, V. D. (1985/86). Toward a general framework of family structure: A review of theory-based empirical research. *Population and Environment, 8,* 143–172.

Rowe, D. C. (1994). *The limits of family influence: Genes, experience, and behavior.* New York: Guilford Press.

Scarr, S. & McCartney, K. (1983). How people make their own environments: A theory of genotype —> Environment effects. *Child Development, 54,* 424–435.

Schooler, C. (1972). Birth order effects: Not here, not now! *Psychological Bulletin, 78,* 161–175.

Schvaneveldt, J. B., & Ihinger, M. (1979). Sibling relationships in the family. In W. R. Burr, R. Hill, F. I. Nye, & I. L. Reiss (Eds.). *Contemporary theories about the family* (Vol. 1). New York: Free Press.

Steelman, L. C. (1985). A tale of two variables: A review of the intellectual consequences of sibship size and birth order. *Review of Educational Research, 55,* 353–386.

Sulloway, F. J. (1996). *Born to rebel.* New York: Vintage.

Velandia, W., Grandon, G., & Page, E. B. (1978). Family size, birth order, and intelligence in a large South American sample. *American Educational Research Journal, 15,* 399–416.

Wachs, T. D. (1983). The use and abuse of environment in behavior-genetic research. *Child Development, 54,* 396–407.

Wachs, T. D. (1993). "Determinants" of intellectual development: Single-determinant research in a multidetermined universe. *Intelligence, 17,* 1–10.

Zajonc, R. B. (1976). Family configuration and intelligence. *Science, 192,* 227–236.

Zajonc, R. B. (1983). Validating the confluence model. *Psychological Bulletin, 95,* 457–468.

Zajonc (1986). The decline and rise of scholastic aptitude scores: A prediction derived from the confluence model. *American Psychologist, 41,* 862–867.

Zajonc, R. B., & Markus, G. (1975). Birth order and intellectual development. *Psychological Review, 82,* 74–88.

Zajonc, R. B., Markus, H., & Markus, G. B. (1979). The birth order puzzle. *Journal of Personality and Social Psychology, 37,* 1325–1341.

Zajonc, R. B., & Mullally, P. R. (1997). Birth order: Reconciling conflicting effects. *American Psychologist, 52,* 685–699.

5

Divorce and Children's Cognitive Ability

John Guidubaldi
John Carroll University

Julie Duckworth
Akron Public Schools

Historically and cross-culturally, parental marriage has been societies' means of ensuring child welfare. As the legally and religiously sanctioned commitment to live together for life, marriage has structured parental roles to optimize stability of financial and emotional resources for children, facilitating children's needs for role models, moral guidance, nurturance, and security. The pervasiveness of this living arrangement across time and culture validates its utility.

Despite its historical success as the primary child socialization unit of most cultures, lifelong marriage is failing in contemporary U.S. society. Divorce and

its common sequelae represent what are arguably the most profound and perva-
sive changes in living arrangements in this century, substantially modifying
such important childrearing factors as parental involvement, extended family
supports, socioeconomic status (SES), residential stability, and coparental har-
mony. These disruptions in children's lives have reasonably raised concern
among social scientists, generating a large number of research studies that address the impact of divorce and single-parenting on various aspects of child adjustment. In this chapter, we examine studies that focus on the potential impact
of divorce on cognitive abilities of children. Children's intellectual functioning
is of primary concern, given that it represents broad-based adaptive capability
and translates into such critical life tasks as school achievement and social
problem solving.

Understanding the divorce phenomenon and its psychological meaning for
child development requires a sensitivity to the rapid escalation of divorce rates
and also to the rates of change in the most frequently related consequences of
divorce, namely father absence and diminished financial resources. These three
disturbing social trends are so intertwined that to consider them separately
would obscure the reality of their aggregate impact on children.

Incidence of Divorce

Reports from the U.S. Department of Health and Human Services (1991) documented that from 1970 to 1990, the number of divorces in the United States increased by 67%. The number of children who experienced parental divorce
each year more than doubled from 1960 to 1990, and now numbers more than 1
million children per year (Nord & Zill, 1996; U.S. Commission on Child and
Family Welfare, 1996). According to Popenoe (1996), the United States has the
highest divorce rate in the industrialized world. He cited estimates that more
than 50% of first marriages occurring today will end in divorce, and that more
than 50% of children born in the past 10 years will not be living with both biological parents by age 17 (U.S Department of Health and Human Services,
1991). When both first marriages and remarriages are considered, the chance of
divorce or permanent separation is estimated to be 60% (Bumpass, 1990).

Incidence of Father Absence

The most salient consequence of divorce is the establishment of two households
where there previously was one. Parents living apart have a logistical dilemma
regarding children's residence that has usually been resolved by preference for
maternal custody. As noted by the director of the National Fatherhood Initia-

tive, Wade Horn (1995), "For nearly one million children each year, the pathway to a fatherless family is divorce.... Perhaps even more troubling is the increasing number of children who experience father flight even before they are born" (p. iii). This alternative source of father absence, unwed motherhood, almost tripled from 1970 to 1993 and currently accounts for 30% of all births (Nord & Zill, 1996; U.S. Commission on Child and Family Welfare, 1996). Popenoe (1996) described the growth of father absent childrearing as follows:

> The trend can be captured in a simple telling statistic: In just three decades, from 1960 to 1990, the percentage of children living apart from their biological fathers more than doubled, from 17 percent to 36 percent. If this rate continues, by the turn of the century nearly 50 percent of American children will be going to sleep each night without being able to say goodnight to their dads. (pp. 2–3)

This projected level of father absence is already evident in divorced mother-custody homes and in unwed motherhood households. In a nationwide study that included 341 divorced family children, Guidubaldi (1988) reported that 51% of children in divorced mother-custody families saw their fathers once or twice per year or never. In another nationwide study, Furstenberg, Nord, Peterson, and Zill (1983) found almost the exact percentage (50%) of father absent divorced-family cases.

The incidence of father absence is even more apparent in studies of high-risk children. For example, one recent study in a large urban center (Guidubaldi et al., 1995) found that 70% of children (mostly boys) with identified severe behavioral handicaps had no father contact at all. In another study that compared boys from regular classrooms with those referred to a child guidance clinic for behavior problems, Tousley (1995) found that fathers in the comparison group were far more involved with their son's lives than fathers in the clinic group.

Family Income and Marital Status

Mother–child households that result from divorce and unwed motherhood have created a large economic underclass. The financial needs of divorced mothers are amply documented by the 1994 Bureau of Labor Statistics reported by the U.S. Commission on Child and Family Welfare (1996). According to these data, 85% of divorced mothers with minor children were employed outside the home in 1994 compared to 68% of married women with a spouse present. The income of two-earner married couples and one-earner married couples surpassed that of mother-headed single-parent families by 300% and 80% respectively. The report further noted that only 9% of families with minor children headed by a married couple were poor, whereas 46% of such families headed by a woman were poor as defined by federal guidelines (U.S. Department of Commerce, 1993). Popenoe's (1996) review of poverty data concluded that an estimated 73% of all children reared by single parents will spend some of their childhood or adolescence at poverty level. Citing Elwood (1988), he described the chronic nature of this poverty, noting that 22% of children from single-parent families will experience poverty for 7 years or more.

THEORETICAL PERSPECTIVES

The Criterion Problem

Traditional psychometric definitions of intelligence have increasingly come under attack as too limited in scope, too tied to Spearman's "g" factor, and not inclusive of other specific adaptive characteristics. For example, Gardner (1983) postulated that additional forms of intelligence exist beyond the linguistic, logical, and spatial abilities typically measured by standardized IQ tests. He identified domains such as interpersonal and intrapersonal intelligence as being equally important to succeed at everyday life. Sternberg's (1985) triarchic definition identified human intelligence within three primary cognitive domains. The analytical domain parallels traditional definitions of intelligence and is the ability most frequently measured by standardized assessments. The creative and practical domains, on the other hand, tap one's ability to problem solve effectively, maintain motivation, and appropriately apply previously learned everyday experiences. In coping with parental divorce or any major life stress, these qualities would appear to be indispensable aspects of resilience.

The application of intelligence to real-life problems, such as resolution of the parental divorce crisis is reflected in definitions by authors of the most prominent intelligence tests. In describing their scale, Binet and Simon (1948) concluded:

> It seems to us that in intelligence there is a fundamental faculty, the alteration or the lack of which is of the utmost importance for practical life. This faculty is judgment, otherwise called good sense, practical sense, initiative, the faculty of adapting one's self to circumstances. To judge well, to comprehend well, to reason well, these are the essential activities of intelligence. (p. 147)

Wechsler (1958) added that IQs reflect "global capacity to act purposefully, to think rationally, and to deal effectively with the environment" (p. 7). Tested IQ, as conceived by the test makers, reflects a personal attribute essential for children's successful resolution of the divorce crisis.

The previous definitions of intelligence that emphasize "interpersonal intelligence," "practical intelligence," "good judgment," or "purposeful, rational dealing with the environment" broaden the definition of cognitive abilities so extensively that they seem to encompass all adaptive behavior. A comprehensive analysis of the effect of divorce on children's cognitive abilities might also include at least a few key indicators of social or emotional competency. As Goleman (1995) stated, "All of us mix IQ and emotional intelligence in varying degrees … still of the two, emotional intelligence adds far more of the qualities that make us more fully human" (p. 45). Clearly, it is not possible to address such breadth of criteria in this review. Yet, if we take a rigid approach to definition whereby the only acceptable criterion of postdivorce child adjustment is a standardized intelligence test, there would in fact be little to review. A reasonable compromise is to extend our examination, with appropriate precaution, to include academic achievement indices as representations of cognitive ability.

The Postdivorce Home Environment

The event of divorce is not our true focus of interest. The sequelae of divorce are, and they are complex indeed. Any comprehensive review of this topic must, at a basic level, consider those life conditions that are both most likely to follow the divorce event and most likely to effect substantial changes in the child's home ecology. Those postdivorce changes that limit the child's interpersonal and material resources, increase anxiety and confusion, and decrease a sense of psychological security, are likely candidates for review because adaptive performance in both academic and interpersonal spheres may be greatly diminished by these psychological challenges. If environmental notions about the genesis of intellectual capability are valid, such major disruptions in the child's primary familial environment must be expected to have some impact, perhaps one that severely limits exercise of genetic potential.

Bioecological theory (Bronfenbrenner & Ceci, 1994; Ceci, 1990; Ceci & Hembrooke, 1995) contends that enduring reciprocal interactions between developing children and their immediate environments, called *proximal processes*, bring about the translation of genotypes into phenotypes. Ceci and Hembrooke further suggested that these "engines of intellectual development" exert a more potent influence on cognitive operations than aspects of the larger environment, such as SES. Bronfenbrenner (1995) explained that in order to be effective, reciprocal interactions, "must occur on a fairly regular basis over extended periods of time" (p. 620). The relevance of this position to family disruption is obvious because the proximal process of father–child interaction is often significantly diminished, and even mother–child interactions may not endure at predivorce levels as the mother responds to postdivorce pressures of role overload.

Another useful theoretical perspective from which to examine outcomes of parental divorce is Coleman's (1988) notion of social capital. He defined social capital in the family as inherent in the relations between children and parents. Whereas the human capital possessed by parents (roughly measured by parents' education according to Coleman) has the potential to create positive learning environments for children, this potential will not be realized if parents are not an important part of their children's lives. Coleman noted that, "The physical absence of adults may be described as a structural deficiency in family social capital. The most prominent element of structural deficiency in modern families is the single-parent family" (p. 89).

METHODOLOGICAL ISSUES

Synthesis of research on the relationship of parental divorce to children's intellectual capability must begin with three important caveats. First, it is clear that most studies of children's adjustment to parental divorce have neglected to include individually administered, or even group administered, intelligence test data. Perhaps because of time costs, especially in the case of individual IQ tests, most references to children's intellectual or cognitive ability have substituted more economical academic achievement tests or teachers' grades in core subject areas. Certainly, these achievement indices incorporate a great deal more than either traditionally defined intelligence or more liberally defined cognitive capability. Achievement motivation, study skills, task persistence, locus of control, family values, and a host of other variables beyond cognitive capability influence final achievement outcomes. Most authorities agree that IQ tests predict, at best, approximately 50% of the variance in school achievement (e.g., Neisser et al., 1996). Consequently, the academic performance criterion cannot be viewed as a definitive test of the impact of parental divorce on children's intelligence, nor can it be strictly defined as an index of cognitive ability.

Second, although father absence creates a great deal of commonality between divorce and unwed motherhood, divorce typically presents some specific dilemmas for children (e.g., coping with heightened parental conflict). Nonetheless, researchers often confound the issue of divorce related child outcomes by including divorced samples and unwed parenthood samples under the common heading of single-parent childrearing. Studies that focus on single parent families often fail to analyze data separately for those created by divorce, unwed motherhood, or death of a spouse, even though the psychological impact on children may be markedly different. Sample descriptions refer to "disrupted" families, "divided" families, and "father absent" families. As Shinn (1978) observed, father absence may be generated by socially approved conditions such as military service, traumatic events such as death, socially stigmatized conditions such as unwed motherhood or imprisonment, and conflict laden events such as divorce or separation.

Third, controls for SES are frequently lacking and reviewers have acknowledged that the performance levels of divorced family children may actually be related to the drop in family income or other SES factors (Amato & Keith, 1991; Demo & Acock, 1988; Shinn, 1978). Svanum, Bringle, and McLaughlin (1982) raised the level of discussion of SES controls from the common assumption that these controls are essential in father-absence studies to a consideration of occasions where such controls would lead to erroneous conclusions. They suggested that controlling for SES may inappropriately remove variance truly attributable to father absence that exerts its effects by reducing income, thereby lowering SES. They also reminded readers that SES may be a relevant variable because it represents parental IQ, which can influence the child both environmentally and genetically. SES tends to correlate rather highly with IQ and the individual differences in IQ, in turn, are thought to be partially attributable to genetic differences. Thus, the correlation with SES might be a reflection of the influence of IQ-involved genes, shared between parents and children.

These authors offered insights surprisingly not raised in prior divorce or father-absence studies; however, they omitted an equally important SES issue. Composition of the SES control is quite variable in divorce or single-parent research, being alternatively based on such disparate measures as school lunch program participation, maternal occupation, father's education level, or some convenient, although muddled, multivariate index. Even family income, as precise as it may seem to be, has inherent ambiguities in research where there are two separate households. Is the nonresident parent's income irrelevant? Court-mandated child support guidelines give evidence to the contrary. Brooks-Gunn (1995) attempted to disentangle income and the human capital resources of parental education and occupational levels. Noting that the latter variables are often used as proxies for poverty, she cautioned that combination SES indices obscure distinctions among family resources.

Considering the complex nature of the SES construct, well-designed research should therefore assess the mediating power of different components of SES, such as mother's and father's education levels and occupational classification, as well as family income. These components may play different roles as environmental influences on children's cognitive performance. For example, compared to family income, parental educational level may be more of a determinant of children's household reading material and educational enrichment. Occupational status of each parent may have a great deal to do with role-modeling potential and amount of available childrearing time. Moreover, the quality of the child's genetic endowment may be better predicted from parents' education and occupational levels than from the family income variable.

In addition to the previously mentioned limitations in divorce research, other methodological concerns include common problems such as nonrepresentative samples (many based on clinical populations); nonstandardized, often crude criterion measures; and short-term rather than longitudinal analyses (a particularly important issue because effects of divorce may be cumulative). Moreover, studies conducted prior to the 1980s may be limited by cohort effects because the psychological and sociological meaning of divorced family status has changed dramatically as a critical mass of single-parent families now exists.

MAGNITUDE OF THE DIVORCE EFFECT

Historical Overview

The relationship between parental divorce and children's cognitive ability was not a research emphasis until the 1980s. A recent analysis of divorce literature was conducted by Kunz (1992), who reviewed 347 empirical studies (only 56 of which dealt with cognitive criteria) from the period 1930 to 1989. Although tabulation and classification errors were apparent, this review offered a rough index of researchers' minimal attention to cognitive outcomes of divorce. The decade of the 1980s signaled an increased sensitivity to issues of parental divorce and child adjustment as evidenced by 198 of the 347 reviewed studies that occurred during this period. The relatively low priority of cognitive criteria continued to be apparent, however, in that only 22 studies were related to cognitive functioning, and most of these used questionnaires, interviews, or academic achievement measures rather than more formal assessments of intelligence. Kunz concluded from this database that children from disrupted homes displayed lower academic performance.

Earlier reviews (Amato & Keith, 1991; Demo & Acock, 1988; Shinn, 1978) also arrived at the same conclusion regarding children's lowered cognitive functioning. For example, Shinn (1978), in a survey of 58 studies of father absence, selected 28 that met minimal methodological requirements regarding sample characteristics and some attempt to control for SES. From this group, only 4 studies separated divorce from other causes of father absence, and Shinn levied specific criticisms about the methodology in each. Nonetheless, these studies concluded that compared to other reasons for father absence, divorce was among the more damaging causes of diminished cognitive performance. Shinn's review concluded that children's interactions with their parents foster cognitive development, and that restricted interaction has detrimental effects.

A review of divorce studies by Demo and Acock a decade later (1988) also reinforced the conclusion that family disruption is related to children's diminished cognitive performance. They examined gender, race, and SES differences in adjustment to family disruption and observed that the weight of evidence regarding cognitive criteria suggests (a) similar effects by gender, (b) little information about effects by race, and (c) substantial influence of SES. They cited studies that illustrated the reduction or elimination of cognitive performance disparities once SES controls were considered (e.g., Hetherington, Camara, & Featherman, 1983; Kinard & Reinherz, 1986; Svanum et al., 1982). In regard to children's academic performance, they noted that it was not possible to determine the impact of family structure because race and social class were not controlled. They did, however, conclude that single-parent children were slightly disadvantaged in school performance.

A more recent review of the effects of parental divorce on child well-being was published by Amato and Keith (1991). Their meta-analysis involved 92 studies that specifically compared the adjustment of divorced family children to intact family children. Selected studies were required to meet several methodological considerations. They had to examine divorce as the specific reason for family disruption and observe its effect on children as opposed to adults. A quantitative measure of child adjustment was required, and data needed to be presented in a way that permitted computation of at least one effect size. These reviewers utilized effect sizes to determine the magnitude of adjustment differences between divorced family and intact family children. Overall findings in regard to children's school achievement revealed a significant effect size of $-.16$, which indicated that across all reviewed studies of academic achievement, children from divorced families scored approximately one sixth of a standard deviation below children from intact families. Moreover, divorce was more negatively related to child academic achievement than family disruption due to the death of a parent. Including all well-being measures (e.g., academic achievement, conduct, psychological adjustment, self-concept, social adjustment, mother–child relations, and father–child relations), the authors concluded that the overall weight of evidence from the meta-analysis supported the hypothesis that parental divorce and its sequelae lower the well-being of children.

Noting that effect sizes were significantly stronger in some studies than in others, these authors added clarification by comparing mean effect sizes based on several research parameters. In an unexpected finding, lower effect sizes on academic criteria were observed if the studies involved random samples, large sample sizes, multiple-item measures of academic criteria, control variables such as SES, and teacher reports of child performance. Each of these research parameters would appear to improve methodology and consequent confidence in results. The authors indicated that "methodologically unsophisticated studies may overestimate the effects of divorce on children" (p. 36).

Thus, the consensus of four extensive literature reviews about divorce or single-parenting confirms the commonly held notion that children's cognitive performance is adversely affected by parental divorce. However, confidence in this conclusion is tempered by reviewers' collective acknowledgment that methodological limitations are substantial. They recommended larger samples, random selection, multifactored, multisourced assessment, use of control variables, and longitudinal designs. Additionally, the possibility of cohort effects in this area of research is considerable because divorce and single-parenting have become so widespread in recent years. What was once stigmatized is now commonplace, and research findings may thus reflect greater acceptance of single parenting by parents and children. This would minimize the relevance of older research such as that reviewed by Shinn in the 1970s, as well as many of the articles examined by the other three reviews. Several relatively recent studies conducted since 1980, are therefore emphasized to clarify the most current findings and trends surrounding these issues.

Contemporary Research Findings

The previously mentioned reviewers consistently verified that studies specifically designed to examine the relationship between parental divorce (rather than other causes of single parenting) and tested child intelligence (rather than academic achievement or social competence) are rare. Therefore, the following recent studies were selected for review because they utilized divorced samples. They are grouped by their various dependent measures of cognitive performance, beginning with the prioritized criterion variable of standardized tested intelligence. These studies are then followed by groupings according to standardized tests of academic achievement and grade point average (GPA).

Divorce And Intelligence Test Performance. Two longitudinal studies that meet above-criteria merit in-depth examination. First, The Virginia Study of Divorce (Hetherington, Cox, & Cox, 1982) specifically examined divorced family status and child cognitive ability. The sample consisted of 72 divorced family children and 72 biologically intact family children. Subjects were matched for age, gender, birth order, and attendance at the same preschool. In addition, parents were matched on age, education, and length of marriage when possible. Two years later, 102 of the original 144 subjects and their families participated in the follow-up study, which was demonstrated to be representative of the original sample on several indices. Data collection occurred at 2 months, 1 year, and 2 years following divorce, and included numerous measures of parent and child functioning. In regard to children's cognitive functioning, the Wechsler Preschool and Primary Scale of Intelligence (WPPSI); Matching Familiar Figures Test, and Embedded Figures Test were administered. Results showed that at both 2 months and 1 year following divorce, there were no significant differences between marital status groups on WPPSI scores. At 2 years following divorce (mean subject age = 5.81), no marital status differences were noted on Full Scale or Verbal IQ; however, children in divorced families scored significantly lower than children in intact families on Performance IQ (M = 97.5 for divorced and 104.4 for intact). Thus, across the three time periods, only one of the nine analyses performed on WPPSI was significant. No differences were noted between the two groupings on the Embedded Figures Test at any of the three time periods. The Matching Familiar Figures Test, on the other hand, revealed that 2 years following divorce, children from divorced families made more errors and had shorter latencies, and were therefore, determined to be more impulsive than children in nondivorced families. When considering the entire array of adjustment criteria, these authors found differences between marital status groups, but posited that on the average, parents and children had adapted to their new situation by 2 years.

Second, the complexity of the linkage between parental divorce and overall child adjustment was illustrated in The National Association of School Psychologists–Kent State University (NASP–KSU) Study of Divorce conducted by Guidubaldi and associates (e.g., Guidubaldi, 1988; Guidubaldi, Cleminshaw, Perry, & McLoughlin, 1983; Guidubaldi & Perry, 1985; Guidubaldi, Perry, & Cleminshaw, 1984; Guidubaldi, Perry, & Nastasi, 1987). Using a geographically stratified random sample of 144 school psychologists from 38 states, this study assessed 699 families and their children with a wide array of measures. The randomly chosen children were evenly distributed from Grades 1, 3, and 5 with one child from each grade selected from a single-parent divorced condition and one from a two-parent household, biologically intact since the child's birth. Among the measures used were three teacher-rating scales of classroom behavior (Hahnemann Elementary School Behavior Rating Scale, [HESB]; Vineland

Adaptive Behavior Scale [VABS]; and Child Behavior Checklist, [CBCL]). Additionally, there were extensive child and parent questionnaires, psychologists' ratings of the child, and most pertinent to this review, standardized psychometric tests of intelligence and achievement (Wechsler Intelligence Scale for Children-Revised, [WISC-R]; Wide Range Achievement Test, [WRAT]). A subsample of 221 children and their families were assessed with a similar battery of instruments 2 to 3 years later, and a second follow-up sample of 81 subjects were studied 7 to 8 years later. The substantial sample size, including 365 males and 334 females divided equally across three grade levels, enabled the researchers to examine relationships between marital status and child outcomes separately for age–gender groupings.

Findings relating to cognitive development were first examined using WISC–R IQ as a criterion. Mean IQ test scores for both intact and divorced family children were at least average, although a small but statistically significant difference that favored the intact sample was observed ($M = 108.3$ for intact, and 105.7 for divorced family subjects). When various SES indicators were used as controls, this significant difference was frequently eliminated. Covariance analyses for educational and occupational levels of each parent eliminated the IQ disparity between marital status groups. A significant Full Scale IQ difference remained between the groups, however, when family income was used as the covariate. Compared to parent education and occupation characteristics, economic disadvantage is thus a less adequate explanation for lower IQs in the divorced population. Considering the number of covariance analyses performed on the three IQ criteria (Verbal, Performance, and Full Scale IQ), the income covariate result represented only one significant finding from 15 analyses. Thus, the IQ variance between the marital status groups appeared to be highly related to nonincome SES indices. If these measures of parents' education and occupation levels represented a rough index of parental intelligence, their use as controls may effectively remove inherited intellectual potential from marital status analyses.

Further examination of the divorce–IQ connection was conducted as part of a second series of analyses of these data according to age–gender groupings (Guidubaldi, 1988; Guidubaldi et al., 1987). Comparing intact and divorced family children separately by first-, third-, and fifth-grade gender groups, no WISC-R Verbal IQ, Performance IQ, or Full Scale IQ differences were found for any of the six comparisons. The absence of significant differences in 18 analyses (three IQ scores for each grade by gender comparison of marital status groups) offered further evidence that parental divorce does not diminish tested intelligence.

A third set of analyses with these data (Jenkins & Guidubaldi, 1997) explored the relationship of divorce and IQ test performance according to gender and race. As found in numerous studies (e.g., Jensen, 1969; Reynolds, Chastain, Kaufman, & McLean, 1987; Thorndike, Hagen, & Sattler, 1986), White and African-American students were substantially different on Verbal, Performance, and Full Scale IQ. When marital status was factored into the analyses, it was clear that racial differences were far more pronounced within the divorced group sample. Whereas, in intact families, White children had better scores than African-American children only on WISC-R Performance IQ, differences by race for the divorced groups included all three IQ criteria as well as WRAT Reading test scores and seven socioemotional measures. More precise analyses that accounted for racial differences by marital status and gender yielded findings that have considerable theoretical importance. Considering IQ and achievement test scores, none were significantly different for racial groups in the female intact or female divorced samples. Only one racial difference was found for the male intact group, where Performance IQ favored Whites. Surprisingly, nine criteria including all three IQ indices, WRAT Reading scores, and five socioemotional criteria were significantly different for the male divorced group racial comparisons. Approximately one third of all possible racial comparisons within the divorced male group showed White males obtained significantly better scores than African-American males. The authors concluded that racial group differences in IQ were attributable to differences in the male and not the female population, and that these differences were more pronounced in disrupted families. These data obviously have bearing on the debate about genetically based racial group differences in IQ.

A fourth examination of this data base conducted by Kraynak (1996) explored differences in postdivorce adjustment between gifted and average IQ children. Subjects included 144 gifted children (defined as 120 to 145 IQ) and 308 average children (defined as 90 to 109 IQ) identified from the NASP–KSU data files. Two- and three-year follow-up data from these files were also examined for these subsamples. Considering academic criteria, gifted intact and gifted divorced family children showed no differences at either time period. In contrast, within the average IQ group, intact family children obtained better academic scores than divorced family children on teacher's ratings of overall academic achievement at Time 1 and on WRAT Reading test scores 2 years later. Comparing gifted and average IQ children within the divorced group, gifted children showed better performance on all four academic indices at Time 1 and 9 of 11 academic criteria at Time 2. These results appear to confirm that the experience of divorce does not deteriorate the academic performance of gifted children. It is interesting to note however, that at the Time 2 period (6.4 years after divorce), gifted intact family children had better scores than gifted divorced family counterparts on quality of relationships with their fathers, as well as better parent and teacher ratings of externalizing, internalizing, and total behavior problems on the CBCL. Thus, although their superior intelligence became manifest in better academic achievement test scores and teacher grades, gifted divorced family children's long-term behavioral and emotional adjustment appeared to be problematic.

A few additional studies that examined the relation between divorce and cognitive functioning add further credibility to the conclusion that divorce does not lead to a diminished IQ, although it does relate strongly to lowered academic achievement test scores and GPA. For example, a study of 115 (89 intact family and 26 divorced single-parent families) suburban kindergarten children (Guidubaldi & Perry, 1984) used multiple regression analyses to examine the relative predictive power of a wide array of family variables, including single-parent status, the Hollingshed Two-Factor Index classification of father's occupational status, mothers' and fathers' level of education, sibling structure, maternal employment, and a number of health-related indices (e.g., birth weight). Multiple intellectual, academic, and social criteria were examined, including the Peabody Picture Vocabulary Test IQ (PPVT IQ), Wide Range Reading and Math Tests, Metropolitan Readiness Tests, and teacher's quartile ranking of the child's general academic readiness for first grade work. As expected, the three SES predictors in combination, significantly predicted PPVT IQ ($r=.34$), WRAT Reading ($r=.38$), WRAT Math ($r=.35$), Metropolitan Total Score ($r=.42$), and teacher's ranking of academic readiness ($r=.34$). Considering all other predictors, single-parent status was the most powerful predictor variable, which related significantly to intellectual, academic, and socioemotional criteria and added significant amounts of independent variance to the SES predictions of achievement and social competency. Despite strong predictions of each academic index (e.g., WRAT Math, $r=.42$), single-parent status did not relate to PPVT intelligence test scores.

Finally, one recent study examined both divorce and father absence variables on standardized IQ scores of inner-city children. The Father Involvement Project (Guidubaldi & Duckworth, 1998) included a sample of 185 at-risk school-aged children identified as either specific learning disabled or severe behaviorally handicapped in a large urban center. Males represented 76% of the sample (typical for these special education classifications). In regard to race, 64% of the subjects were White, and 33% African American. Information was obtained from the child's primary caregivers about satisfaction with the spouse or exspouse's parenting behaviors, the level of conflict in the coparenting relationship, and the amount and quality of biological father involvement with the child. Behavioral and cognitive criteria were assessed, including Wechsler Intelligence Scale for Children–Third Edition (WISC–III) Verbal, Performance, and Full Scale IQ scores. Correlational analyses revealed that high amounts of biological father involvement, high quality of biological father involvement, and low levels of coparental conflict each significantly related to children's higher scores on Verbal, Performance, and Full Scale IQ. Additionally, high parent-role satisfaction significantly related to children's higher scores on Verbal and Full Scale IQ. Approximately 16% to 18% of the variance of Full Scale IQ was accounted for by these independent variables. It is also important to note that intelligence scores were determined to be more influenced by father involvement than marital status. This was evidenced by the absence of significant findings on one-way ANOVA results that compared Full Scale IQ scores for children in the married, divorced, and never married marital status groupings.

Divorce And Standardized Achievement Tests.   Findings that pertain to standardized measures of academic achievement have been inconsistent. Some recent studies reported that there are no significant differences on standardized achievement measures between divorced and intact family children. For example, Kalter, Riemer, Brickman, and Chen (1985) found no differences on Stanford Achievement Tests for girls in Grade 6; and Kinard and Reinherz (1986) found that once controlling for maternal education, no group differences were found for reading or math achievement. A study by Watt, Moorehead-Slaughter, Japzon, and Keller (1990) revealed that intact family children initially had higher reading and math scores on the Iowa Test of Basic Skills. However, once SES controls were imposed, these two marital status groups were not significantly different on standardized measures of achievement or aptitude, as evidenced by scores on the Iowa Test of Basic Skills and the Cognitive Abilities Test. Although most of the aforementioned studies indicated no differences in standardized achievement indices for divorced and intact family children, one study found that there were substantial negative effects of divorce on student achievement tests. Specifically, Kaye (1989) examined divorced and intact family children at two points in time following parental divorce. At Time 1, 238 children were compared on Science Research Associates scores in reading and math obtained during the first 2 years following the divorce. ANOVA results revealed 122 intact family children had significantly higher scores than the 116 divorced family children in both areas. In addition, girls had higher scores than boys. At Time 2, 191 children were compared on the vocabulary, reading, and total math subtest scores of the Iowa Test of Basic Skills, 5 years following paren-tal divorce. ANOVA results showed no main effect for family type, but signifi-cant interactions for family type by child's gender. Specifically, girls had higher scores than boys in divorced families, and boys had higher scores than girls in in-tact families. The aforementioned series of studies by Guidubaldi et al. (1983) also found academic test performance (WRAT) to be substantially better for in-tact family children. When SES was controlled with the use of either the in-come variable or fathers' education and occupation levels, WRAT score differences between the groups were eliminated. However, this was not the case when mothers' educational or occupational levels were used as controls.

Divorce And Student Grade Point Average.   The findings of several re-cent studies reveal that divorce does have a negative impact on student GPA. For example, in a study of 96 middle-school students, Mulholland, Watt, Philpott, and Sarlin (1991) found that even after controlling for scholastic aptitude and so-cial class, divorced family children showed significantly lower GPAs in seventh and eighth grades compared to intact family children. Similarly, Kaye (1989) ex-amined the school records of 234 divorced family children and 223 intact family children. Even after 5 years following the divorce, divorced family children had consistently lower GPAs than their intact counterparts, with boys exhibiting lower GPAs than girls. Congruent findings were also reported by Brubeck and Beer (1992) and Call, Beer, and Beer (1994). The first study, which consisted of 131 high school students, found that divorced family children had significantly lower GPAs than intact family children; and the latter study reported the same findings, in a sample of 116 elementary school children. In both cases, boys had significantly lower GPAs than girls. Finally, Kunz and Kunz (1995) collected data on 169 college men and women and found that parental divorce was significantly related to lower GPAs for this young adult population. Clearly, the weight of re-cent evidence related to parental divorce and student GPA documents that di-vorced family children are earning lower grades in school than intact family children. In the Guidubaldi et al. studies (1983, 1984, 1988) grades in both read-ing and math were considerably higher for intact family children, but once again these differences were eliminated in covariance analyses using income and fa-ther's education level as covariates. Maternal education and occupational con-trols failed to influence these marital status differences.

DISCUSSION

The topics discussed in this chapter—divorce and cognitive ability—are two of the most controversial, emotion laden issues in our contemporary culture. Gender conflicts surrounding divorce reverberate in courtrooms and legislative chambers throughout the country, and the nature–nurture debates about intelligence spill over from scholarly journals to street demonstrations. It is not surprising that empirical findings from research studies on these topics are often exaggerated and politicized to support opposing views. We therefore acknowledge the responsibility to report our conclusions objectively, but we also recognize the responsibility of the scholarly community to provide critically needed guidance to policymakers based on currently available empirical research. The findings summarized here have important implications for policymakers, particularly regarding legislation affecting postdivorce childrearing environments.

The first conclusion to be reached about the relationship between parents' marital status and children's cognitive ability is that tested IQ is not diminished by divorce. There may be a slight IQ advantage in the group of parents who keep their marriages intact, perhaps reflecting more sophisticated problem-solving techniques, and given the high heritability of intelligence, that difference may be manifested in children's tested performance. However, when SES controls for maternal and paternal education and occupational classification are imposed, the minor differences are ordinarily eliminated. Some researchers have suggested that controls for income should diminish or eliminate observed disparities in tested intellectual performance but that was not observed in the NASP–KSU study. The assumption that reduced family income following divorce is the factor responsible for IQ disparities is not supported, but parents' "human capital" of education and occupation levels is identified as a major contributor to variance in tested intelligence.

Taken together, these control variable findings offer some interesting speculations. The fact that parental education and occupational level control variables eliminate marital status IQ differences but income does not, may reveal a strong heritability factor in that the former variables are rough proxies for parental intelligence, and controlling for them eliminates variance attributable to genetic intellectual endowment. In contrast, the income variable is less likely to reflect genetic potential of parents, particularly following divorce. Divorced parents have substantially lower income, but this does not decrease their child's IQ, nor does it reflect lower genetic potential.

The cognitive ability measures most often used in postdivorce research have been either tests of academic achievement or school grades. These are clearly affected by more than inherent intelligence and consequently should be more susceptible to environmental influences. Research findings from numerous studies across recent decades document that intact family children do indeed surpass divorced family children on both achievement tests (e.g., Amato &

Keith, 1991; Guidubaldi, 1988; Guidubaldi et al., 1984; Kaye, 1989; Kinard & Reinherz, 1986) and GPA (e.g., Brubeck & Beer, 1992; Call et al., 1994; Guidubaldi, 1988; Guidubaldi et al., 1984; Kaye, 1989; Mulholland et al., 1991). However, when SES controls are imposed, many of these differences are reduced or eliminated (e.g., Guidubaldi, 1988; Guidubaldi et al., 1984; Kelly, 1993; Kinard & Reinherz, 1986; Watt et al., 1990).

Observed academic achievement differences also vary considerably by gender and age. In the NASP–KSU study, both first-grade boys and girls from intact family homes surpassed their divorced family counterparts on achievement indices. By Grade 5, however, only the boys showed achievement differences between marital status groups. These gender differences are consistent with findings from numerous other studies (e.g., Brubeck & Beer, 1992; Call et al., 1994; Hetherington, Cox, & Cox, 1982; Jenkins & Guidubaldi, 1997; Kaye, 1989).

Findings from the NASP–KSU study that addressed gender and racial IQ differences have relevance for both theoretical and applied psychology. The rare opportunity to analyze marital status differences by gender–race groups revealed that racial differences were accounted for by male but not female subjects. Obviously, this finding contradicts those who posit genetically determined racial group differences in intelligence because both genders share the same gene pool. Moreover, this finding highlights the importance of working with African-American males to enhance achievement motivation and other socioemotional prerequisites for optimal cognitive functioning.

Another conclusion of this chapter is that among the various ecological factors that may affect divorced family children's cognitive performance, none appears to be as powerful an influence as father involvement. A great deal has now been written about this issue beginning with the pioneering works of Biller (1982), Lamb (1976), and others, and currently expressed in excellent volumes by Biller (1993), Popenoe (1996), Lamb (1997), and Amato and Booth (1997). Our studies confirm the salience of not only time of father involvement, but also the quality of that involvement (Guidubaldi & Duckworth, 1998). Path analyses by Whiteside (1996) validated that quality of involvement must be taken into account and this clearly would be a prerequisite to the definition of fathers' social capital.

Increasingly, those who study both divorce and unwed parenthood acknowledge the centrality of regular high-quality father involvement as an overdue intervention for children in distress. Within the past few years, a number of governmental position statements (e.g., Clinton, 1995; National Governors' Association, 1995; U.S. Department of Education, 1997) were issued that generated new initiatives to reconnect children with their fathers. Findings from decades of research on the cognitive performance of divorced family children validate this revived focus on fathering.

REFERENCES

Amato, P. R., & Booth, A. (1997). *A generation at risk: Growing up in an era of family upheaval.* Cambridge, MA: Harvard University Press.

Amato, P. R., & Keith, B. (1991). Parental divorce and the well-being of children: A meta-analysis. *Psychological Bulletin, 110*(1), 26–46.

Biller, H. B. (1982). Fatherhood: Implications for child and adult development. In B. B. Wolman (Ed.), *Handbook of developmental psychology* (pp. 702–725). Englewood Cliffs, NJ: Prentice-Hall.

Biller, H. B. (1993). *Fathers and families: Parental factors in child development.* Westport, CT: Auburn House.

Binet, A., & Simon, T. (1948). The development of the Binet-Simon scale. In W. Dennis (Ed.), *Readings in the history of psychology* (p. 417). New York: Appleton-Century-Crofts.

Bronfenbrenner, U. (1995). Developmental ecology through space and time: A future perspective. In P. Moen, G. H. Elder, & K. Luscher (Eds.), *Examining lives in context: Perspectives on the ecology of human development* (pp. 619–647). Washington, DC: American Psychological Association.

Bronfenbrenner, U., & Ceci, S. J. (1994). Nature–nurture reconceptualized in developmental perspective: A bioecological model. *Psychological Review, 101*, 568–586.

Brooks-Gunn, J. (1995). Children in families in communities: Risk and intervention in the Bronfenbrenner tradition. In P. Moen, G. H. Elder, & K. Luscher (Eds.), *Examining lives in context: Perspectives on the ecology of human development* (pp. 467–519). Washington, DC: American Psychological Association.

Brubeck, D., & Beer, J. (1992). Depression, self-esteem, suicide ideation, death anxiety, and GPA in high school students of divorced and nondivorced families. *Psychological Reports, 71*, 755–763.

Bumpass, L. L. (1990). What's happening to the family? Interactions between demographic and institutional change. *Demography, 27*(4), 483–498.

Call, G., Beer, J., & Beer, J. (1994). General and test anxiety, shyness, and grade point average of elementary school children of divorced and nondivorced parents. *Psychological Reports, 74*, 512–514.

Ceci, S. J. (1990). *On intelligence...more or less: A bioecological treatise on intellectual development.* Englewood Cliffs, NJ: Prentice-Hall.

Ceci, S. J., & Hembrooke, H. A. (1995). A bioecological model of intellectual development. In P. Moen, G. H. Elder, & K. Luscher (Eds.), *Examining lives in context: Perspectives on the ecology of human development* (pp. 303–345). Washington, DC: American Psychological Association.

Clinton, W. J. (1995, June 16). Memorandum for the heads of executive departments and agencies regarding supporting the role of fathers in families. Office of the Press Secretary, The White House. Washington, DC.

Coleman, J. S. (1988). Social capital in the creation of human capital. *American Journal of Sociology, 94*, 95–120.

Demo, D. H., & Acock, A. (1988). The impact of divorce on children. *Journal of Marriage and the Family, 50*, 619–648.

Elwood, D. (1988). *Poor support.* New York: Basic Books.

Furstenberg, F. F., Nord, C. W., Peterson, J. L., & Zill, N. (1983). The life course of children of divorce. *American Sociological Review, 52*(5), 695–701.

Gardner, H. (1983). *Frames of mind: The theory of multiple intelligences.* New York: Basic Books.

Goleman, D. (1995). *Emotional intelligence: why it can matter more than IQ.* New York: Bantum Books.

Guidubaldi, J. (1988). Differences in children's divorce adjustment across grade level and gender: A report from the NASP-KSU nationwide project. In S. Wolchek & P. Karoly (Eds.), *Children of divorce: Perspectives in adjustment* (pp. 185–231). Lexington, MA: Lexington Books.

Guidubaldi, J., Cleminshaw, H. K., Perry, J. D., & Mcloughlin, C. S. (1983). The impact of parental divorce on children: Report of the nationwide NASP study. *School Psychology Review, 12*(3), 300–323.

Guidubaldi, J., & Duckworth, J. (1998). *The influence of father and father surrogate involvement on child behavioral, intellectual, and academic adjustment in an urban special education sample.* Presentation to Domestic Policy Advisor to the President, The White House, Washington, DC.

Guidubaldi, J., & Perry, J. D. (1984). Divorce, socioeconomic status, and children's cognitive–social competence at school entry. *American Journal of Orthopsychiatry, 54*(3), 459–468.

Guidubaldi, J., & Perry, J. D. (1985). Divorce and mental health sequelae for children: A two-year follow-up of a nationwide sample. *Journal of the American Academy of Child Psychiatry, 24,* 531–537.

Guidubaldi, J., Perry, J. D., & Cleminshaw, H. K. (1984). The legacy of parental divorce: A nationwide study of family status and selected mediating variable son children's academic and social competencies. In B. B. Laney & A. E. Kazdin (Eds.), *Advances in clinical child psychology* (Vol. 7, pp. 109–151). New York: Plenum.

Guidubaldi, J., Perry, J., Gagin, J., Pepper, H., Muto, A., & Wells, L. (1995). *Reconnecting the absent parent: An empirical foundation for intervention to promote father involvement with urban special education children.* Symposium presented at the National Association of School Psychologists annual convention, Chicago, IL.

Guidubaldi, J., Perry, J. D., & Nastasi, B. K. (1987). Growing up in a divorced family: Initial and long-term perspectives on children's adjustment. In S. Oskamp (Ed.), Family processes and problems: Social psychological aspects. *Applied Social Psychology Annual* (Vol. 7, pp. 202–235). Newbury Park, CA: Sage.

Hetherington, E. M., Camara, K., & Featherman, D. L. (1983). Achievement and intellectual functioning of children in one-parent households. In J. T. Spence (Ed.), *Child relations* (pp. 205–284). Washington DC: National Association of the Education of Young Children.

Hetherington, E. M., Cox, M., & Cox, R. (1982). Effects of divorce on parents and children. In M. E. Lamb (Ed.), *Nontraditional families: Parenting and child development* (pp. 233–288). Hillsdale, NJ: Lawrence Erlbaum Associates.

Horn, W. F. (1995). *Father facts.* Lancaster, PA: National Fatherhood Initiative.

Jenkins, J. E., & Guidubaldi, J. (1997). The nature–nurture controversy revisited: Divorce and gender as factors in children's racial group differences. *Child Study Journal, 27*(2), 145–160.

Jensen, A. R. (1969). How much can we boost IQ and scholastic achievement? *Harvard Educational Review, 39*(1), 1–123.

Kalter, N., Riemer, B., Brickman, A., & Chen, J. W. (1985). Implications of parental divorce for female development. *Journal of the American Academy of Child Psychiatry, 24,* 538–544.

Kaye, S. H. (1989). The impact of divorce on children's academic performance. *Children of divorce: Developmental and clinical issues*, 283–298.

Kelly, J. B. (1993). Current research on children's postdivorce adjustment. *Family and Conciliation Courts Review, 31*(1), 29–49.

Kinard, E. M., & Reinherz, H. (1986). Effects of marital disruption on children's school aptitude and achievement. *Journal of Marriage and the Family, 48*, 285–293.

Kraynak, A. R. (1996). *The relationship of children's intellectual ability and adjustment to parental divorce*. Unpublished doctoral dissertation, Kent State University, Kent, OH.

Kunz, J. (1992). The effects of divorce on children. In S. J. Bahr (Ed.), *Family research: A sixty-year review, 1930–1990* (Vol. 2, pp. 325–376). New York: Lexington.

Kunz, J., & Kunz, J. P. (1995). Parental divorce and academic achievement of college students. *Psychological Reports, 76*, 1025–1026.

Lamb, M. E. (1976). *The role of the father in child development*. New York: Wiley.

Lamb, M. E. (1997). *The role of the father in child development*. New York: Wiley.

Mulholland, D. J., Watt, N. F., Philpott, A., & Sarlin, N. (1991). Academic performance in children of divorce: Psychological resilience and vulnerability. *Psychiatry, 54*, 268–280.

National Governors' Association. (1995). *Issue brief: The governors' campaign for children*. Washington, DC: Employment and Social Services Policy Studies Division.

Neisser, U., Boodoo, G., Bouchard, T. J., Boykin, A. W., Brody, N., Ceci, S. J., Halpern, D. F., Loehlin, J. C., Perloff, R., Sternberg, R. J., & Urbina, S. (1996). Intelligence: Knowns and unknowns. *American Psychologist, 51*(2), 77–101.

Nord, C. W., & Zill, N. (1996). *Non-custodial parents' participation in their children's lives: Evidence from the survey of income and program participation* (Vol. 1). Prepared for the Office of Human Services Policy, Office of the Assistant Secretary for Planning and Evaluation: U.S. Department of Health and Human Services. Contract NO: DHHS-100-93-0012, Delivery Order No. 11.

Popenoe, D. (1996). *Life without father*. New York: The Free Press.

Reynolds, C. R., Chastain, R. L., Kaufman, A. S., & McLean, J. E. (1987). Demographic characteristics and IQ among adults: Analysis of the WAIS-R standardization sample as a function of the stratification variables. *Journal of School Psychology, 25*, 323–342.

Shinn, M. (1978). Father absence and children's cognitive development. *Psychological Bulletin, 85*(2), 295–324.

Sternberg, R. J. (1985). *Beyond IQ: A triarchic theory of human intelligence*. New York: Cambridge University Press.

Svanum, S., Bringle, R. G., & McLaughlin, J. E. (1982). Father absence and cognitive performance in a large sample of six to eleven year old children. *Child Development, 53*, 136–143.

Thorndike, L. L., Hagen, E. P., & Sattler, J. M. (1986). *Stanford-Binet intelligence scale* (4th ed., Tech. Manual). Chicago: Riverside.

Tousley, D. (1995). *Fathers' involvement and satisfaction in the parenting role as a predictor of their sons' adjustment*. Unpublished doctoral dissertation, Kent State University, Kent, OH.

U.S. Commission on Child and Family Welfare. (1996). *Parenting our children: In the best interest of the nation*. Washington, DC: U.S. Government Printing Office.

U.S. Department of Commerce, Bureau of the Census. Income, poverty, and valuation of noncash benefits: 1993. *Current Population Reports, Consumer Income*, Series P60-18, Table D-6 and D-22, 1995.

U.S. Department of Education, Office of Educational Research and Improvement. (1997). *Father's involvement in their children's schools*. NCES 98-091, by C. Nord, D. Brimhall, & J. West. Washington, DC.

U.S. Department of Health and Human Services, National Center for Health Statistics, *Monthly vital statistics report* (Vol. 39, N.12(s), Table 2, May, 1991).

U.S. Department of Health and Human Services. *Vital statistics of the United States, 1991* (Vol. 1), Natality. Washington, DC: U.S. Government Printing Office.

Watt, N. F., Moorehead-Slaughter, O., Japzon, D. M., & Keller, G. G. (1990). Children's adjustment to parental divorce: Self-image, social relations and school performance. In J. E. Rolf, A. S. Masten, D. Cicchetti, K. H. Nuechterlein, & S. Weintraub (Eds.), *Risk and protective factors in the development of psychopathology* (pp. 281–303). New York: Cambridge University Press.

Wechsler, D. (1958). *The measurement and appraisal of adult intelligence* (4th ed.). Baltimore: Williams & Wilkins.

Whiteside, M. (1996). *The young child's post-divorce adjustment: A meta-analytic review of the literature* (Judicial Council of California Administrative Office of the Courts). Ann Arbor, MI: Ann Arbor Center for the Family.

6

Maternal Employment, Child Care, and Cognitive Outcomes

Margaret R. Burchinal
University of North Carolina

Grace I. L. Caskie
The Pennsylvania State University

Since the 1980s, dramatic increases in the number of working mothers have resulted in marked increases in the number of children who experience regular nonparental care. Today, maternal employment rates range from about 50% for mothers of infants to more than 75% for mothers of school-age children. Correspondingly, the majority of infants and more than 66% of preschoolers in the United States are cared for on a regular basis by someone other than the parent (Lamb, 1998). This increase in the use of nonparental care represents a major societal change in how young children are raised in the United States and has provoked a major controversy among professionals about the impact of early group care on young children's development (Scarr & Eisenberg, 1993). These controversies have, to some extent, shaped the empirical research to date (see Lamb, 1998 for a comprehensive review of these controversies and empirical results).

The most recent estimates regarding the proportions of mothers in the United States who are employed and have children in child care can be found in the National Household Education Survey conducted by National Center for Educational Statistics in 1995 (NCES; 1996). This survey indicated that percentage of children whose mothers who were employed ranged from 48% for mothers of infants under 1 year of age to 57% for mothers of 4-year-olds and preschool-age children, with an additional 6% to 10% of mothers who reported that they were looking for employment. Similarly, 59% of school-age children had employed mothers and an additional 5% had mothers who were looking for employment.

This survey also provided information about child-care experiences. It indicated that the percentage of children who received 10 or more hours per week of regular nonparental care varied from 39% in the child's first year, to 42% in the second year, 45% in the third year, 55% in the fourth year, and 64% in the fifth year. Although the proportion of children who received care by relatives or nonrelatives in the child's home or the adult's home remained relatively consistent across ages, the proportion who attended child-care centers increased dramatically. The proportion of children who were cared for by a relative varied from 18% of infants to 11% of 4-year-olds and by a nonrelative varied from 17% of 2-year-olds to 11% of 4-year-olds. In contrast, the proportion of children who were in center care increased from 6% in the child's first year, 9% in the second year, 14% in the third year, 27% in the third year, to 42% in the child's fifth year.

With so many children experiencing regular nonparental care during the infant and preschool years, controversy has characterized opinions among professionals and parents about the effects of this nonparental care on young children's development. The impact of the timing of nonparental care, amount of care, type of care, and the quality of that care on children's development has been acrimoniously debated. The controversies, in part, have focused on whether differences among families who do and do not use child care and mothers who are and are not employed outside of the home have been adequately considered in analyses.

FAMILY SELECTION OR CONTEXT

Much of the controversy regarding both maternal employment and child care and the impact of these factors on child development has hinged on whether researchers appropriately controlled for differences among mothers who were and were not employed outside of the home and families that did and did not use child care. Much of the early research included few, if any, family or maternal characteristics as covariates to control for such differences. Results from these studies were questioned, especially when early research indicated that extensive maternal employment and, specifically, infant care may harm children, because they ignored the context of the family ecology (Scarr & Eisenberg, 1993).

More recent analyses have been conducted within the framework of ecological or general systems models. Ecological or general systems theory describes human development as influenced by a hierarchy of factors that can facilitate or impair development, which include characteristics of the child, caregivers, family, immediate environment, and the culture in general (Bronfrenbrenner & Crouter, 1983; Sameroff, 1983). The child is seen as embedded in a number of hierarchically structured, interrelated systems ranging from those proximal to the child such as the mother–child relationship to distal systems such as general societal beliefs. They describe developmental patterns as a function of the child's innate characteristics and the proximal and distal environments. Not only do the models identify the levels of influence and risk factors, they also emphasize the dynamic transactions between the child and his or her environment. Development is an iterative process by which the child changes in response to interactions with the environment, which, in turn changes the environment. For example, frequent responsive and stimulating interactions with caregivers are believed to facilitate children's cognitive development because responsive interactions should provide scaffolded learning experiences and evoke more responsiveness in the infant to the caregiver, which make the interactions between infant and caregiver more rewarding, and thus increase the amount of stimulation the infant receives. As this cycle continues, the infants learns increasingly more about his or her world through interactions with the caregiver and by seeking out interactions with others.

Contextual analyses are essential for examining the relations between both maternal employment and child care to children's cognitive development because family and child characteristics known to be related to cognitive outcomes are also related to family choices about maternal employment and child care (e.g., Belsky & Eggebeen, 1991; Burchinal, Ramey, Reid, & Jaccard, 1995; Dunn, 1993; Goelman & Pence, 1987; Hayes, Palmer, & Zaslow, 1990; Kontos

& Fiene, 1987; Kontos, Howes, Shinn, & Galinsky, 1995; NICHD Early Child Care Research Network, 1996; Phillips, McCartney, & Scarr, 1987; Phillips, Voran, Kisker, Howes, & Whitebook, 1994). Mothers who return to the work place tend to be better educated, have higher status occupations, be single, and of color (Burchinal, Roberts, Nabors, & Bryant, 1996; Hoffman, 1989; NICHD Early Child Care Research Network, 1996). Families who select higher quality child care tend to be better educated, have more income, provide more stimulating and responsive home environments, and espouse childrearing beliefs and practices that have been linked to better child outcomes (Lamb, 1997; NICHD Early Child Care Research Network, 1996). All current child-care research must attend to issues of family context and include family selection variables to be credible (Scarr & Eisenberg, 1993).

More recently, researchers have extended this contextual approach by asking whether associations between either maternal employment or child-care experiences and child development vary as a function of child or family characteristics. At least three sets of hypotheses regarding interactions between child-care experiences and child outcomes were generated. Some hypothesized that differences in developmental patterns will be found when a discrepancy exists between the quality of care at home and in child care, with good quality child care enhancing development for children with less responsive home environments and poor quality care impairing development for children with more responsive home environments (Caughy, DiPietro, & Strobino, 1994). For example, researchers have argued that maternal employment and associated child care is the most harmful for the most advantaged children. They worry that cognitive development may be impaired for children from households with high incomes, highly educated parents, and stimulating home environments because child care is unlikely to provide comparable levels of stimulation as would full-time care by the mother (Greenstein, 1995). Still others have hypothesized that development is impaired if children experience discontinuities between home and child care, and argue that what constitutes appropriate child care should vary across children depending on the values and beliefs of their home environment (Garcia-Coll, 1990; Lamb, 1998). Such analyses have focused on identifying child and family factors that serve as risk or protective factors for children who receive child-care of varying quality. Of particular interest has been determining whether children from stimulating and responsive home environments are buffered from the negative effects of low quality child care and whether children from stressed families are at increased risk for experiencing negative effects of low quality care. Finally, others have questioned whether the impact of aspects of child care, such as quantity and quality, will vary as a function of ethnicity or culture because of cultural differences in child-care practices and beliefs. They argue that what constitutes high quality and quantity of care may be different for children of color than for White/non-Hispanic children because of differences in the history of societal discrimination and cultural practices (Garcia-Coll et al., 1996).

MATERNAL EMPLOYMENT

Studies of associations between maternal employment and children's cognitive outcomes produced mixed findings (Beyer, 1995; Hoffman, 1989). Almost separate literatures have examined the association between maternal employment and cognitive development for preschool-age and school-age children. Early studies indicated that IQ and academic achievement scores tended to be higher among school-age children whose mothers were employed than among children whose mothers were not employed (Heyns, 1982; Hoffman, 1989). Studies of preadolescents and adolescents found either no association or that maternal employment was positively related to cognitive and academic achievement scores among low-income, working-class, and middle-class girls and among low-income and working-class boys, but negatively related for middle-class boys (Hoffman, 1989; Moore & Driscoll, 1997; Vandell & Ramanan, 1992). More recent studies demonstrated that other factors such as parental stress, attitudes, and parenting styles mediate these associations between maternal employment and child outcomes. For example, agreement between parental attitudes about maternal employment and whether the mother worked predicted children's academic grades in a study of 240 ninth graders (Paulson, 1996) in analyses that adjusted for social class and gender. Other studies have linked maternal employment to higher cognitive and academic achievement among girls, due in part, to less stereotyped gender roles within families in which mothers were employed (Hoffman, 1989). In a review of this literature, Beyer (1995) concluded that "despite years of study, no definitive answer regarding the effect of maternal employment on children's academic achievement has emerged" due to lack of focus on the role of parenting styles as mediating variables (p. 213).

An almost separate literature has examined the associations between maternal employment and cognitive development in the child's first 5 years of life, which reflects the dramatic increase during the past 20 years in maternal employment among women with infants and preschool-age children. The original studies hypothesized that early, regular separation from the mother impair social, but not cognitive, development, and few of those studies measured children's cognitive development. Recent studies have employed contextual analyses of cognitive development that take the family ecology into account. Many of these studies used the analyses of the National Longitudinal Survey of Youth (NLSY), a nationally representative labor survey of youths who were between 14 and 21 years-of-age in 1979. These youths were followed prospectively, along with their children. Analyses of the first wave of child outcome data collected in 1986 indicated that maternal employment beginning during the child's first year was related to lower Peabody Picture Vocabulary Test (PPVT) scores at 3 to 4 years (Baydar & Brooks-Gunn, 1991), especially for middle-class boys (Desai, Chase-Lansdale, & Michael, 1989). Greenstein (1995) used the first three waves of data to test the hypothesis that maternal employment disproportionately impairs the cognitive development of the most advantaged children due to the generally poorer quality of care provided in child care than by the mother. She did not find evidence of a main effect for maternal employment or the hypothesized interaction between maternal employment and family income. Other studies also found no consistent pattern of evidence that maternal employment during the first year was related to cognitive development among middle-class children at 18 months old (Weinraub, Jaeger, & Hoffman, 1988) or during middle childhood (Burchinal et al., 1995). Part-time employment, compared with full-time employment, has been both positively (Beyer, 1995) and negatively (Baydar & Brooks-Gunn, 1991) related to cognitive development.

In summary, studies of maternal employment during early childhood and children's cognitive development have led researchers to conclude that it is family and child-care factors associated with maternal employment, not employment itself, that are linked to child outcomes. Hoffman (1989) summarized this literature by saying, "maternal employment is not so robust a variable that it can be linked to child outcomes. It operates through its effects on the family environment and the child care arrangements, and these are moderated by parental attitudes, family structure, and other variables" (p. 289). Most researchers are now focusing on factors such as the timing, amount, and quality of child care, the family environment, and parental attitudes instead of maternal employment as the primary predictors of interest.

TIMING OF CHILD CARE

The most vigorous debate about child-care concerns the potential influence of early nonparental care—especially in the first year of life—on later social and emotional development. Only a few studies have examined whether infant child care, irrespective of quality of care, is linked to cognitive development, and the results have been conflicting. Two sets of studies reported poorer cognitive development associated with infant child care. One study involved 8-year-olds in Texas who received extensive infant day care of dubious or poor quality (Vandell & Corasaniti, 1990). Among these children, full-time nonparental care that began during infancy was related to poorer academic and social skills. Two analyses of the NLSY mother–child data addressed the question of correlates of routine nonmaternal care during infancy in this national sample. Caughy et al. (1994) examined the association between child-care experience in the first 3 years and achievement scores of 867 White, Hispanic, and African-American children at 5 to 6 years of age. They found that initiation of child care during the first year of life was related positively to reading achievement at 5 to 6 years for children from less stimulating and responsive home environments and negatively for children from more optimal home environments. Baydar and Brooks-Gunn (1991) focused on 3- to 4-year-old White/non-Hispanic children and reported that children whose mothers return to work full-time during the child's first year tended to score lower on IQ and behavioral adaptation assessments than other children. However, questions about the dubious quality of care of the children in Texas and about the representativeness of the 1986 NLSY child sample (i.e., the children included in the 1986 sample were disproportionately from poor, young, undereducated mothers—for example, the mean level of education of mothers was less than a high school degree in the NLSY studies) limit the ability of these studies to address the question about the long-term effects of infant care among middle-class children.

Other studies have reported no or positive associations between children's long-term cognitive development and infant child care. Results from early intervention projects in which either high-quality center care or no treatment was randomly assigned to children at risk for poorer cognitive development due to poverty indicated that intervention beginning early in infancy may produce larger, more enduring cognitive gains than intervention beginning during the preschool years (Campbell & Ramey, 1994). A retrospective study of middle-class White and African-American families in the Seattle area suggested that entering care during the child's first year was neither positively nor negatively related to measures of social, emotional, or cognitive development during middle childhood (Burchinal et al., 1995). In contrast, Fields (1991) and Andersson (1989, 1992) reported better social, behavioral, and academic adjustment among middle-class U.S. and Swedish children who began attending high-quality child-care centers during infancy than among comparable children who began attending center child care later.

In summary, the most comprehensive and recent studies suggest that full-time child care during infancy is not linked to impaired cognitive development during early or middle childhood. It appears that earlier findings linking infant care to positive or negative outcomes were due to existing differences between families who elected to use or not to use infant child care and to the presumably poor quality of infant care in several studies and the high quality in other studies.

CHILD CARE QUALITY

Poor quality child care is of concern because developmental theories are based on the assumption that infants and preschoolers need responsive and stimulating interactions with adults to enhance cognitive and language development in early childhood (Sameroff, 1983). In particular, it is believed that adults who take turns in interactions with young children and share periods of joint focus provide young children with the linguistic scaffolding needed to facilitate language and cognitive development (Bradley et al., 1989; Tomasello & Farrar, 1986). Accordingly, children in group care are unlikely to experience such interactions unless there are relatively few children per adult and have teachers who provide developmentally appropriate interactions with each child in the class. Two almost distinct research literatures have examined the relations between child-care experiences and children's development, the early intervention and the community child-care literatures.

Early Intervention Child Care

Center-based early childhood interventions have been provided for children from families living in poverty, based on the assumption that their family settings too often did not provide sufficient early learning opportunities. The assumption that underlies these programs is that frequent, responsive, and stimulating interactions with caregivers and exposure to a variety of educational materials and experiences through their center-based experiences will enhance children's cognitive development over time. Most of these early intervention projects were implemented between 1964 and 1980 and provided child care at research child-care centers. At least some studies randomly assigned children to either treatment (child care) or control groups. Most of these programs were operated by university-based research teams, employed well-trained staff with high levels of supervision, and were presumed to be of high quality. Consistent with these underlying assumptions, cognitive gains among treated children appear to be due, in part, to increased infant responsiveness in interactions with people and objects associated with contingent, responsive interactions with caregivers within the child-care center (Burchinal, Campbell, Bryant, Wasik, & Ramey, 1997).

Program evaluations have provided clear support that these child-care experiences enhanced children's cognitive and language development, at least for the duration of the intervention (cf. Haskins, 1989; IHDP, 1990; Lazar & Darlington, 1982; O'Connell & Farran, 1982). Differences between treatment and control group IQ means were as large as a standard deviation during treatment (Campbell & Ramey, 1994). Lazar and colleagues conducted a comprehensive evaluation of many of the early intervention programs. Compared with those in the control groups, low-income children who attended high-quality child-care centers displayed higher cognitive scores during the preschool years (Burchinal, Lee, & Ramey, 1989; IHDP, 1990; Lazar & Darlington, 1982). For the most intensive early childhood programs, such benefits endured into adolescence and adulthood (Campbell & Ramey, 1994; Garber, 1988), which revealed treatment differences as large as one third of a standard deviation on cognitive and achievement tests during adolescence. In addition, compared with control children, children who received early interventions were more likely to be promoted in school, graduate from high school, and become productive young adults (Lazar & Darlington, 1982; Schweinhart, Weikart, & Larner, 1986). In contrast, control children were more likely to be retained in a grade, be placed in special education, and drop out of school (Lazar & Darlington, 1982).

Community Child Care

Other researchers have examined the relations between quality of child care and children's development among families using child care available in their communities. An extensive literature exists relating child-care quality to cognitive and language development. Most studies have indicated that preschool-age children display better cognitive and language development if they experience higher than lower quality care. This literature has demonstrated that factors such as parental education and beliefs about childrearing are related both to the type of care that families select for their child and to child outcomes, which creates a potential confound that must be considered in analyses. Much of the current research examined the quality of center-based child care and developmental outcomes, although a few studies examined quality of care in other settings.

Using standard measures of child-care quality, researchers have found that child-care quality was related to language and cognitive development, even after controlling for family selection factors such as socioeconomic status (SES), maternal education, or family structure in the large multisite studies (NICHD Early Child Care Research Network, 1997a; Peisner-Feinberg & Burchinal, 1997; Whitebook, Howes, & Phillips, 1989) and in smaller single-site studies (Dunn, 1993; Phillips et al., 1987; Schliecker, White, & Jacobs, 1991). In most of these studies, children who attended higher quality child care tended to display better cognitive and language development than children who attended lower quality child care, although the magnitude of these associations were generally modest. However, these associations between child care quality and child outcomes were not always observed (Clarke-Stewart, Gruber, & Fitzgerald, 1994; Goelman & Pence, 1987; Kontos, 1991), perhaps because of relatively small samples or restricted range of observed child-care quality.

The impact of quality of care on infant development has not been examined as extensively. At least two studies related infant care quality to infant language and cognitive development. Infants who experience higher quality care were more likely to demonstrate better cognitive and language skills in a large multisite study that included children in a wide variety of care settings (NICHD Early Child Care Research Network, 2000) and in a sample of 89 African-American infants who began attending a child-care center during their first year (Burchinal et al., 1996). Other studies indirectly suggest that quality of infant care is related to infant cognitive and language development. Melhuish, Lloyd, Martin, and Mooney, (1990) found that language development was poorer among infants who experienced lower quality care in child-care centers than among infants who received better quality care at home, with relatives, or in family child care in a middle-class sample. Similarly, preschoolers who experienced high-quality child care beginning during infancy showed better progress on tests of language and cognitive functioning than preschoolers without such child-care experiences (Burchinal et al., 1989; Roberts et al., 1989).

Based in part on the early intervention literature, it is assumed that high-quality community-based child care can serve as a protective factor for children at risk for impaired development due to risk factors such as low parental education, minority ethnic background, single-parent homes, and poverty (Lamb, 1998). At least two variations of this conceptual model have been presented. Some researchers argue that family factors and child-care factors interact such that positive child-care experiences can serve to protect or buffer at-risk children from the negative impact of these risk factors, whereas positive family factors protect the child from the impact of negative child-care factors. These investigators point to the large intervention effects for poor children and small or nonsignificant child-care effects among middle-class children observed in many studies of children attending community child-care centers (cf.

Lamb, 1997). Other researchers believe that both family and child-care factors are important in development, but child-care factors are more important for the child from at-risk family environments. The second set of beliefs is based on the growing literature from large multisite studies of community child care that find modest associations between child outcomes and child-care experiences for children from middle-class families. Several studies reported differential effects of child care on cognitive or language development related to SES or family structure (Baydar & Brooks-Gunn, 1991; Bryant, Burchinal, Lau, & Sparling, 1994; Caughy et al., 1994; Peisner-Feinberg & Burchinal, 1997; Vandell & Corasaniti, 1990), ethnicity (Bryant, Peisner-Feinberg, & Clifford, 1993; Burchinal et al., 1995), gender (Baydar & Brooks-Gunn, 1991; Bryant et al., 1994; Vandell & Corasaniti, 1990), and mother's education (Peisner-Feinberg & Burchinal, 1997). Most found that the effects of child care are stronger for preschool children from less advantaged circumstances. However, several recent studies failed to find evidence for moderating effects on cognitive or language development when examining parent education, family income, quality of home environment, or child gender (Burchinal et al., 1996; NICHD Early Child Care Research Network, 2000; Stipek, Feiler, Daniels, & Milburn, 1995).

Among the studies that examined the association between child-care quality and cognitive and language development and tested whether child-care effects are differentially related to child outcomes for children from varying family backgrounds, are two large recent studies. These are presented in more detail as they are likely the most comprehensive studies to date.

The Cost, Quality, and Child Outcomes study examined 100 child-care centers in each of four states (California, Colorado, Connecticut, and North Carolina) selected to represent variation in economic and regulatory climates. Preschool-aged children in observed classrooms were recruited, and cognitive, language, and social development was assessed for 757 children (Peisner-Feinberg & Burchinal, 1997). A composite quality measure was created from a measure of global quality, teacher sensitivity, teacher responsiveness, and child-centeredness. In addition, teacher ratings of the closeness of his or her relationship with the target child was included as a separate measure of child-care quality. Hierarchical linear models examined the association between these measures of quality and standardized measures of receptive vocabulary and preacademic skills and the teacher's perceptions of behavior problems and cognitive and attentional skills. Analyses adjusted for maternal education, the child's gender and ethnicity, and classroom effects related to selecting multiple children from the same classroom. Results indicated that child-care quality was positively, albeit modestly, related to higher vocabulary and prereading scores on standardized tests and to the teacher's ratings of the child's cognitive skills. Tests of interactions between the two child-care quality measures and mother's education, ethnicity, and child gender were conducted. An interaction between maternal education and care quality indicated the quality composite was related to children's prereading skill only for children whose mothers had less education. Child-care quality was modestly correlated ($.15 < r < .30$) with these outcomes prior to adjusting for covariates, with somewhat smaller associations after adjustment. Follow-up assessments indicated that this measure of child-care quality was related to the child's vocabulary and math skills when longitudinal analyses were conducted on data collected through kindergarten (Peisner-Feinberg et al., 1998). These analyses indicated that children who had experienced higher quality child care tended to perform better across time on measures of vocabulary and math skills. Neither the anticipated interaction between maternal education and reading skills nor between rates of change over time and child-care quality were observed in these analyses.

The second study examined the association between child-care quality and cognitive and language assessments in the 10-site NICHD Study of Early Child Care (NICHD Child Care Network, 2000) for more than 1,100 children. Quality of care for children in a wide variety of settings (centers, child-care homes, babysitters in child's home, and care by relatives which included grandparents and fathers) was observed when the children were 6, 15, 24 and 36 months of age, with the Observational Record of the Caregiving Environment (ORCE) (NICHD Early Child Care Research Network, 1996). Children's cognitive development was measured with two standardized assessments and language development was measured with parent ratings at 15 and 24 months and with a standardized assessment at 36 months. Hierarchical regressions examined each outcome as a function of selection variables, child gender, parenting variables, global child-care variables (average hours of nonmaternal child care per week, number of child-care centers attended, number of child-care homes attended, and total rating of quality from ORCE), and a specific child-care variable (amount of language stimulation in child-care environment from the ORCE). Blocks of variables were entered in this order into the hierarchical regressions. Analyses indicated that children who experienced higher quality child care tended to score higher on the cognitive tests at 15, 24, and 36 months and on the language tests at 36 months and had mothers who reported more receptive and expressive vocabulary at 15 and 24 months. Comparisons of models that included and excluded the specific measure of child-care quality (i.e., language stimulation), indicated that language stimulation in the child care accounted for most of the association between the 15- and 24-month outcomes and overall global child-care quality. Tests of interactions between child-care quality and the quality of family environment, income, ethnicity, and gender did not yield consistent findings that indicated the child-care quality was differentially related to these cognitive or language outcomes for children with varying home environments, family income, ethnic backgrounds, or gender.

In summary, most studies have indicated that children who attend higher quality child care have better cognitive and language development. In general, these associations appear to be modest for children who do not experience major risk factors such as poverty, with child outcomes more strongly related to family characteristics than to child-care quality in hierarchical analyses that enter demographic and family characteristics first.

TYPE OF CHILD CARE

A few studies have compared child outcomes for children attending different types of child care. Preschool or center-based child care is linked to both positive and negative developmental outcomes, but these associations may not continue after children begin attending primary schools. In an extensive earlier review, Clarke-Stewart and Fein (1983) concluded that center-based child care related with remarkable consistency to better intellectual performance, at least while children were attending centers. Furthermore, this relationship was maintained regardless of children's gender, ethnicity, social class, or temperament. Later, Clarke-Stewart (1989) reviewed the greatly expanded literature and concluded that attendance at a high-quality center/preschool correlated positively in the early years with higher intelligence, as well as more self-confidence, independence, extroversion, and assertiveness for almost all children during preschool years. In contrast, several studies reported no reliable differences between infants who attended center or child-care home (Barglow, Vaughn, & Moliter, 1987; Clarke-Stewart, 1992; Moore, Snow, & Poteat, 1988). In contrast, a longitudinal study of Swedish children indicated that children who attended child-care homes engaged in more positive and competent play with peers in their child-care setting than children who attended centers (Lamb, Sternberg, Knuth, Hwang, & Broberg, 1994) and a retrospective study of U.S. middle-class children indicated that White and Black children who attended centers tended to display better receptive vocabularies in middle childhood when compared with children who did not attend child-care centers (Burchinal et al., 1995).

Such differences that favor preschool-age children with center care were reported in comprehensive, recent, two studies. In a study that compared six types of child-care arrangements experienced by 150 predominantly middle-class 2- to 4-year-olds (Clarke-Stewart, 1992). Children who experienced care in a center or preschool, whether full or part time, demonstrated greater competence in verbal ability, cognition, social competence, cooperation with peers, and social cognition compared to those who experienced home-based care, either with their parents, sitters, or day care providers. The NICHD Study of Early Child Care found that children in center care scored higher on 24- and 36-month measures than children in other types of care after adjusting for the quality and quantity of child care and selected family and child characteristics (NICHD Child Care Network, 1997a). These advantages, however, weren't always detected in middle childhood for middle-class children in the United States (cf. Clarke-Stewart, 1989). In fact, one of the NLSY studies found that center child-care experience of unknown quality was negatively related to math achievement score at 5 to 6 for children from more optimal home environments, whereas center experience was positively related for children from more impoverished home environments (Caughy et al., 1994). In contrast, longer term follow-up studies in Sweden (Andersson, 1989, 1992) and West Germany (Tietze, 1987) reported from large population-based cohorts that children who attended high quality child-care centers had significantly better academic performance and social adjustment at 8 to 13 years of age.

In conclusion, limited evidence exists to suggest that center care during the preschool years may be related to slightly better cognitive outcomes. Reassuringly, these findings were obtained from studies that measured both type and quality of care as well from studies that did not measure quality of care.

QUANTITY OF CHILD CARE

Linked to concerns about childcare are concerns about full-time or extensive child care (Lamb, 1997) on children's social development. Developmentalists express concerns that time away from parents may result in more time in less stimulating and responsive environments, which can impair cognitive development for children from stimulating and responsive home environment (Paulson, 1996). Somewhat different conclusions are drawn from studies that did and did not measure child-care quality. Continuous full-time care beginning in infancy was negatively related to academic achievement (Vandell & Corasanti, 1990) and vocabulary scores for girls (Burchinal et al., 1995) among predominantly middle-class children and positively related to academic achievement among low-income children (Moore & Driscoll, 1997; Vandell & Ramanan, 1992) in studies that did not adjust for quality of care. In contrast, extensive care in high quality child-care centers has been related more positive cognitive and academic outcomes into middle childhood in the United States (Fields, 1991) and Sweden (Andersson, 1989, 1992). Amount of care was not related positively or negatively to cognitive and language development in the multisite NICHD study of child care either before or after adjusting for care quality (NICHD Early Child Care Research Network, 2000). In conclusion, evidence that links extensive care to negative child outcomes appear to emerge primarily from studies that did not measure quality of care.

CONCLUSIONS AND PUBLIC POLICY IMPLICATIONS

After 30 years of research into the relations between children's cognitive development and both maternal employment and child-care experiences, it appears that some aspects of child-care experiences are related to some developmental outcomes for at least some children. Maternal employment appears to have indirect effects only and operates through factors such as parental attitudes, parenting style, and child-care experiences. Of the various components of child care, child-care quality shows the strongest and most consistent associations with cognitive and social development. These associations tend to be modest, at least for middle-class children, with characteristics of the family showing stronger associations with all outcomes than characteristics of child care. In contrast, studies of early intervention for children from families living in poverty have suggested that high quality child care, beginning during infancy, can have large and long-term effects on cognitive development. Other aspects of the child-care experience such as timing, quantity, and type of care appear to less related to development outcomes in studies that also considered child-care quality and family selection factors, although some evidence exist to suggest that center care may be modestly positively related to cognitive outcomes.

At least some developmentalists have argued that the modest effects associated with child-care quality implies that quality really doesn't matter (Scarr, 1998). This view is not widely accepted. Some developmentalists argue, based on the few studies that have followed children into middle childhood, that child-care quality may have long-term effects indirectly, not directly, because of its impact on children's expectations regarding the teacher–child relationship (Howes, Hamilton, & Phillipsen, 1998). Howes argued that children who experience poor relationships with teachers are likely to develop lower, more problematic expectations regarding relationships with teachers and other adults in general. These expectations make it difficult for the child to adjust and learn within the classroom environment. Other developmentalists argue that it is unreasonable to expect large associations when analyses are conducted using a general systems or ecological models. These models suggest that the child's development is a function of interconnected systems such as the parent–child relationship, the family, the child care, and the community. Overlapping systems will lead to smaller portions of variance that will be uniquely accounted for by any one component of the child's life. Indeed, comparisons of individual regression coefficients from the full regression model, not the hierarchical model, suggest that child-care quality can be as strongly related to outcomes such as cognitive development to characteristics such as the mother's IQ or the quality of mother–child interactions (NICHD Early Child Care Research Network, 2000). Further work is clearly needed to identify and clarify the mechanisms by which these global measures of quality are related to children's cognitive and social development, and to determine whether these mechanism operate similarly or differently for children from diverse backgounds (Lamb, 1997).

If one concludes that child-care quality does matter, then there are public policy implications. Characteristics of child care such as child–adult ratios, class sizes, and caregiver education and training that can be regulated have been linked child care quality (Arnett, 1989; Berk, 1985; Howes, 1983; Howes & Rubenstein, 1985; Kontos & Fiene, 1987; Phillipsen, Burchinal, Howes, & Cryer, 1997) and directly to child outcomes. Children's cognitive and social developmental outcomes are more positive (Burchinal et al., 1996; Howes, 1997; Howes & Olenick, 1986; Howes, Rodning, Galuzzo, & Myers, 1988; Ruopp, Travers, Glantz, & Colen, 1979) in classrooms with a smaller than a larger number of children per caregiver. In classrooms with smaller group sizes, children have been found to behave more positively (Howes, 1983; Howes & Rubenstein, 1985; Kontos & Fiene, 1987; Ruopp et al., 1979), and their language and intellectual development is enhanced (Kontos & Fiene, 1987; Ruopp et al., 1979) when compared to children in classrooms with larger group sizes. Children placed in the care of teachers with more education and training have been found to have better child development outcomes (Howes, 1997; Howes & Olenick, 1986; Ruopp et al., 1979; Vandell & Powers, 1983; Whitebook et al., 1989) than children with less educated teachers. To provide more information relevant for policymakers, several studies demonstrated that children's cognitive and social development is enhanced when classrooms meet professional recommendations regarding teacher education and caregiver–child ratios (Burchinal et al., 1996; Howes, 1992; Howes, Phillips, & Whitebook, 1998; NICHD Early Child Care Research Network, 1997b). The NICHD study revealed that children's cognitive and social outcomes at 36 months was linked linearly to the number of recommendations met in that child's classroom.

In conclusion, maternal employment and nonparental child care is the norm, not the exception, for children in the United States. The mediocre quality of much of the child care in the United States (Lamb, 1998) raises concerns about maternal employment and the associated child care on the cognitive development of young children because quality of care is a fairly consistent, albeit modest, correlate of these developmental outcomes. Public policies that promote fewer children per caregiver and better educated and trained caregivers are likely to enhance child outcomes by increasing child-care quality.

REFERENCES

Andersson, B. E. (1989). Effects of public day care: A longitudinal study *Child Development, 60*, 857–866.

Andersson, B. E. (1992). Effects of day-care on cognitive and socio–emotional competence in 13-year-old Swedish school children. *Child Development, 63*, 20–36.

Arnett, J. (1989). Caregivers in day-care centers: Does training matter? *Journal of Applied Developmental Psychology, 10*, 541–552.

Barglow, P., Vaughn, B. E., & Moliter, N. (1987). Effects of maternal absence due to employment on the quality of infant–mother attachment in a low-risk sample. *Child Development, 58*, 945–954.

Baydar, N., & Brooks-Gunn, J. (1991). Effects of maternal employment and child care arrangements on preschoolers' cognitive and behavioral outcomes: Evidence from the children of the national longitudinal survey of youth. *Developmental Psychology, 27*, 932–945.

Belsky, J., & Eggebeen, D. (1991). Early and extensive maternal employment and young children's socioemotional development: Children of the National Longitudinal Survey of Youth. *Journal of Marriage and Family, 53*, 1083–1110.

Berk, L. (1985). Relationship of caregiver training to child-oriented attitudes, job satisfaction, and behaviors towards children. *Child Care Quarterly, 14*, 103–129.

Beyer, S. (1995). Maternal employment and children's academic achievement: Parenting styles as mediating variables. *Developmental Review, 15*, 212–253.

Bradley, R. H., Caldwell, B. M., Rock, S. L., Ramey, C. T., Barnard, K. E., Gray, C., Hammond, M. A., Mitchell, S., Gottfried, A. W., Siegel, L., & Johnson, D. L. (1989). Home environment and cognitive development in the first three years: A collaborative study involving six sites and three ethnic groups in North America. *Developmental Psychology, 25*, 217–235.

Bryant, D. M., Burchinal, M. R., Lau, L. B., & Sparling, J. J. (1994). Family and classroom correlates of Head Start children's developmental outcomes. *Early Childhood Research Quarterly, 9*, 289–309.

Bryant, D. M., Peisner-Feinberg, E. S., & Clifford, R. M. (1993). *Evaluation of public preschool programs in North Carolina: Final report*. Chapel Hill, NC: Frank Porter Graham Child Development Center.

Burchinal, M. R., Campbell, F. A., Bryant, D. M, Wasik, B. A., & Ramey, C. T. (1997). Early intervention and mediating processes in cognitive performance of children of low-income African-American families. *Child Development, 68*, 935–954

Burchinal, M. R., Lee, M. W., & Ramey, C. T. (1989). Type of day-care and preschool intellectual development in disadvantaged children. *Child Development, 60,* 128–137.

Burchinal, M. R., Ramey, S. L., Reid, M. K., & Jaccard, J. (1995). Early child care experiences and their association with family and child characteristics during middle childhood. *Early Childhood Research Quarterly, 10,* 33–61.

Burchinal, M. R., Roberts, J. E., Nabors, L. A., & Bryant, D. (1996). Quality of center child care and infant cognitive and language development. *Child Development, 67,* 606–620.

Campbell, F., & Ramey, C. T. (1994). Effects of early intervention on intellectual and academic achievement: A follow-up study of children from low-income families. *Child Development, 65,* 684–698.

Caughy, M. O., DiPietro, J. A., & Strobino, D. M. (1994). Day-care participation as a protective factor in the cognitive development of low-income children. *Child Development, 65,* 457–471.

Clarke-Stewart, K. A. (1989). Infant day care: Maligned or malignant? *American Psychologist, 44,* 266–273.

Clarke-Stewart, K. A. (1992). Consequences of child care for children's development. In A. Booth (Ed.), *Child care in the 1990s: Trends and consequences* (pp. 63–83). Hillsdale, NJ: Lawrence Erlbaum Associates.

Clarke-Stewart, K. A., & Fein, G. C. (1983). Early childhood programs. In P. H. Mussen (Series Ed.) and M. M. Haith & J. J. Campos (Vol. Eds.), *Handbook of child psychology:* Vol. 2. *Infancy and developmental psychobiology,* 4th ed., (pp. 917–999). New York: Wiley.

Clarke-Stewart, K. A., Gruber, C. P., & Fitzgerald, L. M. (1994). *Children at home and in day care.* Hillsdale, NJ: Lawrence Erlbaum Associates.

Desai, S, Chase-Lansdale, P. L., & Michael, R. T. (1989). Mother or market? Effects of maternal employment on the intellectual ability of 4-year-old children. *Demography, 4,* 545–561.

Dunn, L. (1993). Proximal and distal features of day care quality and children's development. *Early Childhood Research Quarterly, 8,* 167–192.

Fields, T. (1991). Quality infant day-care and grade school behavior and performance. *Child Development, 62,* 863–870.

Garber, H. L. (1988). *The Milwaukee project: Preventing mental retardation in children at risk.* Washington, DC: American Association on Mental Retardation.

Garcia-Coll, C. T. (1990). Developmental outcome of minority infants: A process-oriented look into our beginnings. *Child Development, 61,* 270–289.

Garcia-Coll, C. T., Lamberty, G., Jenkins, R., McAdoo, H. P., Crnic, K., Wasik, B. H., & Garcia, H. V. (1996). An integrative model for the study of developmental competencies in minority children. *Child Development, 67,* 1891–1914.

Goelman, H., & Pence, A. R. (1987). Effects of child care, family, and individual characteristics on children's language development: The Victoria day care research project. In D. Phillips (Ed.), *Quality in child care: What does the research tell us?* (pp. 89–104). Washington, DC: National Association for the Education of Young Children.

Greenstein, T. N. (1995). Are the "most advantaged" children truly disadvantaged by early maternal employment? Effects on child cognitive outcomes. *Journal of Family Issues, 16,* 149–169.

Haskins, R. (1989). Beyond metaphor: The efficacy of early childhood education. *American Psychologist, 44,* 274–282.

Hayes, C. D., Palmer, J. L., & Zaslow, M. J. (Eds.), (1990). *Who cares for America's children?: Child care policy for the 1990's.* Washington, DC: National Academy Press.

Hoffman, L. W. (1989). Effects of maternal employment in the two-parent family. *American Psychologist, 44,* 283–292.

Howes, C. (1983). Caregiver behavior in center and family day care. *Journal of Applied Developmental Psychology, 4,* 99–107.

Howes, C. (1997). Children's experiences in center-based child care as a function of teacher background and adult: Child ratios. *Merrill-Palmer Quarterly, 43,* 404–425.

Howes, C., Hamilton, C. E., & Phillipsen, L. C. (1998). Stability and continuity of child–caregiver and child–peer relationships. *Child Development, 69,* 418–426.

Howes, C., & Olenick, M. (1986). Family and child care influences on toddler compliance. *Child Development, 57,* 202–216.

Howes, C., Phillips, D. A., & Whitebook, M. (1992). Threshholds of quality: Implications for the social development of children in center-based child care. *Child Development, 53,* 449–460.

Howes, C., Rodning, C., Galluzzo, D. C., & Myers, L. (1988). Attachment and child care: Relationships with mother and caregiver. *Early Childhood Research Quarterly, 3,* 403–416.

Howes, C., & Rubenstein, J. (1985). Determinants of toddlers' experiences in care: Age of entry and quality of setting. *Child Care Quarterly, 14,* 140–151.

IHDP. (1990). Enhancing the outcomes of low-birth-weight, premature infants - A multisite, randomized trial. *Journal American Medical Association, 263,* 3035–3042.

Kontos, S. J. (1991). Child care quality, family background, and children's development. *Early Childhood Research Quarterly, 6,* 249–262.

Kontos, S., & Fiene, R. (1987). Child care quality, compliance with regulations, and children's development: The Pennsylvania study. In D. Phillips (Ed.), *Quality in child care: What does research tell us?* (pp. 57–80). Washington, DC: National Association for the Education of Young Children.

Kontos, S., Howes, C., Shinn M., & Galinsky, E. (1995). *Quality in family child care and relative care.* New York: Teachers College Press.

Lamb, M. E. (1998). Nonparental child care: Context, quality, correlates. In W. Damon, I. E. Sigel, & K. A. Renninger (Eds.), *Handbook of child psychology: Vol. 4. Child psychology in practice 5th ed.,* (pp. 73–134). New York: Wiley.

Lamb, M. E., Sternberg, K. J., Knuth, N., Hwang, C. P., & Broberg, A. G. (1994). Peer play and nonparental care experiences. In H. Goelman & E. V. Jacobs (Eds.), *Children's play in childcare settings* (pp. 37–52). Albany: State University of New York Press.

Lazar, I., & Darlington, R. (1982). Lasting effects of early education: A report from the consortium for longitudinal studies. *Monographs of the Society for Research in Child Development, 47* (2–3), Serial No. 195.

Melhuish, E. C., Lloyd, E., Martin, S., & Mooney, A. (1990). Type of child care at 18 months—II. Relations with cognitive and language development. *Journal of Child Psychology and Psychiatry and Allied Disciplines, 316,* 861–870.

Moore, K. A., & Driscoll, A. K., (1997). Low-wage maternal employment and outcomes for children: A study. *The Future of Children, 7,* 122–127.

Moore, M. S., Snow, C. W., & Poteat, M. (1988). Effects of variant types of child care experience on the adaptive behavior of kindergarten children. *American Journal of Orthopsychiatry, 58,* 297–303.

National Center for Educational Statistics. (1996). *1995 National household education survey.* Washington, DC: U.S. Department of Education Office of Educational Research and Improvement.

NICHD Early Child Care Research Network. (1996). Characteristics of infant child care: Factors contributing to positive caregiving. *Early Childhood Research Quarterly, 11,* 269–306.

NICHD Early Child Care Research Network. (2000). *The relationship of child care to cognitive and language development. Child Development, 17,* 958–978.

O'Connell, J. C., & Farran, D. C. (1982). Effects of day care experience on the use of intentional communicative behaviors in a sample of socio-economically depressed infants. *Developmental Psychology, 18,* 22–29.

Peisner-Feinberg, E. S., & Burchinal, M. R. (1997). Relations between preschool children, child care experiences, and concurrent development: The Cost, Quality, and Outcomes Study. *Merrill-Palmer Quarterly, 43,* 451–477.

Peisner-Feinberg, E., Clifford, R., Yazejian, N., Culkin, M., Howes, C., & Kagan, S.L. (1998, April). *The longitudinal effects of child care quality: Implications for kindergarten success.* Paper presented at the annual meeting of the American Education Research Association, Anaheim, CA.

Paulson, S. E. (1996). Maternal employment and adolescent achievement revisited: An ecological perspective. *Family Relations, 45,* 201–208.

Phillips, D. A., McCartney, K., & Scarr, S. (1987). Child care quality and children's social development. *Developmental Psychology, 23,* 537–543.

Phillips, D. A., Voran, M., Kisker, E., Howes, C., & Whitebook, M. (1994). Child care for children in poverty: Opportunity or inequity? *Child Development, 65,* 472–492.

Phillipsen, L. C., Burchinal, M. R., Howes, C., & Cryer, D. (1997). The prediction of process quality from structural features of child care. *Early Childhood Research Quarterly, 12,* 281–303.

Roberts, J. E., Rabinowitch, S., Bryant, D. M., Burchinal, M. R., Koch, M. A., & Ramey, C. T. (1989). Language skills of children with different preschool experiences. *Journal of Speech and Hearing Research, 32,* 773–786.

Ruopp, R., Travers, J., Glantz, F., & Coelen, G. (1979). *Children at the center.* Cambridge, MA: Abt Associates.

Sameroff, A. J. (1983). Developmental systems: Contexts and evolution. In P. H. Mussen (Series Ed.) & W. Kessen (Vol. Ed.), *Handbook of child development: Vol. 1. History, theories, and methods* (pp. 237–294). New York: Wiley.

Scarr, S. (1998). American child care today. *American Psychologist, 53,* 95–108.

Scarr, S., & Eisenberg, M. (1993). Child care research: Issues, perspectives, and results. *Annual Review of Psychology, 44,* 613–644.

Schliecker, E., White, D. R., & Jacobs, E. (1991). The role of day care quality in the prediction of children's vocabulary. *Canadian Journal of Behavioral Science, 23,* 12–24.

Schweinhart, L. J., Weikart, D. P., & Larner, M. B. (1986). Consequences of three preschool curriculum models through age 15. *Early Childhood Research Quarterly, 1,* 15–45.

Stipek, D., Feiler, R., Daniels, D., & Milburn, S. (1995). Effects of different instructional approaches on young children's achievement and motivation. *Child Development, 66,* 209–223.

Tietze, W. (1987). A structural model for the evaluation of preschool effects. *Early Childhood Research Quarterly, 2,* 133–153.

Tomasello, M., & Farrar, J. (1986). Joint attention and early language. *Child Development, 57,* 1454–1463.

Vandell, D. L., & Corasaniti, M. A. (1990). Child care and the family: Complex contributors to child development. In K. McCartney (Ed.), *New directions in child development* (pp. 23–37). San Francisco: Jossey-Bass.

Vandell, D. L., & Powers, C. P. (1983). Day care quality and children's free play activities. *American Journal of Orthopsychiatry, 53,* 489–500.

Vandell, D. L., & Ramanan, J. (1992). Effects of early and recent maternal employment on children from low-income families. *Child Development, 63,* 938–949.

Weinraub, M., Jaeger, E., & Hoffman, L. (1988). Predicting infant outcome in families of employed and nonemployed mothers. *Early Childhood Research Quarterly, 3,* 361–378.

Whitebook, M., Howes, C., & Phillips, D. (1989). *Who cares? Child care teachers and the quality of care in America.* Oakland, CA: National Child Care Staffing Study, Child Care Employee Project.

7

Parental Beliefs, Parenting Style, and Children's Intellectual Development

Lynn Okagaki
Purdue University

I recently lost my mother, and it was one of the hardest things I've ever gone through. I could never minimize or discount what she gave to me. My mother gave me everything that's best in me. All of my survival skills. I went into the same profession. My mom was in my corner cheering me on or providing a shoulder to cry on, loving me unconditionally throughout my life. How can that be minimized? Peers are fickle, and so are spouses. They can leave. But most parents are there for life.

—Mia Farrow (quoted by Begley, 1998)

Parents have a profound influence on their children. They want the best for their children. They would like their children to be the best. When my students

141

have asked parents what kinds of goals they have for their child, invariably some of the goals were related to the child's intellectual development. Parents want their children to be bright, curious, good problem solvers, and good students. Parents want their children to develop their intellectual potential, but what is it that parents do to facilitate their children's intellectual development?

This chapter is an exploration of research on the relations between children's intellectual development and parenting. Darling and Steinberg (1993) proposed that parenting is comprised of at least three distinct aspects: (a) the goals and values parents have for their children (e.g., wanting children to do well in school); (b) the strategies or behaviors parents employ to encourage their children's development toward those goals (e.g., helping children study for spelling tests); and (c) *parenting style*, which they define as "a constellation of attitudes toward the child that are communicated to the child and that, taken together, create an emotional climate in which the parent's behaviors are expressed" (p. 488). According to this model, parental goals and values influence both parenting style and the behaviors and strategies parents exercise to meet their goals. Parental behaviors and strategies are hypothesized to directly affect child outcomes. Parenting style, which is comprised of those behaviors that communicate the parent's attitudes and emotions about the child to the child, is hypothesized to directly affect the child's willingness to embrace the parent's goals and thereby indirectly affects child outcomes. Moreover, they proposed that parenting style moderates the relation between parenting behaviors and child outcomes because the emotional climate of the parenting style will shape the way in which a parenting strategy is carried out. In addition to goals and values that influence parents' behaviors and parenting style, there is evidence that parents also have specific beliefs—for example, beliefs about child development, intelligence, and education—that help to shape their goals and behaviors. In this chapter the relations between children's intellectual development and parents' beliefs, expectations, and childrearing style are examined. To begin, let's consider research on the relation between the content of parents' beliefs and children's intelligence.

PARENTAL BELIEFS AND CHILDREN'S INTELLECTUAL DEVELOPMENT

Beliefs About Child Development

Parents have ideas about children's development—how they develop, when they develop, and what constitutes favorable outcomes of development. These informal or implicit theories of child development enable parents to assess the progress their child is making vis-à-vis an expected standard of development (Goodnow, 1976; Hess, Kashiwagi, Azuma, Price, & Dickson, 1980). In this chapter, the focus is on ideas related to intellectual development. Among these ideas are notions about intelligence. According to Sternberg (1985), people invent theories of intelligence that are relevant to their cultural context. What constitutes intelligent behavior depends on culturally relevant demands. Consequently, the construct of intelligence varies across groups. For example, in contrast to most Western psychological theories of intelligence (Gardner's, 1983, multiple intelligences theory is one exception), implicit theories of intelligence among many groups include a social dimension (e.g., Dasen, 1984; Serpell, 1984; Wober, 1974). For the Baoulé of the Ivory Coast, a willingness to serve one's family and community is considered an important aspect of intelligence (Dasen, 1984). Within a culture, Siegler and Richards (1982) observed that dimensions of intelligence vary according to the age of the population to which one is ascribing intelligence. For example, motor coordination was one of the five characteristics most frequently mentioned by American college students to describe both an intelligent 6-month-old and an intelligent 2-year-old. For older children and adults, the characteristics associated with intelligence included verbal ability, learning ability, reasoning, problem solving, and creativity, but not attributes related to physical ability.

In a study of immigrant parents from Cambodia, Mexico, the Philippines, and Vietnam and U.S.-born parents of Mexican descent and European-Americans, Okagaki and Sternberg (1993) found that motivation was an important component of the Asian parents' understanding of intelligence. A child who is intelligent is one who works to achieve good grades. The European-American parents placed more emphasis on creativity as a dimension of intelligence than other parents. For parents of Mexican descent, good social skills was considered an important aspect of intelligence.

Given that parents' notions about intelligence differ, it seems plausible that parents may desire, expect, and encourage different intellectual skills in their children. For example, parents' ideas about when children should develop specific skills and abilities may vary across groups. In a comparison of mothers from Japan and Caucasian mothers from the United States, Hess and his colleagues (Hess et al., 1980) observed that Japanese mothers expected their children to develop emotional maturity, compliance, and social courtesy with adults at an earlier age than their U.S. counterparts. In contrast, U.S. mothers expected their children to mature more quickly in the areas of verbal assertiveness and social skills with peers. In both countries, developmental expectations were related to children's cognitive development. In particular, mothers who expected their child to develop verbal assertiveness at an earlier age had children who did better on a variety of cognitive tasks.

In an Australian study of Australian-born mothers and Lebanese-born immigrant mothers, Goodnow, Cashmore, Cotton, and Knight (1984) replicated the developmental timetable comparison that was conducted by the Japanese and U.S. research team led by Hess and Azuma (Hess et al., 1980). In the same way that U.S. mothers expected earlier development of verbal assertiveness and ability to relate to peers than the Japanese mothers, Australian-born mothers expected their children to develop in these two domains at an earlier age than Lebanese-born mothers. The Lebanese immigrant mothers set a later age for their children to exhibit independence from their parents (e.g., to play outside without supervision, to entertain him or herself). Although Goodnow and her colleagues did not examine the relation between mothers' developmental expectations and children's intellectual development, they observed that when mothers had earlier expectations for the development of a skill they were more likely to report helping the child to develop that skill. Taken together, these two studies demonstrated that parental expectations are related to parents' self-reported childrearing strategies (Goodnow et al., 1984) and to children's intellectual development (Hess et al., 1980).

Although most research on parental expectations has focused on children's development, Feldman and her colleagues (e.g., Feldman & Quatman, 1988; Feldman & Wood, 1994) examined parents' expectations for early adolescents. In the United States, granting autonomy is one of the critical dimensions of the evolving parent–adolescent relationship. Feldman and Wood (1994) hypothesized that giving young adolescents freedom and responsibility too early is analogous to a permissive parenting style, which has been associated with less desirable child outcomes (e.g., poor school achievement, Dornbusch, Ritter, Leiderman, Roberts, & Fraleigh, 1987). In a study of White, middle-class, early adolescent boys, Feldman and Wood (1994) found that fathers' expectations for granting autonomy to their sons at Time 1 (when the boys were in the sixth grade) were related to the boys' academic achievement 4 years later at Time 2.[1] Fathers who anticipated granting privileges (e.g., attending boy–girl parties, going to rock concerts, not having a curfew when out at night) to their sons at later ages, had sons who achieved higher grades and reported putting more effort into their school work. Fathers' developmental expectations for granting privileges

---

[1]When referring to other research, I adopted the terms the authors used to identify different ethnic or cultural groups.

to their sons were positively related to the boys' school achievement. Mothers' expectations, however, were not related to their sons' school achievement.

In summary, for both young children and adolescents, parents' beliefs about child development—in particular, their beliefs about the timing of the development of specific skills—have been correlated with children's intellectual development. There is some evidence to suggest that the relation between parental expectations and children's cognitive development may be mediated by parents' childrearing strategies.

Expectations for Children's Academic Achievement

One of the most widely documented observations is that parents' expectations for their children's academic achievement are related to children's school performance (e.g., Entwisle & Hayduk, 1978; Okagaki & Frensch, 1998; Okagaki, Frensch, & Gordon, 1995; for a review, see Seginer, 1983). For example, in a study of economically disadvantaged African-American families, Halle, Kurtz-Costes, and Mahoney (1997) found that parents' expectations for their children's educational attainment were positively related to children's (8- to 10-year-olds) math and reading achievement test scores.

In my research group, we found that parents differ across ethnic groups in their expectations for children's school achievement and that these expectations are related to children's school performance. In a study of Asian-American, Latino, and European-American families with fourth- and fifth-grade children (Okagaki & Frensch, 1998), we found that across all three groups, parents' expectations for their child's educational attainment were related to the child's school grades. The more schooling parents expected their child to obtain, the higher the child's grades were. In addition, for the European-American and the Latino families, parents' expectations for the grades children receive on school assignments were also related to the child's grades.

In a related study of high-achieving and low-achieving (as determined by school achievement test scores) children of Mexican descent, we again found that parents' expectations were related to school performance. Although parents of both high-achieving and low-achieving children valued education, wanted their children to obtain good educations and held similar expectations for the amount of schooling they expected their children to obtain, parents of high-achieving and low-achieving children differed in the minimum educational attainment level that they set for their children and in their responses to grades of Cs and Ds (Okagaki et al., 1995). Parents of high achievers set a higher minimum boundary for their children's grades and educational attainment. Although about half of the parents in each group wanted their child to at least complete college, of those who would be satisfied with less than a college degree, the parents of high achievers were more likely to want their child to complete at least some college or vocational training after high school. Parents of high achievers were also less satisfied with Cs and Ds than parents of low achievers. A difference in reactions to lower grades is not surprising given that parents' reactions to Cs and Ds are likely to be contingent on children's past performances. However, when only the responses of parents who reported that their children normally received As and Bs were examined, parents of low achievers were still more likely to be satisfied with Cs and Ds than parents of high achievers.

In her review of research on parents' educational expectations, Seginer (1983) observed that although a majority of studies obtained a positive correlation between parents' expectations for their children's school achievement and children's performance, the causal direction of the relation is unclear. Along these lines, Entwisle and Hayduk (1978) found that parents adjusted their expectations for their child's grades as they received feedback from previous year's grades. In my research group, we obtained some evidence that suggested, at least for some populations, parental expectations are not solely a function of children's previous school performance. In our study of fourth- and fifth-grade children (Okagaki & Frensch, 1998), parents' expectations for their child's school attainment differed across ethnic groups with Asian-American parents having higher expectations for their child's school performance. In a hierarchical regression in which the previous year's grades and parents' perceptions of their child's ability were used to partial out differences in actual and perceived school performance, we still obtained ethnic group differences in parents' expectations for their child's school attainment, a finding consistent with the hypothesis that parental expectations are not simply a response to children's prior achievements.

Differing expectations for children's school performance, along with general beliefs about the value and role of education, have been posited as factors contributing to cross-national differences in children's school achievement. In an extensive program of cross-national research, Stevenson and his colleagues completed several multinational comparisons of student achievement and parental beliefs (e.g., Stevenson, Chen, & Lee, 1993; Stevenson & Lee, 1990; Stevenson, Lee, & Stigler, 1986). They argued that the poor performance of U.S. school children in math relative to the performance of children in other countries is due in part to parents' satisfaction with the effectiveness of U.S. schools and with their overestimation of their child's abilities. For example, in a comparison of Chinese, Japanese, and U.S. kindergarten, first-, and fifth-grade children, and their parents' beliefs, Stevenson et al. (1986) reported that although U.S. children's math scores were lower than Japanese students' scores at all three grades and lower than Chinese students' scores in first and fifth grades, U.S. mothers rated their child's math abilities as being above average when compared to other children his or her age. Their ratings were higher than the ratings of Chinese mothers and about the same as the ratings of the Japanese mothers. In addition, U.S. mothers were more likely to be satisfied with what their child's school was doing than Japanese and Chinese mothers. In a 10-year follow-up study, Stevenson et al. (1993) found that the math scores of U.S. first, fifth, and eleventh graders were still lower than the scores of their Japanese and Chinese counterparts. Even though the U.S. parents were aware that U.S. children did not do as well in math as children in several other industrialized nations, the U.S. parents were still more satisfied with their child's math performance than Asian parents. They were also still more likely to rate their child's school as doing a good job in educating their child. Stevenson and his colleagues observed that U.S. parents are neither likely to encourage their children to work harder to achieve more in school nor to demand that schools do more to facilitate children's learning as long as they are satisfied with the performances of their children and of the schools.

With respect to differences between Chinese and U.S. children's math and reading test scores, Chen and Uttal (1988) suggested that specific values within the Chinese culture and aspects of Chinese society lead parents to place a higher value on education and to have higher expectations for their children's school performance as compared to U.S. parents. In their study of approximately 700 U.S. children and 400 Chinese children, Chinese first, third, and fifth graders scored higher on math tests than their U.S. counterparts. In reading, Chinese first and third graders scored higher than the U.S. children, but at fifth grade there was no difference between the groups. Despite the high performance of Chinese youngsters, Chinese parents were much less satisfied with their children's academic performance than U.S. parents. Although 76% of U.S. mothers were satisfied or very satisfied with their child's performance, only 36% of the Chinese mothers indicated that they were satisfied or very satisfied with their child's school performance. In addition, the level of performance with which Chinese mothers indicated they would be satisfied was higher than the level of performance that they expected their child to achieve. When asked to indicate what grade they would expect their child to obtain on a 100-point math test in which the average score was 75 points, Chinese and U.S. mothers indicated a grade between 80 and 85 points. The Chinese mothers reported that they would be satisfied if their child obtained a score about 10 points higher than the expected grade. In contrast, U.S. mothers would be satisfied if their child's score was an average of 7 points lower than the expected score. Chen and Uttal argued that Chinese parents set high expectations for their children's intellectual performance because of the high value placed on education both historically and in contemporary China, the cultural emphasis on self-improvement, and the strong cultural belief in human malleability. They suggested that these beliefs and values along with the collectivist orientation of the society produce a climate in which children value educational achievement and are intrinsically motivated to work hard in school.

Bacon and Ichikawa (1988) posited that parents must be realistic in their expectations for their children's intellectual achievement. In their attempt to explain why Japanese kindergartners outperform U.S. youngsters in math, they examined both parental beliefs and kindergarten classroom practices. Consistent with other research on parenting of young children in Japan, mothers of the Japanese kindergartners were more concerned with their child's social and emotional development than with their child's intellectual achievement. For example, compared to American mothers, Japanese mothers were much less likely to spend time teaching their child beginning literacy and numerical skills (e.g., counting and addition). Japanese mothers were more likely to believe that kindergarten teachers should not assign homework to their students. As other researchers observed (e.g., Azuma, 1994), Bacon and Ichikawa found that Japanese mothers of young children were less demanding than their U.S. counterparts. For example, 68% of the U.S. mothers indicated that they would force their child to go to school if the child refused to go to school, but only 37% of the Japanese mothers reported that they would force the child to go.

Bacon and Ichikawa's observations of the kindergarten classrooms revealed that children in Japan spend more time in free play activities and less time in academic instruction than children in U.S. kindergarten classrooms. If neither classroom instruction nor parental instruction emphasizes development of academic skills, what contributes to the Japanese children's advantage in math skills at the kindergarten level? Bacon and Ichikawa suggested that the Japanese mothers may have had more realistic expectations for their children and that realistic expectations may yield more effective mother–child interactions. This hypothesis is consistent with the notion that parents who have more accurate perceptions of their child's cognitive ability are better able to encourage and support their child's development (e.g., Hunt & Paraskevopoulos, 1980; Miller, 1986). The importance of developing an accurate understanding of the child's ability level is in accord with the Vygotskian concept of scaffolding within the zone of proximal development and is supported by evidence that mothers who more accurately predict their child's performance on cognitive tasks have children who perform better on these tasks (Hunt & Paraskevopoulos, 1980; Miller, 1986).

Thus, in contrast to Chen and Uttal's hypothesis that Chinese youngsters do better than U.S. children because their parents have higher expectations, Bacon and Ichikawa posited that Japanese kindergartners do better in math because their mothers have more realistic expectations for them. There is, however, an alternative, or perhaps complementary, explanation for the math performance of the Japanese kindergartners. It is possible that the Japanese children are learning about math from their mothers via incidental learning. Azuma (1994) described parenting of young children in Japan as parenting by osmosis, rather than parenting by direct instruction. Mothers do not intentionally teach their young child values and skills. Observations of mother–child interactions during a task in which mothers were asked to teach their child how to sort a group of blocks indicated that Japanese mothers did not use verbal messages to explain how to do the task in a step-by-step fashion. The mothers modeled how to complete the task and used verbal messages to encourage the child to become involved in the activity and to try to do it correctly. According to Azuma, incidental learning occurs as the child observes what the mother does and, in an effort to maintain the close connection with the mother, attempts to engage in the activity. A strength of developing this motivational bond between the mother and child is that the mother's expectations for the child continue to be important to the child as the child progresses through school. Azuma and his colleagues (Azuma, Kashiwagi, & Hess, 1981) found that Japanese mothers' expectations for their child's school attainment at age 3 were related to the child's school readiness at age 5 to 6 years and, with school readiness partialed out, were still significantly related to the child's school performance at age 11 to 12 years. For U.S. mothers, expectations for school attainment were related to school readiness, but with school readiness partialed out, there was no direct relation between maternal expectations at age 3 and school performance at 11 to 12 years.

The data previously presented support the hypothesis that parents' beliefs about child development and their expectations for their child's development influence their child's intellectual development. Because it is not the focus of this chapter, studies designed to demonstrate that childrearing strategies act as the mediator between parental beliefs and child outcomes were not reviewed. However, a few of the studies (e.g., Goodnow et al., 1984) provided some evidence that suggests childrearing strategies may be the mechanism by which parental beliefs and values are transmitted to the child. In the remainder of this chapter, I examine the role of parental style on intellectual development.

PARENTING STYLE AND CHILDREN'S INTELLECTUAL DEVELOPMENT

Since the 1940s or 1950s, the construct of parenting style has encompassed the overall pattern of childrearing practices, parental beliefs and attitudes, and the emotional quality of the parent's interactions with the child. The notion of parenting style emerged as researchers, theorists, and practitioners observed that the effects of specific parenting strategies on children's development were nearly impossible to measure because the strategies do not occur in isolation. Rather, they occur within the context of a conglomeration of childrearing strategies and parental attitudes toward the child. For example, high expectations for school performance in the context of parental behaviors that support a warm, nurturing parent–child relationship are likely to mean something different from high expectations surrounded by parental behaviors which are cold, unresponsive to child needs, and unencouraging. Consequently, researchers suggested that the effects of parenting on child outcomes could best be understood in terms of global patterns of childrearing practices and the emotional tone of the parenting behavior. Baumrind (1968, 1971) is one of the theorists who is most often associated with current conceptualizations of parenting style. She originally described three types of parenting style—authoritative, authoritarian, and permissive—and contrasted the use of control in each of these styles of parenting. Permissive parenting is child-oriented, responsive, and nurturing with few demands placed on the child. In sharp contrast to the permissive parent, the authoritarian parent values obedience to and respect for authority, places high demands on the child, does not include the child in decision making, and is not warm and nurturing. The authoritative parent is responsive to and nurtures the child, while at the same time, sets clear expectations for the child and is willing and able to explain the reasons behind those expectations. Both authoritative and authoritarian parents monitor their children's behaviors but authoritarian parents are more restrictive and coercive in their use of power to maintain control than are authoritative parents. Authoritative parents expect their child to observe their standards, but use rational arguments to explain their decisions rather than appealing to position or external authorities. In Baumrind's (1989) terms, authoritative parents are psychologically differentiated. They use "reason to obtain compliance and [encourage] exploratory behavior and verbal assertiveness" (p. 352).

In their classic review of research on socialization, Maccoby and Martin (1983) proposed two basic dimensions of parenting: (a) parental demandingness, which is the degree to which parents establish high expectations for their children's behaviors and monitor what their children actually do; and (b) parental responsiveness, which is the degree to which parents are warm, nurturing, and sensitive to their children's cues. Maccoby and Martin's typology yielded the four types of parenting style generally acknowledged today by adding indifferent or neglectful parenting (i.e., low demands and low responsiveness) to Baumrind's original three parenting categories. In general, developmental researchers have found that authoritative parenting is associated with positive psychosocial and cognitive outcomes for children (for reviews, see Baumrind, 1991a, 1991b; Maccoby & Martin, 1983). The following discussion begins with an exploration of the relation between parenting style and intellectual development, and concludes with an examination of factors that moderate the relation between parenting style and intellectual development and factors that mediate the relation between them.

Relation Between Parenting Style and Intellectual Performance

Researchers who examine the relation between parenting styles and intellectual performance have typically found parenting style to be related to intellectual performance … at least for European-American adolescents (Dornbusch et al., 1987; Steinberg, Dornbusch, & Brown, 1992; Steinberg, Lamborn, Dornbusch, & Darling, 1992). For example, in a study of approximately 7,800 high school students, Dornbusch and his colleagues (Dornbusch et al., 1987) examined the relations between parenting styles and academic achievement. Students indicated the degrees to which their parents were authoritative, authoritarian, and permissive. For this study, the authoritarian items emphasized compliance with adult authority (e.g., the parent expects the student not to argue with or question the parent's decisions) and low responsiveness of parents (e.g., when the student received a good grade, the parents responded by indicating that the student should do even better). The permissive items centered on the lack of parental monitoring and involvement in the adolescent's life (e.g., parents didn't care if the student earned good grades or poor grades). The authoritative scale included items that assessed democratic parenting strategies and parental responsiveness and encouragement. Overall the degrees to which parents were authoritarian or permissive in their parenting were negatively related to adolescents' academic achievement for both males and females. Authoritativeness was significantly and positively related to school grades for both males and females.

In a study that included approximately 4,100 14- to 18-year-old adolescents, Lamborn, Mounts, Steinberg, and Dornbusch (1991) examined the relations between parenting styles and multiple aspects of adolescent development, including school achievement. This diverse sample included 61% non-Hispanic White, 15% Hispanic, 14% Asian-American, and 11% African-American youngsters and was part of their Wisconsin-California longitudinal study of 20,000 high school students. Using adolescents' ratings of (a) parents' acceptance of the adolescent and involvement in the adolescent's life and (b) parents' strictness and monitoring of the adolescent's behaviors, adolescents were divided into four parenting style groups—authoritative, authoritarian, indulgent, and neglectful. Authoritative parents were those whose ratings on both dimensions were in the upper third. Neglectful parents were in the bottom third on both dimensions. Authoritarian parents were in the upper third on monitoring and in the bottom third on acceptance, whereas indulgent parents were the opposite. School competence was assessed with grade point average (GPA), students' ratings of academic competence, and students' orientation or attitude toward school. Adolescents who perceived their parents as authoritative had significantly higher ratings on measures of school competence than adolescents from the other three types of families. However, with respect to GPA, adolescents from authoritative homes did not significantly differ from adolescents with authoritarian parents. This finding is counter to the Dornbusch et al. (1987) finding in which authoritarian parenting was negatively related to grades. The lack of consistency in the findings may in part be explained by the measures used. First, in the Lamborn et al. study, students were classified into four distinct parenting groups (i.e., authoritarian, permissive, authoritative, neglectful); whereas in the Dornbusch et al. study, the degrees to which students perceived their parents as authoritative, authoritarian, and permissive were rated. Second, examination of the items used in the Dornbusch et al. study suggested that their scale primarily focused on the parent's lack of warmth and encouragement rather than on the parent setting high expectations for the adolescent and monitoring the adolescent's behaviors. In fact, in one of our own studies, we found that the Dornbusch et al., authoritarian parenting scale was negatively correlated with parental warmth for college students' perceptions of their mothers and fathers but was not related to a separate measure of parental monitoring (Okagaki, Hammond, & Seamon, 1999). Consequently, it may be the case that the earlier study did not actually tap the aspect of authoritarian parenting that may be most important to achievement (i.e., setting high expectations and monitoring of behaviors).

Lamborn and her colleagues (1991) also found that adolescents who perceived their parents as neglectful were significantly lower on measures of academic competence than adolescents from authoritative homes. There was, however, no difference on ratings of perceived academic competence between adolescents from neglectful homes and adolescents from authoritarian homes. Similarly, adolescents from neglectful homes did not differ from adolescents with indulgent parents on GPA or school orientation. The implication of these results is that high parental supervision is associated with better academic performance, whereas high parental acceptance is associated with more positive self-perceptions of academic competence.

Critical evidence regarding the direction of the relationship between authoritative parenting and school achievement was obtained by Steinberg, Lamborn, Dornbusch, and Darling (1992). Approximately 6,300 ninth-, tenth-, and eleventh-grade students participated in the 1987 and 1988 data collections. Students' 1987 ratings of their parents' authoritativeness were positively related to their 1988 school performance (e.g., grades, time spent on homework, expected educational attainment) and to 1988 school engagement (e.g., classroom engagement, relationship with teachers, school misconduct). These relations were significant even when 1987 school performance and school engagement were partialed out. Thus, this study provided evidence that authoritative parenting influences adolescents' intellectual performance, rather than simply being a correlate of intellectual achievement.

Other research has addressed the relations between specific aspects of parenting style (e.g., warmth, control, or monitoring) and intellectual development. For example, beliefs related to authoritarian control have been associated with poor intellectual performance. Schaefer and Edgerton (1985) found that authoritarian childrearing beliefs (e.g., parents have absolute authority over their children, children will misbehave if allowed to) and parental valuation of conformity (e.g., emphasis on neatness, having good manners, obedience) were negatively related to kindergarten and first-grade children's achievement test scores and teachers' ratings of their creativity and curiosity. In my research, conformity was negatively related to intellectual performance in kindergarten through second-grade children (Okagaki & Sternberg, 1993) and in fourth and fifth graders (Okagaki & Frensch, 1998). In contrast to the relation between intellectual performance and authoritarian control, higher intellectual performance was associated with parental press for independence in a sample of 800 Australian sixth graders (Marjoribanks, 1996) and with psychological autonomy-granting among early adolescents (Linver & Silverberg, 1997).

Parental monitoring, a key aspect of parenting style, was found to be positively related to school achievement for 9- to 12-year-old boys (Crouter, MacDermid, McHale, & Perry-Jenkins, 1990), for early adolescent boys and girls (Linver & Silverberg, 1997), and for European-American fourth and fifth graders (Okagaki & Frensch, 1998). Parental warmth has also been related to intellectual performance. Linver and Silverberg (1997) reported that higher school achievement was associated with greater maternal warmth among early adolescent boys and girls. Among 5-year-old Scandinavian boys, but not girls, maternal warmth was associated with higher verbal and performance IQ scores (Andersson, Sommerfelt, Sonnander, & Ahlsten, 1996).

In summary, parenting style is related to the individual's intellectual development. Steinberg et al.'s (1992b) research demonstrated that authoritative parenting influences subsequent school achievement. The relation between parenting style and intellectual performance has been observed across multiple samples and in children and adolescents. In addition, when both parents are perceived to be authoritative in their parenting, adolescents perform better in school as compared to when both parents are permissive or one parent is authoritarian and one parent is moderately responsive and autonomy granting (Johnson, Shulman, & Collins, 1991). Finally, in some studies (e.g., Dornbusch et al., 1987; Okagaki & Frensch, 1998), differences in the relations between parenting style and school achievement across ethnic groups emerged. In the next section, I review what researchers have discovered about the interaction between parenting styles and cultural context within the United States.

Ethnicity and the Relation Between Parenting Style and Intellectual Development

In the Dornbusch study (Dornbusch et al., 1987), differences in parenting styles emerged across ethnic groups. For both boys and girls, White parents had lower authoritarian scores than other parents. White parents were more authoritative than Hispanic and Asian parents of both boys and girls and Black parents of females. In general, White parents were less permissive than Hispanic and Asian parents; however, Black parents had lower permissiveness scores than did White parents.

Ethnic differences were also obtained in the relations between parenting styles and academic performance. For White families, authoritarian and permissive parenting were negatively related to school achievement; authoritative parenting was positively correlated with school achievement. For Black families, which was the smallest subgroup, none of the parenting styles were significantly related to school achievement. For Hispanic adolescents, authoritative parenting was positively correlated with school achievement. Although authoritarian parenting scores were negatively related to the grades of Hispanic females, authoritarian parenting was not related to grades for Hispanic males. Finally, the researchers observed that differences in parenting styles did not explain the academic achievement of Asian students very well. Neither authoritativeness nor permissiveness was related to the grades of Asian students. Prior to this study, there was an abundance of research on cross-national variation in parenting (e.g., Dickson, Hess, Miyake, & Azuma, 1979; LeVine, 1974). Minimal research within the United States, however, had addressed cultural or ethnic variation in parenting styles and in the relations between parenting style and child outcomes—even though Baumrind (1972) suggested that some important differences might exist. The study by Dornbusch and his colleagues (1987) opened the doors for an examination of the interaction between parenting processes and social contexts.

Steinberg, Mounts, Lamborn, and Dornbusch (1991) examined the effects of ethnicity and social class on the relation between authoritative parenting and school achievement using a sample of approximately 10,000 9th through 12th grade students from the Wisconsin–California data set. This sample was comprised of 9% Black, 14% Asian, 12% Hispanic, and 60% White students (5% of the students were from other groups). If parents had completed a college education, adolescents were classified as middle class. Adolescents whose parents had less than a baccalaureate degree were classified as working class. Family status was divided into two groups: two-parent, biologically intact and nonintact (e.g., single-parent families, blended families). In this analysis, to be classified as having authoritative parents, students had to score above the median on all three of the parenting scales: (a) parental acceptance and involvement in child's life, (b) firm control (including parental monitoring and setting standards), and (c) psychological autonomy (i.e., the degree to which parents use democratic parenting strategies and allow adolescent to express individuality). All other students were grouped together in the nonauthoritative category. As one might expect, authoritative parenting was more common among White families than minority families and more common among middle-class families than working-class families. In addition, consistent with the findings of the Dornbusch et al. (1987) study, the effect of authoritative parenting on school achievement was greater for White students than for African-American or Asian-American students.

Not all studies have obtained ethnicity × parenting style interactions. In a study of nearly 4,000 ninth-grade students, Radziszewska, Richardson, Dent, and Flay (1996) questioned whether ethnicity, gender, and income moderate the relation between parenting style and academic achievement. In their study, parenting style was assessed with a single item in which students indicated whether their parents were authoritarian (i.e., parents make decisions without the adolescent's input), authoritative (i.e., parents and adolescents discuss decisions, but parents have the ultimate authority for making the decision), permissive (i.e., adolescents have more say in decisions than parents do), or unengaged (i.e., parents let the adolescent make decisions on his or her own). They found that students who described their parents as authoritative reported having higher grades than other students. There was no difference in the self-reported grades of adolescents from permissive and authoritarian families and adolescents with unengaged parents reported the lowest grades. (Again, the lack of effect of authoritarian parenting on grades may have been due to the emphasis on lack of psychological autonomy rather than setting expectations and monitoring behaviors.) In this study, there were main effects of gender and ethnicity, but no interactions between parenting style and gender, ethnicity, or income. Thus, in contrast to previous studies, the relation between parenting style and grades was not significantly moderated by ethnicity. The fact that assessment of parenting styles was comprised of a single question, however, may have limited the ability to detect ethnic differences in the relations between parenting style and grades.

In a study of fourth- and fifth-grade Asian-American, Latino, and European-American children, we observed that the relations between parental beliefs and children's school performance differed across ethnic groups (Okagaki & Frensch, 1998). For example, we examined the relations between children's school performance and three aspects of childrearing that are related to parenting style—parental encouragement of autonomous behaviors, parental encouragement of conformity to external standards, and parental monitoring. There were significant belief × ethnicity interactions for conformity and parental monitoring. The relation between encouraging conformity and grades was negative for European-American parents, but there was virtually no relation between conformity and grades for Asian-American parents. We obtained a positive relation between parental monitoring of children's behaviors and children's grades for European-American parents and again no such relation for Asian-American parents. Just as Steinberg, Dornbusch, and their colleagues observed, we also found that the constructs that have defined dimensions of parenting in Western psychological theories do not explain well the relation between parenting and children's school achievement in Asian-American families. In this study, we examined the relations between children's school performance and four aspects of parenting—parents' expectations for their children's school attainment, expectations for children's grades, general childrearing beliefs, and school-related behaviors. All four parenting domains were significantly related to school performance for European-American and Latino parents. For Asian-American parents, only the educational attainment cluster significantly predicted children's school performance.

Using their Wisconsin–California data set including African-American, Asian-American, Hispanic, and White adolescents, Steinberg et al. (1992a) compared parental and peer influences on academic achievement across ethnic groups. As reported earlier (Steinberg et al., 1991), analysis of this data set indicated that although Asian-American students maintained the highest grades, authoritative parenting was least common among Asian-American families. In addition, Asian-American students did not gain as much from authoritative parenting as other students. According to Steinberg, Dornbusch, and Brown, the key to the success of Asian-American students lies in their peers. They suggested that peers have a stronger impact on Asian-American and African-American students than on other students. For Asian-American students, their Asian-American peers support academic achievement. For African-American students, the African-American peer group is not as school oriented and does not encourage individual African-American students to perform well in school. Thus, the lack of authoritative parenting among Asian-American families is compensated for by peers who support academic goals. On the other hand, African-American adolescents do not gain from the advantage of having authoritative parents in their homes because their peers do not support educational goals. Steinberg and his colleagues concluded that peers have a stronger influence on Asian-American and African-American adolescents than parents.

Using the National Survey of Family and Household data set, Taylor, Hinton, and Wilson (1995) examined the relations between parenting styles and parents' reports of their child's school achievement in a subsample of 566 African-American children ages 5 to 18. Parents were classified as permissive if they were high in nurturance and low on control, authoritarian if they were high on control and low on nurturance, and authoritative if they were high on both control and nurturance. In this study, children with authoritative parents had higher reported grades than children from other families. This study opened the possibility that Steinberg and his colleagues were premature in their pronouncement that parenting style is not as important to school achievement in African-American adolescents as it is for other adolescents.

Contrary to Steinberg et al. (1992a), Schneider, Hieshima, Lee, and Plank (1994) maintained that the academic success of Asian-American children emerges from their family's values. For example, they observed, "Japanese-American parents stress particular values at home that forge a tripartite relationship between cultural continuity, family obligation, and academic performance. This relationship is strengthened by specific educational activities undertaken at home that are directly connected to academic performance and high educational aspirations" (p. 346). Similarly, Chao (1994) took exception to the Steinberg et al. (1992a) conclusion that Asian-American parents did not influence their children's academic performance. She argued that the notion of authoritarian parenting is not an appropriate construct to apply to Asian parenting and contrasted authoritarian parenting with the Chinese view of training a child. In her study of Chinese immigrant and European-American parents of preschoolers, she replicated the findings that Chinese parents scored higher on measures of authoritarian parenting and parental control and lower on authoritative parenting than European-American parents. However, Chinese parents also scored higher on several aspects of parenting arising from a Chinese cultural perspective. Compared to European-American mothers, Chinese mothers more strongly agreed with statements such as, "Mothers primarily express love by helping child succeed, especially in school," "A mother's sole interest is in taking care of her child," and "Mothers must train child to work very hard and be disciplined" (Chao, 1994, p. 1116). Chao rightly reasoned that if Western psychological constructs do not capture the essence of parenting born out of other cultural perspectives, we should not be surprised if these constructs do not adequately explain child outcomes.

Clearly from the research to date, behavioral scientists need to more carefully consider cultural influences on parenting if we are going to understand the relations between parenting and children's intellectual development in the United States. Current research is consistent with the hypothesis that dimensions of parenting that contribute to intellectual development may vary across cultural groups and should motivate researchers to develop measures which better capture culturally relevant expressions of parenting.

Parenting Style as Process and Context

How does parenting style affect intellectual development? Steinberg et al. (1992b) posited that specific parenting behaviors—parental involvement in school and parental encouragement of academic achievement—mediate the relation between authoritative parenting and adolescents' school achievement. Path analyses indicated that the relation between authoritative parenting and school performance was mediated by parental involvement in schooling. Parental encouragement, however, did not appear to play a significant role in adolescents' school performance or school engagement once parental involvement was considered. In short, authoritative parenting is associated with better school performance because authoritative parents are more involved in their child's schooling.

In addition to examining parental involvement as a mediator between authoritative parenting and school achievement, Steinberg and his colleagues (1992b) considered whether authoritative parenting moderated the influences of parental involvement and parental encouragement on school achievement. That is, greater parental involvement may improve adolescents' school achievement in general, but is that effect more powerful in the context of authoritative parenting? If, for example, authoritative parenting yields warmer parent–adolescent relationships, adolescents in authoritative families may do better in school because they have a stronger desire to please their parents. According to their analyses, authoritative parenting influenced the relation between parental involvement and school performance such that the relation between parental involvement and school performance was weaker for the nonauthoritative parents than for other parents. Similarly, the relation between parental encouragement and school engagement was weaker for the nonauthoritative group. These data support Darling and Steinberg's (1993) model in which parenting style was posited to moderate the relations between specific parenting strategies and developmental outcomes.

In a study of 120 adolescents (mean age = 13 years, 1 month), Steinberg, Elmen, and Mounts (1989) examined the relation between young adolescents' perceptions of the authoritativeness of their parents' childrearing strategies and the adolescents' school achievement 1 year later. The sample was comprised of equal numbers of males and females, was 88% White, and included 39% blue-collar, 37% white-collar, and 24% professional families. The young adolescents indicated the degrees to which their parents were warm and accepting, controlled their behaviors (i.e., made decisions regarding their adolescent's behaviors vs. allowing the adolescent to make decisions independently), and granted psychological autonomy. In this study, the degrees to which parents exerted more control over young adolescents' behaviors and granted more psychological autonomy were positively related to adolescents' school performance in the following year. Further analyses indicated that the effects of authoritative parenting were mediated through the adolescent's psychosocial maturity. That is, parental acceptance, granting of psychological autonomy, and behavioral control were each positively related to adolescents' psychosocial maturity, which in turn was positively related to school performance. Because parental behaviors are, in part, a response to children's behaviors, Steinberg and his colleagues questioned whether degree of parental authoritativeness was ac-tually a response to adolescents' prior levels of psychosocial maturity or a con-tributor to subsequent psychosocial maturity. Because of the longitudinal nature of their data, they were able to conduct a path analysis which indicated that parental acceptance was a correlate of psychosocial maturity, but did not affect later psychosocial maturity. However, both parental control and granting of psychological autonomy were positively related to subsequent psychosocial maturity in the adolescent, which in turn was positively related to school perfor-mance. Finally, the researchers examined which aspects of psychosocial matu-rity were most affected by authoritative parenting. In this study, psychosocial maturity was assessed using the work orientation, self-reliance, and identity subscales of the Psychosocial Maturity Inventory (Greenberger, Josselson, Knerr, & Knerr, 1974). The analysis indicated that all three aspects of authori-tative parenting positively contributed to young adolescents' work orientation, which in turn was related to school performance. In short, then, Steinberg, Elmen, and Mounts' research suggested that the relation between authoritative parenting and school performance is mediated through young adolescents' work orientation. Young adolescents who have authoritative parents have a stronger desire to work hard to achieve goals. Thus, authoritative parenting may not influence the development of children's cognitive processes per se. Rather, authoritative parenting may affect intellectual performance and intel-lectual achievement through children's ability or desire to focus on and perse-vere in intellectual tasks.

Conclusions Regarding Parenting Style and Intellectual Development

The research to date has shown that parenting style is related to intellectual de-velopment. In general, authoritative parenting is associated with higher aca-demic achievement (e.g., Dornbusch et al., 1987; Lamborn et al., 1991; Steinberg et al., 1992b). Conversely, neglectful parenting is associated with lower intellectual achievement (e.g., Lamborn et al., 1991). The effect of au-thoritarian parenting is not as clear. Studies that emphasize the compliance and control aspect of authoritarian parenting (e.g., Dornbusch et al., 1987) and studies that examine the effect of parental beliefs about control and conformity (e.g., Okagaki & Frensch, 1998; Okagaki & Sternberg, 1993; Schaefer & Edgerton, 1985) found these variables to be negatively correlated with school achievement. On the other hand, measures of authoritarian parenting which have focused on parental monitoring and lack of warmth in the parent–child relationship were not associated with lower intellectual performance (e.g., Lamborn et al., 1991). Parental monitoring appears to be a key factor in children's school achievement (e.g., Crouter, MacDermid, McHale, & Perry-Jenkins, 1990; Linver & Silverberg, 1997).

There is evidence that authoritative parenting influences adolescents' school achievement and is not simply a parental response to responsible behavior by the adolescent (Steinberg et al., 1992b). Authoritative parenting may have a stronger effect on intellectual performance for White and Hispanic adolescents than for Asian-American and African-American adolescents (Dornbusch et al., 1987; Steinberg et al., 1991), but current research has not yet considered in-depth how parental beliefs and strategies which are rooted in the cultural backgrounds of minority families might contribute to this finding. Finally, it appears that the relation between parenting style and intellectual achievement is mediated by specific parenting behaviors, such as parental involvement in school (Steinberg et al., 1992b), and by characteristics in the adolescent, such as work orientation (Steinberg, Elmen, & Mounts, 1989).

Two interesting studies of mesosystem influences on intellectual development also shed light on how parenting style might influence children's intellectual achievement. Paulson, Marchant, and Rothlisberg (1998) examined the effect of congruence between parenting style and teaching style on fifth and sixth graders' school achievement. The majority of the 230 students in this study were White, with approximately 50% from middle-class homes and 50% from working-class homes. The children rated the degrees to which they perceived their parents to be demanding, responsive, and involved in their schooling and their teachers to be demanding and responsive. Using a hierarchical clustering strategy, children were divided into four groups: (a) congruent authoritative, in which students perceived both parents and teachers to be authoritative; (b) congruent moderate styles, in which both parents and teachers were viewed as moderately demanding and moderately responsive to the child; (c) incongruent-authoritarian parents, in which parents were perceived as authoritarian and teachers were seen as moderately demanding and responsive; and (d) incongruent-authoritarian teachers, in which children perceived teachers to be authoritarian and parents were described as "relatively neglecting" (low responsiveness, low involvement in schooling, and moderately demanding). Highest school achievement was obtained by children in the congruent authoritative cluster, followed by children in the moderate congruent and incongruent-authoritarian parents groups. Children in the incongruent-authoritarian teachers category had the lowest grades. This study provided evidence that suggested congruence between parenting style and teaching style may facilitate children's intellectual performance. Taken with the Johnson et al., (1991) report on congruence in parenting styles between mother and father, these findings implied that consistent authoritative adult–child interaction styles may prove most beneficial for children.

Fletcher, Darling, Steinberg, and Dornbusch (1995) used the Wisconsin–California data to examine the potential influence of the presence of authoritative parenting in the adolescent's social network on the adolescent's development. The adolescents in the study identified the names of their closest friends. To be included in the analysis, the target adolescent had to have identified at least three friends who also participated in the study. This resulted in a subsample of 4,431 students (57% female) including 65% non-Hispanic White, 14% Asian-American, 9% African-American, 10% Hispanic-American, and approximately 2% comprised of Native American, Middle Eastern, and Pacific Islander students. Using data from the target adolescent's friends' questionnaires, the presence of authoritative parenting in the target adolescent's social network was determined on a scale of 1 to 5. For example, if at least half of the identified friends had nonauthoritative parents and none of the friends had authoritative parents, then the social network was classified as nonauthoritative (equal to 1). Conversely if at least half of the friends reported having authoritative parents, then the social network was classified as mostly authoritative (equal to 5).

This study was designed to answer two specific questions. First, does the presence of authoritative parenting in the adolescent's social network contribute to the adolescent's development over and above the influence of the adolescent's own parents? Second, does the presence of authoritative parenting in the adolescent's social network influence the adolescent directly (e.g., by providing an additional adult role model for the adolescent) or indirectly (e.g., through the friend's behaviors)? To address the first question, hierarchical regression analyses were conducted with adolescent outcomes (e.g., grades, self-perception of academic competence, school orientation) as the dependent variables (DVs) and home authoritativeness (i.e., level of authoritative parenting by the target adolescent's parents) as the first independent variable (IV) and authoritativeness of the social network as the second IV. Analyses were conducted separately for boys and girls. For both boys and girls, the presence of authoritative parenting among the parents of the target adolescent's friends positively contributed to the adolescent's grades and other school-related outcomes (e.g., orientation to school, perception of academic competence, time on homework, and relationship with teachers) beyond the contribution of authoritative parenting in the target adolescent's home.

To examine whether the authoritativeness of a friend's parents directly influenced the target adolescent or indirectly influences the adolescent through the friend's behaviors, a second set of hierarchical regression analyses was conducted with home authoritativeness as the first IV, network authoritativeness as the second IV, and a measure of the friends' behaviors on the outcome of interest (e.g., friends' grades) as the third IV. Fletcher et al. reported that, in general, the relations between network authoritativeness and academic outcomes were mediated by the behaviors of the target adolescent's friends.

It is important to note that although the sample was ethnically diverse, only 8% of the students were from lower or working-class families. Fletcher and her colleagues reported that there was reluctance among students from nonmiddle-class and nonprofessional families to identify their friends. Consequently inferences drawn from the results of these analyses do not apply to these groups. So with this caveat in mind, the conclusion is that adolescents from middle-class and professional families benefit academically from having friends whose parents engage in authoritative parenting. This study elegantly links adolescent development across three contexts—home, school, peer group—and highlights the influence of authoritative parenting on intellectual achievement.

As previously noted, Steinberg and his colleagues (Fletcher et al., 1995; Steinberg et al., 1992a) suggested that peers play an influential role in adolescents' school achievement. Harris (1995, 1998) went beyond this position in her proposal of group socialization theory as an explanation of individual differences in psychological characteristics. Although Harris focused on the development of personality, she also attributed individual differences in intellectual development and performance to peer group socialization rather than to parental socialization. According to Harris (1995), "children would develop into the same sort of adults if we left them in their homes, their schools, their neighborhoods, and their cultural or subcultural groups, but switched all the parents around" (p. 461). She theorized that children's attitudes toward school and intellectual achievement are shaped by their peers. If a child is a member of a group of children who like school and do well in school, he or she will also like school and do well in school. Children conform to the norms of their peer group.

Two fundamental assumptions of group socialization theory make clear the hypothesized relation between parental socialization and peer socialization: (a) "Parents do not transmit their culture directly to their children. Culture is transmitted from the parents' peer group (and from other cultural sources) to the children's peer group" (Harris, 1995, p. 267), and (b) "Children transfer behavior learned at home to the peer group only if it is shared by, and approved by, the majority of members of the peer group" (Harris, 1995, p. 267). For example, individuals may, by birth, be part of and subsequently identify with a group that is not perceived to do well in school (e.g., children from low-income families) or in a particular intellectual domain (e.g., women and math). Harris proposed that these individuals are more likely to underachieve in school because they do not want to break the norms of their group. Understanding these group norms and the motivation for internalizing them are assumed to come from peers and not from parents. But is it the case that children's beliefs and values develop out of their peer groups or do children choose peers who are like themselves? Rubin and his colleagues (Rubin, Lynch, Coplan, Rose-Krasnor, & Booth, 1994) observed 7-year-old children who played together for the first time in assigned play groups during a 20-minute play session. Afterward, children rated how much they liked playing with each child in their play group. Children who expressed a clear preference for one child over another child in their group, liked the child whose behavior was most similar to their own. Others (see Epstein, 1989) also interpreted existing data to indicate that children are attracted to those whose beliefs and attitudes are similar to their own. Unfortunately, most studies are simply not designed to show the direction of the causal relationship. Based on her review of the research, Epstein (1989) contended that children select those who are similar to themselves and that children are influenced by their friends' beliefs and behaviors.

Let's consider the assumption that beliefs are transmitted from the parents' peer group to the children's peer group rather than directly from parent to child. If children's peer groups are not randomly assembled and similarly, parents' peer groups are not randomly formed, then in fact, children from different families within the same community may hear similar messages from their parents. If a child espouses a particular belief held by both peers and parents, how does one tell whether that belief emerged from the family context or the peer context? Adolescent development researchers maintain that on issues related to education, occupation, religion, and morality adolescents' beliefs are related to their parents' beliefs, but that on issues related to popular culture (e.g., music, clothes), adolescents are more likely to be influenced by their peers (see Brown, 1990). Even if children evaluate their family beliefs and values in light of their friends' beliefs and values, one might reasonably hypothesize that children's beliefs will still bear some semblance to their parents' beliefs. In our own research (Okagaki, Frensch, & Dodson, 1996), within a sample of Mexican-American children, parents' beliefs about the existence of racial prejudice were related to children's beliefs about prejudice. Although our data do not rule out the possibility that children's beliefs were derived from their peers' beliefs rather than

from their parents' beliefs, our data indicated that some of the variation in beliefs within a group of Mexican-American children can be accounted for by differences in their parents' beliefs. Because Harris (1995) recognized that
behavior can be contextually specific (e.g., what children do at home may be
different from what they do at school), it is important to note that in this study
the children's beliefs were assessed at school, not in their homes.

As Harris (1998) noted, genetic variation accounts for much of the variation
in individual IQ scores. According to behavioral geneticists, heritability estimates (h^2) of intelligence among samples of children are about .45 with between-family (c^2) variance around .35 (Neisser et al., 1996). In samples of older
adolescents and adults, however, heritability is around .75 and between-family
variance is minimal. Neisser and his colleagues (1996) cautioned that the samples on which these estimates were obtained do not represent all populations. In
particular, the lowest SES groups have been underrepresented in studies. The
high heritability estimates in adult samples do not mean that the environment
has no effect on intelligence. After all, most physical traits have high heritability
estimates, but environmental factors (e.g., nutritional resources) have a powerful effect on these traits (see Bronfenbrenner, 1972a; Ceci, Rosenblum, de
Bruyn, & Lee, 1997; Neisser et al. 1996). In addition, Harris (1998) and others
(e.g., Bronfenbrenner, 1972a) observed that in behavioral genetic models, the
variance attributed to heredity includes both direct genetic effects and indirect
effects (i.e., the covariance of genetic and environmental effects), thereby in-
flating heritability estimates. Finally, when the range of environmental differences is reduced, the potential environmental effect is also reduced
(Bronfenbrenner, 1972a; Harris, 1998), making it more difficult to obtain a substantial environmental effect.

Harris (1995, 1998) did not claim that environmental factors were unimportant. Rather, she purported that the effect of the environment on psychological
traits comes via the individual's peer groups rather than from the individual's
parents. Noting the ineffectiveness of intervention programs to produce lasting
changes in children's IQ scores, she contended that intervention programs
must target the attitudes and behaviors of groups of children to be effective.
Why is it so difficult for early intervention programs to change children's intellectual achievement? One answer comes from the longitudinal study of 42
American families conducted by Hart and Risley (1995). The researchers observed young children in their homes each month for a period of 2½ years, beginning when the children were between 7 and 12 months old. The families
ranged in SES from upper income to welfare. Hart and Risley found incredible
differences in the children's linguistic environments. For example, the average

number of utterances directed by parents in the professional families to the infant was 487 per hour compared to 178 utterances per hour in the families on welfare and 301 utterances per hour in the working-class families. During the period when the infants were 11 to 18 months old, the range in the average number of parent utterances to the child was from a low of 56 utterances per hour to a high of 793 utterances per hour. What was most striking to the researchers was the consistency in family talk over time. In their words:

> [W]e found that characteristics such as the gender of the child, birth order, family size, and parent employment affected the allocation of family talk but not its amount. Children learning to talk, new babies being born, changes in jobs or residence, and other substantial changes in family life had only small effects on the amount of talking in the homes relative to the large and stable differences among the families.... The consistency we saw in family amounts of talk has grave implications. In an average 14-hour waking day, a child spoken to 50 times per hour will hear 700 utterances; a child spoken to 800 times per hour will hear more than 11,000 utterances. (p. 70)

Over the course of a year, Hart and Risley projected the difference for these two children to be 250,000 utterances versus 4 million utterances. By age 3, the quality of the language environment surrounding the child was related to children's IQ scores. When the children were in third grade, school achievement and intellectual ability test scores were obtained for 29 of the children. Measures of parenting when the children were 1 and 2 years old predicted children's third-grade achievement and ability scores. When one considers the cumulative difference in family environments, it is little surprise that early interventionists find it difficult to obtain lasting improvements in children's intellectual achievement. It appears that intensive intervention, such as that provided by the Carolina Abecedarian Project (Campbell & Ramey, 1994), in which the mean age for program entry was 4.4 months and continued through preschool at 8 hours per day, 5 days per week, and 50 weeks per year, is needed to achieve lasting results.

Adoption is, perhaps, the quintessential intervention program. Harris (1998) noted that in the French adoption study (Capron & Duyme, 1989) children placed in middle-class homes scored higher on IQ tests than children with working-class adoptive parents. According to Harris' theory, the reason for this difference is because the children became members of different peer groups with different attitudes toward schooling. Unfortunately, there is no way to separate the effects of peer groups from family environments in this study. It is just as plausible that differences in family environments accounted for the differences in children's achievement.

Few studies have been designed to tease apart the contributions of parents and peers to children's intellectual achievement. As previously mentioned, Fletcher et al. (1995) reported that the presence of authoritative parenting in the adolescent's peer group contributed to the adolescent's intellectual achievement after the variation explained by the parenting style of the adolescent's own parents was accounted for in a hierarchical regression. Certainly these data could be analyzed to determine if parents and peers account for unique portions of the variance in adolescents' achievement. The bottom line is that those who examine parental socialization can no longer ignore alternative hypotheses such as those offered by group socialization theorists and by behavioral genetic theorists. If researchers want to claim that parents or peers or genetics makes a difference, they should design studies that simultaneously consider the potential effects of parental socialization, peer socialization, and genetic contributions to children's development.

CONCLUSIONS

The studies reviewed in this chapter provide evidence that parental beliefs, expectations for children's development and achievement, and parenting style are related to children's intellectual development. An underlying theme in this research is that context affects development. First, context affects parents' development. Variation in cultural context is associated with differences in parents' beliefs about child development (e.g., when should children be able to control their emotions or express their needs verbally), ideas about intelligence, expectations for children's school performance, evaluations of children's performance, and parenting style. Second, Darling and Steinberg (1993) introduced the concept of parenting style as a context that influences adolescents' motivation to accept their parents' goals and values. In their research, (Steinberg et al., 1992b) demonstrated that the effect of parental involvement in adolescents' schooling is weaker for nonauthoritative parents than for other parents. In my research group (Okagaki & Bevis, 1999; Okagaki et al., 1999), we found that young adults who perceived their parents to be more authoritative and who enjoyed warmer, more securely attached relationships with their parents expressed a greater desire to share their parents' religious beliefs than other young adults. Our work supports Darling and Steinberg's hypothesis that authoritative parenting style may be associated with higher school performance, not because it affects development of cognitive skills, but because it creates a context in which adolescents are more willing to work to achieve the goals that their parents value.

This review highlights at least three needs in the field. First, the ability to syn-thesize research on parenting styles is limited because researchers have operationalized parenting styles in different ways and have focused on different aspects of each style. Some of the inconsistencies in results may be related to these differences in the operationalization of parenting styles. Second, research following Darling and Steinberg's model of the relations among parental goals and values, parenting style, parenting strategies, and child outcomes could be a fruitful endeavor if researchers can make a clear distinction between specific parenting strategies (i.e., behaviors) and parenting style, which is communi-cated to the child through parental behaviors and verbalizations. Finally, at some point, researchers who study the relations between child outcomes and parental beliefs and behaviors need to answer the challenge of behavioral ge-neticists and peer socialization theorists. That is, we need to conduct studies which seriously consider alternative explanations to parental socialization. We need to go back to what we learned in our first research methods course—"[a] causal hypothesis is not proved so long as an alternative hypothesis can be of-fered to explain the same findings" (Bronfenbrenner, 1972b, p. 12).

REFERENCES

Andersson, H. W., Sommerfelt, K., Sonnander, K., & Ahlsten, G. (1996). Maternal child-rearing attitudes, IQ, and socioeconomic status as related to cognitive abilities of five-year-old children. *Psychological Reports, 79*(1), 3–14.

Azuma, H. (1994). Two modes of cognitive socialization in Japan and the United States. In P. M. Greenfield & R. R. Cocking (Eds.), *Cross-cultural roots of minority child development* (pp. 275–284). Hillsdale, NJ: Lawrence Erlbaum Associates.

Azuma, H., Kashiwagi, K., & Hess, R. D. (1981). *The influence of attitude and behavior upon the child's intellectual development*. Tokyo: University of Tokyo Press.

Bacon, W. F., & Ichikawa, V. (1988). Maternal expectations, classroom experiences, and achievement among kindergartners in the United States and Japan. *Human Development, 31,* 378–383.

Baumrind, D. (1968). Authoritarian vs. authoritative parental control. *Adolescence, 3,* 255–272.

Baumrind, D. (1971). Current patterns of parental authority. *Developmental Psychology Monograph, 4* (1, Pt. 2).

Baumrind, D. (1972). An exploratory study of socialization effects on Black children: Some Black–White comparisons. *Child Development, 43,* 261–267.

Baumrind, D. (1989). Rearing competent children. In W. Damon (Ed.), *Child development to-day and tomorrow* (pp. 349–378). San Francisco: Jossey-Bass.

Baumrind, D. (1991a). Effective parenting during the early adolscent transition. In P. A. Cowan & E. M. Hetherington (Eds.), *Family transitions. Advances in family research series* (pp. 111–163). Hillsdale, NJ: Lawrence Erlbaum Associates.

Baumrind, D. (1991b). The influence of parenting style on adolescent competence and sub-stance use. *Journal of Early Adolescence, 11*(1), pp. 56–95.

Begley, S. (1998, September 7). The parent trap. *Newsweek*, 52–59.

Bronfenbrenner, U. (1972a). Is 80% of intelligence genetically determined? In U. Bronfenbrenner (Ed.), *Influences on human development* (pp. 118–127). Hinsdale, IL: Dryden Press.

Bronfenbrenner, U. (1972b). The structure and verification of hypotheses. In U. Bronfenbrenner (Ed.), *Influences on human development* (pp. 2–30). Hinsdale, IL: Dryden Press.

Brown, B. B. (1990). Peer groups and peer cultures. In S. S. Feldman & G. R. Elliott (Eds.), *At the threshold: The developing adolescent* (pp. 171–196). Cambridge, MA: Harvard University Press.

Campbell, F. A., & Ramey, C. T. (1994). Effects of early intervention on intellectual and academic achievement: A follow-up study of children from low-income families. *Child Development, 65*, 684–698.

Capron, C., & Duyme, M. (1989). Assessment of the effects of socio-economic status on IQ in a full cross-fostering study. *Nature, 340*, 552–554.

Ceci, S. J., Rosenblum, T., de Bruyn, E., & Lee, D. Y. (1997). A bio-ecological model of intellectual development: Moving beyond h². In R. J. Sternberg & E. Grigorenko (Eds.), *Intelligence, heredity, and environment* (pp. 303–322). New York: Cambridge University Press.

Chao, R. K. (1994). Beyond parental control and authoritarian parenting style: Understanding Chinese parenting through the cultural notion of training. *Child Development, 65*, 1111–1119.

Chen, C., & Uttal, D. H. (1988). Cultural values, parents' beliefs, and children's achievement in the United States and China. *Human Development, 31*, 351–358.

Crouter, A. C., MacDermid, S. M., McHale, S. M., & Perry-Jenkins, M. (1990). Parental monitoring and perceptions of children's school performance and conduct in dual- and single-earner families. *Developmental Psychology, 26*, 649–657.

Darling, N., & Steinberg, L. (1993). Parenting style as context: An integrative model. *Psychological Bulletin, 113*(3), 487–496.

Dasen, P. R. (1984). The cross-cultural study of intelligence: Piaget and the Baoulé. *International Journal of Psychology, 19*, 407–434.

Dickson, W. P., Hess, R. D., Miyake, N., & Azuma, H. (1979). Referential communication accuracy between mother and child as a predictor of cognitive development in the United States and Japan. *Child Development, 50*(1), 53–59.

Dornbusch, S. M., Ritter, P. L., Leiderman, P. H., Roberts, D. F., & Fraleigh, M. J. (1987). The relation of parenting style to adolescent school performance. *Child Development, 58*, 1244–1257.

Entwisle, D. R., & Hayduk, L. A. (1978). *Too great expectations: The academic outlook of young children*. Baltimore, MD: John Hopkins University Press.

Epstein, J. L. (1989). The selection of friends: Changes across the grades and in different school environments. In T. J. Berndt & G. W. Ladd (Eds.), *Peer relationships in child development* (pp. 158–187). New York: Wiley.

Feldman, S. S., & Quatman, T. (1988). Factors influencing age expectations for adolescent autonomy: A study of early adolescents and parents. *Journal of Early Adolescence, 8*, 325–343.

Feldman, S. S., & Wood, D. N. (1994). Parents' expectations for preadolescent sons' behavioral autonomy: A longitudinal study of correlates and outcomes. *Journal of Research on Adolescence, 4*(1), 45–70.

Fletcher, A. C., Darling, N. C., Dornbusch, S. M., & Steinberg, L. (1995). The company they keep: Relation of adolescents' adjustment and behavior to their friends' perceptions of authoritative parenting in the social network. *Developmental Psychology, 31* (2), 300–310.

Gardner, H. (1983). *Frames of mind*. New York: Basic Books.

Goodnow, J. J. (1976). The nature of intelligent behavior: Questions raised by cross-cultural studies. In L. Resnick (Ed.), *The nature of intelligence* (pp. 169–188). Hillsdale, NJ: Lawrence Erlbaum Associates.

Goodnow, J. J., Cashmore, J. A., Cotton, S., & Knight, R. (1984). Mothers' developmental timetables in two cultural groups. *International Journal of Psychology, 19*, 193–205.

Greenberger, E., Josselson, R., Knerr, C., & Knerr, B. (1974). The measurement and structure of psychosocial maturity. *Journal of Youth and Adolescence, 4*, 127–143.

Halle, T. G., Kurtz-Costes, B., & Mahoney, J. L. (1997). Family influences on school achievement in low-income, African American children. *Journal of Educational Psychology, 89*, 527–537.

Harris, J. R. (1995). Where is the child's environment? A group socialization theory of development. *Psychological Review, 102*(3), 458–489.

Harris, J. R. (1998). *The nurture assumption*. New York: Free Press.

Hart, B., & Risley, T. R. (1995). *Meaningful differences in the everyday experience of young American children*. Baltimore, MD: Brookes.

Hess, R. D., Kashiwagi, K., Azuma, H., Price, G. G., & Dickson, W. P. (1980). Maternal expectations for mastery of developmental tasks in Japan and the United States. *International Journal of Psychology, 15*, 259–271.

Hunt, J. McV., & Paraskevopoulos, J. (1980). Children's psychological development as a function of the inaccuracy of their mother's knowledge of their abilities. *Journal of Genetic Psychology, 136*, 285–298.

Johnson, B. M., Shulman, S., & Collins, W. A. (1991). Systemic patterns of parenting as reported by adolescents: Developmental differences and implications for psychosocial outcomes. *Journal of Adolescent Research, 6*(2), 235–252.

Lamborn, S. D., Mounts, N. S., Steinberg, L., & Dornbusch, S. M. (1991). Patterns of competence and adjustment among adolescents from authoritative, authoritarian, indulgent, and neglectful families. *Child Development, 62*, 1049–1065.

LeVine, R. A. (1974). Parental goals: A cross-cultural view. *Teachers College Record, 76*(2), 226–239.

Linver, M. R., & Silverberg, S. B. (1997). Maternal predictors of early adolescent achievement-related outcomes: Adolescent gender as moderator. *Journal of Early Adolescence, 17*(3), 294–318.

Maccoby, E. E., & Martin, J. A. (1983). Socialization in the context of the family: Parent–child interaction. In P. H. Mussen (Series Ed.) & E. M. Hetherington (Vol. Ed.), *Handbook of child psychology: Vol. 4. Socialization, personality, and social development* (4th ed., pp. 1–101). New York: Wiley.

Marjoribanks, K. (1996). Ethnicity, proximal family environment, and young adolescents' cognitive performance. *Journal of Early Adolescence, 61*(3), 340–359.

Miller, S. A. (1986). Parents' beliefs about their children's cognitive abilities. *Developmental Psychology, 22*, 276–284.

Neisser, U., Boodoo, G., Bouchard, T. J., Jr., Boykin, A. W., Brody, N., Ceci, S. J., Halpern, D. F., Loehlin, J. C., Perloff, R., Sternberg, R. J., & Urbina, S. (1996). Intelligence: Knowns and unknowns. *American Psychologist, 51*, 77–101.

Okagaki, L., & Bevis, C. (1999). Transmission of religious values: Relations between parents' and daughters' beliefs. *Journal of Genetic Psychology, 160*(3), 303–318.

Okagaki, L., & Frensch, P. A. (1998). Parenting and children's school achievement: A multi-ethnic perspective. *American Educational Research Journal, 35*(1), 123–144.

Okagaki, L., Frensch, P. A., & Dodson, N. E. (1996). Mexican-American children's self-perceptions and school achievement. *Hispanic Journal of Behavioral Sciences, 18*(4), 469–484.

Okagaki, L., Frensch, P. A., & Gordon, E. W. (1995). Encouraging school achievement in Mexican-American children. *Hispanic Journal of Behavioral Sciences, 17*(2), 160–179.

Okagaki, L., Hammond, K. A., & Seamon, L. (1999). Socialization of religious beliefs. *Journal of Applied Developmental Psychology, 20*(2), 273–294.

Okagaki, L., & Sternberg, R. J. (1993). Parental beliefs and children's early school performance. *Child Development, 64*(1), 36–56.

Paulson, S. E., Marchant, G. J., & Rothlisberg, B. A. (1998). Early adolescents' perceptions of patterns of parenting, teaching, and school atmosphere: Implications for achievement. *Journal of Early Adolescence, 18*(1), 5–26.

Radziszewska, B., Richardson, J. L., Dent, C. W., & Flay, B. R. (1996). Parenting style and adolescent depressive symptoms, smoking, and academic achievement: Ethnic, gender, and SES differences. *Journal of Behavioral Medicine, 19*(3), 289–305.

Rubin, K. H., Lynch, D., Coplan, R., Rose-Krasnor, L., & Booth, C. L. (1994). "Birds of a feather … ": Behavioral concordances and preferential personal attraction in children. *Child Development, 65*, 1778–1785.

Schaefer, E. S., & Edgerton, M. (1985). Parent and child correlates of parental modernity. In I. E. Sigel (Ed.), *Parental belief systems: The psychological consequences for children* (pp. 287–318). Hillsdale, NJ: Lawrence Erlbaum Associates.

Schneider, B., Hieshima, J. A., Lee, S., & Plank, S. (1994). East-Asian academic success in the United States: Family, school, and community explanations. In P. M. Greenfield & R. R. Cocking (Eds.), *Cross-cultural roots of minority child development* (pp. 323–350), Hillsdale, NJ: Lawrence Erlbaum Associates.

Seginer, R. (1983). Parents' educational expectations and children's academic achievements: A literature review. *Merrill-Palmer Quarterly, 29*(1), 1–23.

Serpell, R. (1984). Research on cognitive development in sub-Saharan Africa. *International Journal of Behavioral Development, 7*, 111–127.

Siegler, R. S., & Richards, D. D. (1982). The development of intelligence. In R. J. Sternberg (Ed.), *Handbook of human intelligence* (pp. 897–974). New York: Cambridge University Press.

Steinberg, L., Dornbusch, S. M., & Brown, B. B. (1992a). Ethnic differences in adolescent achievement: An ecological perspective. *American Psychologist, 47*(6), 723–729.

Steinberg, L., Elmen, J. D., & Mounts, N. S. (1989). Authoritative parenting, psychosocial maturity, and academic success among adolescents. *Child Development, 60*, 1424–1436.

Steinberg, L., Lamborn, S. D., Dornbusch, S. M., & Darling, N. (1992b). Impact of parenting practices on adolescent achievement: Authoritative parenting, school involvement, and encouragement to succeed. *Child Development, 63*, 1266–1281.

Steinberg, L., Mounts, N., Lamborn, S., & Dornbusch, S. (1991). Authoritative parenting and adolescent adjustment across various ecological niches. *Journal of Research on Adolescence, 1*, 19–36.

Sternberg, R. J. (1985). *Beyond IQ: A triarchic theory of intelligence.* New York: Cambridge University Press.

Stevenson, H. W., Chen, C., & Lee, S.-Y. (1993). Mathematics achievement of Chinese, Japanese, and American children: Ten years later. *Science, 259*(1), 53–58.

Stevenson, H. W., & Lee, S.-Y. (1990). Contexts of achievement. *Monographs of the Society for Research in Child Development, 55*(1-2, Serial No. 221).

Stevenson, H. W., Lee, S.-Y., & Stigler, J. W. (1986). Mathematics achievement of Chinese, Japanese, and American children. *Science, 321*, 693–699.

Taylor, L. C., Hinton, I. D., & Wilson, M. N. (1995). Parental influences on academic performance in African-American students. *Journal of Child and Family Studies, 4*(3), 293–302.

Wober, M. (1974). Towards an understanding of the Kiganda concept of intelligence. In J. W. Berry & P. R. Dasen (Eds.), *Culture and cognition: Readings in cross-cultural psychology* (pp. 261–280). London: Methuen.

8

Sources of Environmental Influence on Cognitive Abilities in Adulthood

Deborah Finkel
Indiana University Southeast

Nancy L. Pedersen
Karolinska Institute
University of Southern California

Twin studies are usually thought of as providing information about genetic in-fluences. They can, with equal validity, be used to examine environmental in-fluences on cognitive abilities in adulthood. Clearly, in partitioning variance into genetic and environmental components, twin studies demonstrate not only heritability; environmental influences are also documented and further partitioned into shared and nonshared components. Behavioral genetic research that examined environmental influences on behavior has shown that shared environmental effects are important for specific cognitive abilities, especially during childhood (Plomin & Daniels, 1987). Although studies of adolescents (Scarr & Weinberg, 1978) and adults (Bouchard, Lykken, McGue, Segal, & Tellegen, 1990) failed to find significant evidence for shared environmental influences on cognitive abilities, results from studies of older adult twins affirm their importance (Pedersen, Plomin, Nesselroade, & McClearn, 1992; Tambs, Sundet, & Magnus, 1984). Evidence from both cross-sectional and longitudinal studies converges on the conclusion that heritability for general cognitive ability increases from infancy through childhood and adolescence, plateaus in adulthood, and decreases late in life (Pedersen & Lichtenstein, 1997). As Fig. 8.1 illustrates, the proportion of variance in cognitive abilities explained by environmental influences, both shared and nonshared, is largest during childhood and late adulthood. The aim of this chapter is to focus on the environmental portion of variance in cognitive abilities during adulthood within the context of genetically informative designs.

ENVIRONMENTAL COMPONENTS OF VARIANCE

It is important to begin by noting that *shared environment* and *family environment* are not synonymous terms with regard to behavioral genetic analyses. You could say that behavioral geneticists define components of variance from the top down. Shared environmental influences are parametrized as environmental variance that is perfectly correlated ($r = 1.00$) for a pair of individuals. In contrast, nonshared environmental influences are parametrized as environmental variance that is perfectly uncorrelated ($r = 0.00$) for a pair of individuals. Shared environmental influences result in similarities among family members, whereas nonshared environmental influences produce differences between family members. All experiences that produce similarities do not occur in the family context, and experiences within the family context often affect family members differently (Goldsmith, 1993; Plomin & Daniels, 1987). Thus, the distinctions between shared and nonshared environmental effects in behavioral genetic designs do not map well onto some issues that concern the effects of the family environment. For that reason, both shared and nonshared environmental components of variance are considered in our review of environmental sources of variance in cognitive abilities.

Studies of adult twins have consistently reported significant genetic influences on cognitive abilities, across cultures and across the entire adult life span (Bouchard et al., 1990; Finkel, Pedersen, McGue, & McClearn, 1995; Jarvik, Blum, & Varma, 1972; Kallmann, Feingold, & Bondy, 1951; McClearn et al., 1997; Pedersen et al., 1992; Swan et al., 1990; Tambs et al., 1984). Heritability of general cognitive ability is high in adulthood; between 60% and 80% of the total variance can be attributed to genetic influences. Consequently, these studies indicate that between 20% and 40% of the variance in cognitive abilities results from environmental influences. Most of these studies concluded that the environmental variance was largely nonshared. Only a few studies reported significant shared environmental influences on cognitive abilities in late adulthood.

Theories of crystallized and fluid abilities would probably predict greater importance of shared environmental influences for crystallized than for fluid measures (Cattell, 1957). Twin studies that reported shared environmental effects on cognitive abilities in adulthood, however, have found them for both types of measures. Tambs et al. (1984) reported more shared environmental influences for Performance IQ (27%) than for Verbal IQ (9%) in a sample of Norwegian twins ranging in age from 30 to 57 years. In a sample of Japanese twins who ranged in age from 50 to 78 years, Hayakawa, Shimizu, Ohba, and Tomioka (1992) reported large shared environmental effects for measures of memory and perceptual speed. Pedersen et al. (1992) found shared rearing environmental effects for measures of crystallized abilities and fluid abilities in a sample of Swedish twins aged 50 to 80. Even in Swedish twins over 80, small but significant shared environmental effects were reported for both crystallized and fluid measures (McClearn et al., 1997). These studies demonstrated that shared environmental influences can affect not only learning of facts (crystallized) but also problem-solving skills (fluid). However, shared environmental influences are not important sources of individual difference for all measures of cognitive abilities. What is also striking about these findings is the suggestion that shared environmental influences can cast a long shadow; the effects are observed decades after twins have left the families in which they were reared and presumably begun to live separate lives. Now the task is to move beyond anonymous components of variation to an investigation of measurable experiences in the family environment. In other words, researchers have begun to identify specific components of environmental variation using "bottom-up" methods, much like molecular geneticists are identifying quantitative trait loci that account for a portion of the genetic component of variation.

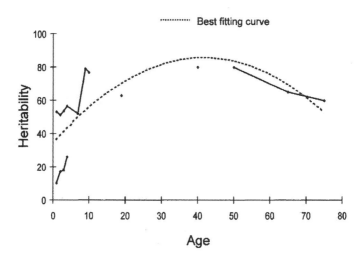

FIG 8.1   Summary of heritability estimates for general cognitive abilities across the lifespan.
Longitudinal data for ages 1 to 4 are from the Louisville Twin Study (Wilson, 1985) and for
ages 1 to 10 from CAP, MALTS, and TIP (Cherny, Fulker, & Hewitt, 1996; Fulker, Cherny, &
Cardon, 1993). The single point at age 20 is based on twin data from Tambs et al. (1989) and
at 40 on data from Tambs, Sundet, & Magnus, 1986 and Bouchard et al., 1990. Longitudinal
data from 50 and above are from SATSA (Finkel, Pedersen, Plomin, & McClearn, 1998).
The dotted line is the polynomial regression line fitted to all the points. From Pedersen and
Lichtenstein (1997). Reprinted with permission.

SPECIFIC SOURCES OF ENVIRONMENTAL INFLUENCES

In response to the lack of evidence for shared family effects often reported by behavior genetic studies, environmentally oriented researchers assert that behavioral geneticists seldom use direct measures of the environment
(Bronfenbrenner, 1986; Hoffman, 1991; Wachs, 1983, 1993). Rowe and
Waldman (1993) contended that much of the disagreement arises from the emphasis by behavioral geneticists on anonymous variance components rather
than specific measures of the environment. Having identified the extent of environmental influences on individual differences in cognitive abilities in adulthood, behavior geneticists must now begin to identify specific measures of the
environment that underlie environmental components of variance. Part of this
effort must be better and more standardized measurements of the environment
(Horowitz, 1993).

Decades of research have proposed many "environmental" variables that may account for variance in cognitive abilities. Mascie-Taylor (1993) documented numerous correlations between environmental factors and intelligence. The correlations are difficult to interpret, however, because of the inevitable confusion between genetics and environment in nuclear families: Does the correlation arise from shared environment or shared genes? Genetic and shared environmental effects are confounded in nuclear families. It is not enough to demonstrate that a variable that is considered a measure of the environment accounts for some of the variance in cognitive abilities. So-called environmental variables are not always what they seem. Converging evidence suggests that many measures of the environment, including measures of the family environment during childhood, reflect genetic influences (Plomin, 1994; Plomin & Bergeman, 1991; Plomin, McClearn, Pedersen, Nesselroade, & Bergeman, 1988; Rowe, 1994). In other words, genetic factors often influence how people recall and describe their family environment. Furthermore, several researchers investigated the effects of environmental indices, such as socioeconomic status (SES), on cognitive abilities (Marjoribanks, 1977; Wolf, 1964) without regard to whether these effects are shared or nonshared among relatives. An implicit premise in many developmental studies has been that if environmental influences are of importance during childhood, they contribute to sibling similarity, and thus are shared (McCall, 1983).

As we stated in the introduction, the environmental variance need not be treated as a unitary concept, but can be partitioned into shared and nonshared components. A growing number of behavioral genetic studies of cognitive abilities are focusing attention on identifying specific environmental influences of importance for behavior within the components of variance paradigm. For example, a major effort was directed toward identifying nonshared environmental influences that cause differences among siblings (Hetherington, Reiss, & Plomin, 1994; Reiss, Neiderhiser, Hetherington, & Plomin, 2000). In contrast, little research has concentrated on specifying experiences that lead to sibling similarity and thus may be considered aspects of shared environmental effects for cognitive abilities (Coon, Fulker, DeFries, & Plomin, 1990; Hoffman, 1991; Rowe & Waldman, 1993; Spuhler & Vandenburg, 1978). As we describe later, behavior genetic methods allow us to determine whether an "environmental" variable actually explains the environmental, as opposed to genetic, variance in cognitive abilities.

Several analytical methods are available within the behavioral genetic armentarium that focus on specific sources of environmental variation. Multivariate biometric and multiple regression techniques can be used to determine whether specific environmental measures account for the environmental components of variance in cognitive abilities. Co-twin comparisons provide a method for comparing the cognitive outcomes for genetically identical twins who are discordant for a specific environmental variable. Studies of twins who were reared separately since early childhood provide additional insights into the influences of environmental variables. Finally, the possibility of gene–environment interaction effects can be explored by examining monozygotic intrapair differences and sums.

MULTIPLE REGRESSION ANALYSIS

A modified version of the DeFries and Fulker (DF; 1985) multiple regression analysis, as described by Rowe and Waldman (1993), can be used to determine whether specific measures of the environment explain portions of the environmental variance in a trait. The DF regression involves regressing the score for one twin on the score for the co-twin. The regression equation takes the following form:

$$P_1 = b_0 + b_1 P_2 + b_2 R + b_3 P_2 R, \text{ (1)}$$

where P_1 is the phenotype of one twin, P_2 is the phenotype of the co-twin, R is the coefficient of genetic relationship. Monozygotic (MZ) twins share all of their genetic material, thus their coefficient of relationship is 1.0. Dizygotic (DZ) twins share, on average, one half of their segregating genes, which results in a coefficient of relationship of 0.5. The unstandardized regression coefficient, b_3, directly estimates heritability because it indicates the degree to which twin similarity on the phenotype differs by level of genetic relatedness. The coefficient for the co-twin's phenotype, b_1, is a direct estimate of shared environmental influences because it indicates the portion of twin similarity not due to genetic influences. Rowe and Waldman (1993) suggested adding to the DF regression equation a measured environmental variable (M) that affects both twins' phenotypes similarly. The augmented equation would be:

$$P_1 = b_0 + b_1 P_2 + b_2 R + b_3 P_2 R + b_4 M. \text{ (2)}$$

The significance of b_4 indicates the extent to which the specific environmental measure accounts for some of the abstract shared environmental variance. For example, evidence suggests SES is an aspect of the home environment that is relevant to cognitive abilities. If application of equation 1 to the data produces a statistically significant estimate of anonymous shared environmental influences

(b_1), we can test the ability of SES to explain part of that shared environmental variance. If adding each pairs' SES level during childhood to the DF regression equation as variable M results in a significant reduction in the shared environmental parameter and a significant value for b_4, then we can conclude that SES accounts for some portion of the shared environmental variance in cognitive abilities. To date, this method remains an untapped resource for the investigation of specific sources of environmental variance in cognitive abilities during adulthood; to our knowledge, no report of use of the DF regression for this purpose has appeared in press.

MULTIVARIATE BIOMETRIC ANALYSIS

Multivariate biometric analysis can determine the extent to which cognitive abilities and specific measures of the environment are influenced by the same environmental factors, or whether there are environmental factors for cognitive abilities independent of these measures of the environment. As with the multiple regression analysis, if the environmental variance for cognitive abilities can be attributed to specific measures of the environment, the latter can be considered as sources of environmental influences for cognitive abilities. One behavioral genetic model that can address these issues involves a Cholesky decomposition of the covariance between the cognitive measure and the measures of the environment (Neale & Cardon, 1992).[1] As presented in Fig. 8.2, the Cholesky model decomposes the variance in measures of cognition and the environment into genetic (G), shared environmental (Es), and nonshared environmental (Ens) components. The variance in cognition is divided into portions that are shared with the environmental measures and portions independent of the environmental measure. Thus, the total shared environmental influence on the cognitive measure can be estimated $(w^2 + y^2)$, as well as the shared environmental variance that is common to both the environmental and cognitive measures (w^2). If the w parameter is significant, then we can conclude that the specific measure of the environment explains a portion of the abstract shared environmental variance. The Cholesky model can be extended to include three or more variables. Other multivariate models, such as the common factor model, can provide information about environmental variance common to measures of cognition and the environment using similar calculations (Neale & Cardon, 1992).

---

[1] We present this model as it is the model most frequently applied. However, Neale (1996) and others are developing methods to incorporate directly environmental measures within the variance components design (Martin, Boomsma, & Machin, 1997).

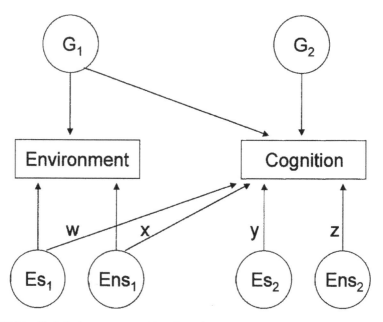

FIG 8.2   Cholesky decomposition of the relationship between cognition and a measure of
the environment.

Few studies have been conducted that use multivariate biometric models
specifically to determine the particular environmental measures that underlie
the environmental variance in cognitive abilities in adulthood (Pedersen &
Lichtenstein, 1997). However, some studies that used multivariate models to
focus on the genetic relationship between cognitive abilities and possible environmental measures provide information concerning the extent to which the
environmental measures share environmental variance with cognition (and
hence, may be considered specific environmental sources of variance for cognition). The results of these studies vary, as the summary in Table 8.1 indicates.
Total shared ($w^2 + y^2$) and nonshared ($x^2 + z^2$) environmental variance for each
cognitive measure are reported in the columns headed Total Es and Total Ens,
respectively. The amount of variance attributable to shared environmental
variance (w^2) and nonshared environmental (x^2) variance common to both the
cognitive and environmental measures is reported in the columns labeled Common Es and Common Ens, respectively. For each row in Table 8.1, if Common
Es or Common Ens percentages are significant, then the data indicate that the
specific environmental measure does explain some or all of the abstract environmental variance in the cognitive measure. Consider the results of Pedersen,

Lichtenstein, Plomin, and McClearn (1996). They found that 10% of the total variance in performance on the Information test was attributable to anonymous shared environmental effects. Applying the Cholesky model to the covariance between Information and the Culture & ATE factor indicated that nearly one third of the abstract shared environmental variance in Information (3% of total variance) was in common with the shared environmental variance for the Culture & ATE factor. From these data we can conclude that one third of the shared environmental variance in Information can be attributed to a specific measure of the environment: Culture & ATE.

In some cases, variables that may be considered measures of the environment account for little of the environmental variance, either shared or nonshared, in the cognitive measure (e.g., Figure Memory and Social Class; Finkel & McGue, 1993). For the most part, if there is evidence of shared environmental variance for the cognitive measure, some or all of that abstract variance can be explained by environmental variance in common with a specific environmental measure. However, significant shared environmental variance was reported for less than half of the cognitive measures. The findings based on the Swedish Adoption/Twin Study of Aging (SATSA; Pedersen et al., 1996) are noteworthy in that only five of the eight Moos Family Environment subscales were associated with any of the 13 measures of cognitive abilities, and no single correlation accounted for more than 4% of the variation in the cognitive measure. Nonetheless, all of the shared environmental variance for Block Design and Thurstone's Figure Memory was in common with shared environmental variance for Culture & ATE.

There is no overlap of cognitive measures used in the different studies reported in Table 8.1. We need more analyses that incorporate the same cognitive measures to provide replication of these results before strong conclusions can be drawn. Finding variables that explain nonshared environmental variance is more difficult. Only one comparison in Table 8.1 reported an environmental variable that explained a significant portion of the nonshared environmental variance for a cognitive measure: Word Recall and Social Class in Finkel and McGue (1993). The co-twin control method may be a superior method for identifying sources of nonshared environmental variance in cognitive performance.

CO-TWIN CONTROL METHOD

Comparing the cognitive performance of MZ twin pairs provides a method for holding genetic influences constant while allowing environmental influences to vary. Typically, researchers compare the cognitive performance of MZ twins

TABLE 8.1

Studies Reporting Multivariate Behavior Genetic Analysis of Cognitive and Environmental Measures

Study	Cognitive Measure	Environmental Measure	Total Es	Common Es	Total Ens	Common Ens
Finkel and McGue (1993)	Word recall	Social class	0%	0%	44%	25%
	Word recall	Physical activity	0%	0%	44%	0%
	Word recall	Intellectual activity	0%	0%	44%	0%
	Text recall	Social class	0%	0%	43%	3%
	Text recall	Physical activity	0%	0%	43%	1%
	Text recall	Intellectual activity	0%	0%	43%	0%
	Figure memory	Social class	0%	0%	36%	0%
	Figure memory	Physical activity	0%	0%	36%	7%
	Figure memory	Intellectual activity	0%	0%	36%	1%
Finkel et al. (1995)	Cognitive factor[a]	Physiological factor[b]	21%	21%	20%	0%
	Cognitive factor	Speed factor[c]	21%	0%	20%	0%
Pedersen et al. (1996)	Information	Culture & ATE[d]	10%	3%	29%	0%
	Block design	Culture & ATE	9%	9%	34%	0%

Thurstone	Culture & ATE	6%	6%	61%	1%
Digit symbol	Culture & ATE	0%	0%	39%	0%
Tambs et al. (1989)[e]	IQ	Occupation	45%	45%	18%	0%
	IQ	Education	45%	45%	18%	0%

Note. Es = Shared Environment, Ens = Nonshared Environment. Total Es or Ens indicates the amount of variance in the cognitive measure explained by Es or Ens effects. Common Es or Ens indicates the amount of environmental variance in the cognitive measure that is shared with the environmental measure.

[a] The Cognitive factor includes verbal IQ, performance IQ, text recall, block design, and forward digit span.

[b] The Physiological factor includes systolic blood pressure, diastolic blood pressure, and pulse.

[c] The Speed factor includes simple reaction time, choice reaction time, digit symbol, and inductive reasoning.

[d] ATE is the acronym for attitudes towards education.

[e] Data for the oldest cohort from Tambs et al. (1989) are reported.

who are discordant for exposure to the environmental variable of interest. If the "exposed" twin differs significantly from the "nonexposed" twin, the intrapair difference in cognitive performance can be attributed to the effects of the environmental variable. By definition, the only type of environment in which MZ pairs can be discordant is nonshared environment. It is possible, however, for MZ pairs to be discordant on some measure of the family environment, especially MZ pairs who were reared separately. Again, few studies of cognitive performance in adult twins have taken advantage of this method.

One difficulty associated with using the co-twin control method is finding a sufficient sample of MZ twins who are discordant for the environmental measure (see Table 8.2). In a sample of 76 MZ pairs, Hayakawa et al. (1992) found 11 pairs discordant for occupation, 24 pairs discordant for alcohol consumption, and 7 pairs discordant for school career. Only one comparison produced a statistically significant intrapair difference in performance on the Digit Symbol task. Twins engaged in light labor scored half a standard deviation higher than their co-twins who worked in heavy labor occupations. In an investigation of the effects of smoking on cognitive performance, Kasl-Godley, Pedersen, and Gatz (1998), found 11 pairs discordant for smoking, out of a sample of 86 pairs. Even in that small sample, Kasl-Godley et al. (1998) found that nonsmokers scored significantly better than their smoking co-twins on measures of acculturated knowledge, visual memory, and perceptual speed. Kasl-Godley et al. combined both reared-apart and reared-together twins in their co-twin control analysis. In the next section, we discuss the unique information that analyses of reared-apart twins can provide.

REARED-APART TWINS

Investigation of the similarity of twins who were reared apart since early childhood adds to our understanding of environmental influences in two important ways. First, including both reared-together and reared-apart twins allows separation of shared environmental variance into estimates of the importance of rearing environments (Es) and other forms of correlated environment (Ec). Correlated environment refers to all twin similarity that cannot be attributed to either genetic or shared environmental influences. It can include prenatal influences and similarities in adult life experiences. For example, if both twins win the lottery, it would not be considered a rearing environmental effect, but it is an environmental event that the twins share. Correlated environment includes such shared environmental effects that are not part of the rearing environment. Whereas only twins reared in the same household can share Es effects, both

TABLE 8.2

Studies Reporting Co-twin Control Analysis of Cognitive
and Environmental Measures.

Study	Cognitive Measure	Environmental Measure	Number of Discordant Pairs	Significant Intrapair Difference?[a]
Hayakawa et al. (1992)	Digit symbol	Occupation	11	Yes
	Digit symbol	Alcohol consumption	24	No
	Digit symbol	Education	7	No
Kasl-Godley et al. (1998)	Information	Smoking	11	Yes
	Names and faces	Smoking	11	Yes
	Figure identification	Smoking	11	Yes
	Synonyms	Smoking	11	No
	Analogies	Smoking	11	No
	Figure logic	Smoking	11	No
	Block design	Smoking	11	No
	Card rotation	Smoking	11	No
	Digit symbol	Smoking	11	No
	Digit span	Smoking	11	No
	Thurstone	Smoking	11	No

Note. [a]Indicates whether or not intrapair differences on the cognitive measure attained statistical significance.

reared-apart and reared-together twin pairs may share Ec effects. Thus, inclusion of reared-apart twins allows us to decompose environmental influences into three components: shared rearing environment, correlated environment, and nonshared environment. Pedersen et al. (1992) reported significant Ec effects for measures of fluid ability and memory (i.e. shared effects that could not be attributed to the rearing situation). Further research is necessary to isolate the specific sources of the correlated environmental influences.

The second way in which reared-apart twins can aid our understanding of environmental influences involves analysis of the effect of age at separation. Reared-apart twins are not necessarily separated a birth. Most studies report great variability in the age at which the twins were separated and in the total length of the separation. Comparing twin similarity by age at separation, degree of separation, and number of years separated is an effective method for evaluating the influence of the rearing environment. In her review of data on reared-apart MZ twins, Farber (1981) found no decrease in the similarity of MZ twins she classified as "highly separated" when compared with the entire sample. Hayakawa et al. (1992) reported that intrapair similarity on measures of Digit Symbol, Digit Span, and Block Design increased significantly as the age at separation increased. Intrapair similarity for occupation, sports activities, and food preferences was also positively correlated with age at separation. These results suggested the influence of lifestyle factors, if not the rearing environment per se, on cognitive performance in adulthood. In contrast, other studies of reared-apart twins have reported no relationship between age at separation and twin similarity on cognitive measures. Pedersen et al. (1992) found little or no effect of age of separation, degree of separation, or number of years separated on twin similarity for cognitive abilities for the reared-apart twins from the SATSA. Furthermore, similarities in the SES of the rearing home were not associated with similarity for cognition. This result is in contrast to the results for alcohol consumption, for which there was a significant association with degree of separation (Pedersen, McClearn, Plomin, & Nesselroade, 1992). Bouchard (1997) reported similar negative results from the Minnesota Study of Twins Reared Apart. The preponderance of evidence suggests little effect of any of the various indicators of separation on twin similarity for cognitive abilities.

GENE–ENVIRONMENT INTERACTION

Until now, we discussed environmental influences as if their action is independent of the organism—as if environmental variables affect all genotypes in exactly the same way. We know that reality is much more complex. *Genotype–environment* (GE) *interaction* refers to nonlinear combinations of genetic and environmental influences (Jinks & Fulker, 1970). In other words, an environmental variable may have a different impact on different genotypes, or genotypes may be differentially susceptible to the influence of the environment (Falconer, 1960). In the classic demonstration of GE interaction effects (Cooper & Zubeck, 1958), rats bred to perform well in running a maze (maze bright) were compared with rats bred for poor maze running performance (maze dull). When the two different genotypes (maze-bright and maze-dull) were exposed to the same novel environment influence (an enriched environment including a cage filled with stimulating toys), only the maze-dull rats were affected: Their maze running performance improved. Thus, the two genotypes reacted differently to the influence of that particular environmental effect.

Jinks and Fulker (1970) presented methods for testing for GE interactions for both shared and nonshared environmental effects using twin data. Correlating intrapair sums with absolute intrapair differences for MZ twins provides a measure of whether twin similarity varies with level of performance. *Intrapair sum* (or average) indicates the level of performance of the twin pair and, indirectly, provides an assessment of the genotype. One could say twin pairs who score high on measures of cognitive performance are analogous to maze-bright rats and low scoring pairs are analogous to maze-dull rats. Assessing the absolute intrapair difference provides an indication of the extent of environmental influences on the pair. Recall that only environmental influences can cause differences between MZ twins. Large intrapair differences must result from a greater impact of the environment. If a positive correlation between intrapair sums and differences results, then low scoring twins are more similar than high scoring twins. By extension, high scorers are more susceptible to environmental influences. A negative correlation, on the other hand, indicates that low scorers are less similar and thus more susceptible to environmental influences. For example, a negative correlation would indicate that the similarity of "maze-bright" twins is not affected by environmental influences, whereas "maze-dull" twins are less similar. Their performance is more variable, which indicates greater susceptibility to the environment.

Calculating the intrapair sum/intrapair difference correlation separately for MZ twins reared together (MZT) and MZ twins reared apart (MZA) allows for the identification of GEns interactions versus GEs interactions, respectively. Both genetic and shared environmental influences add to the similarity of MZT pairs; only Ens effects can cause differences between MZT pairs. Therefore, if the correlation between sums and differences for MZT pairs is significant, then an interaction between G and Ens influences is indicated. Only genetic factors can underlie the similarity of MZA pairs, whereas both Ens and Es effects can cause differences. Thus, a significant sums/differences correlation for MZA pairs may indicate GEns and GEs interactions. Without further information, we cannot determine whether one or both possible interactions exist. If the MZA correlation is significant (support for GEns and GEs interactions) and the MZT correlation is not (evidence against GEns interaction), then an interaction between G and Es influences is indicated.

This method for identifying GEs and GEns interactions was applied to data from SATSA; the results are presented in Table 8.3. The correlations between intrapair sums and intrapair differences are presented separately for MZT and MZA pairs for each of 12 cognitive measures. A measure of general cognitive ability was also created. Individuals' scores on the first principal component of all the measures were obtained (e.g., Pedersen et al., 1992). With the exception of Forward Digit Span, all measures loaded higher than .50 on the first principal component, which accounted for 45% of the total variance. As in Jinks and Fulker (1970), we found no evidence for either GEs or GEns interactions for general cognitive ability. In contrast, interaction effects were indicated for five of the 12 measures of specific cognitive abilities. Significant MZT intrapair sum/difference correlations suggested GEns interaction effects for Information, Digit Symbol, Names and Faces, and Thurstone's Picture Memory. Surprisingly, the interaction effects were not all in the same direction. The significantly negative correlations for Information, Digit Symbol, and Thurstone's Picture Memory represent more susceptibility to nonshared environmental effects for low scorers. According to Jinks and Fulker (1970), low scorers are more at the mercy of environmental effects and thus may be less likely to reach their potential. One might also imagine that the low scorers in this sample of elderly twins are those in a period of cognitive decline, which perhaps later results in dementia. The timing of this decline may differ for members of a pair and hence intrapair differences reflect environmental effects on timing of decline. This hypothesis is consistent with dementia research which indicates that environmental influences are greater for age of onset than for the occurrence of Alzheimer's disease (Gatz et al., 1997; Posner, Pedersen, & Gatz, 1999).

A significant positive correlation was found for the Names and Faces task, which was replicated by the delayed recall version of the task (MZT sums/differences correlation = .44, $p < .01$). For this task, high scorers appear to be more susceptible to nonshared environmental variation. Significant MZA intrapair sum/difference correlations were found for nearly the same set of variables, making it difficult to disentangle GEns and GEs interactions. The one exception was Figure Logic. A significant negative correlation was found, which indicated that shared environmental effects play a larger role in the performance of low scorers. Similar associations were evaluated for not only MZ but also DZ pairs on the Army General Classification Test (AGCT) by Plassman and colleagues (Plassman et al., 1995). Intrapair sums and differences were negatively correlated for DZ pairs, whereas no association was found for MZ pairs. Thus, the criteria for GE interaction suggested by Jinks and Fulker (1970) were not fulfilled. However, a consequence of the differential associations by zygosity was

TABLE 8.3

Correlation of Intrapair Differences and Intrapair Sums
for MZT and MZA Twins in SATSA.

Variable	MZT (67 pairs)	MZA (46 pairs)
Information	−.33 **	−.43 **
Synonyms	−.09	−.22
Analogies	.12	.07
Figure logic	.01	−.31*
Block design	−.11	.03
Card rotation	.05	.29
Digit symbol	−.37 **	.05
Figure identification	.22	−.22
Forward digit span	.20	−.03
Backward digit span	−.03	−.06
Names and faces	.39**	.57**
Thurstone	−.31*	−.22
General cognitive ability	−.11	−.09

Note. MZT = monozygotic reared together; MZA = monozygotic reared apart. Significant correlation for MZT indicates GEns interaction. Significant correlation for MZA indicates GEns and/or GEs interaction.

$*p < .05; **p < .01$

lower heritability estimates for lower ACGT scorers. These data would suggest that, in contrast to the older twins where lower performers may have been more susceptible to environmental effects, genetic effects may be greater for these younger, lower scorers. On the other hand, comparisons of heritability estimates across ability levels from other studies of adult twins have not replicated this finding (Saudino, Plomin, Pedersen, & McClearn, 1994; Sundet, Eilertsen, Tambs, & Magnus, 1994).

The comparison of MZT and MZA intrapair sums and differences correlations can only be considered a first step in the investigation of GE interactions. The previously mentioned analysis serves to indicate whether GE interactions exist, but does not identify which environmental measures are the source of the interactions. To find specific environmental measures responsible, researchers could stratify the twin sample on the basis of exposure to the environmental variable or variables of interest. If differences in heritability result, then support for a specific source of the GE interaction would be provided (Bronfenbrenner & Ceci, 1993; Heath, Neale, Hewitt, Eaves, & Fulker, 1989).

CONCLUSIONS

There is a paucity of empirical evidence concerning the influence of specific environmental effects within the variance components model often used in behavioral genetic analyses. Nevertheless, methodological techniques are being developed to encompass not only anonymous variance components, but also measured, identified influences (Martin, Boomsma, & Machin, 1997; Neale, 1996). We have demonstrated that behavioral genetic designs can be used to identify specific sources of environmental variance. Co-twin control designs directly address the importance of specific environmental influences, although by definition, the relative influence of genetic influences can not simultaneously be evaluated. Regression techniques have been proposed, but not applied. Multivariate biometric techniques have been applied, but few have focused interpretations on environmental influences. Perhaps the most intuitively appealing are GE interaction effects. Indications of GE interaction are obtainable in any twin study, albeit almost never evaluated. GE interactions through evaluations of differential heritability as a function of environmental exposure have not been explored for cognitive abilities. There is a continuing effort toward developing methodologies to incorporate measured environments (as well as measured genotypes) in genetically informative designs (Martin et al., 1997). Application has not yet caught up with methodological development. The bottom line is that the techniques are available, but that they have not yet been put into practice.

It is important to note that environmental influences are likely to be "polyenvironmental" and pleiotropic; in other words, myriad environmental factors may be important for a behavior, and interactions among these factors may exist. Therefore, the effect of any single measure of the environment is likely to be small. Analyses of measures of specific environmental influences may be considered an analog to molecular genetic techniques that search for quantitative trait loci (Cardon, Smith, Fulker, & Kimberling, 1994). In both cases, the aim is to identify specific effects (genetic loci or measured environments) that may account for a moderate amount of the total phenotypic variation previously attributed to anonymous genetic and environmental components of variance.

Despite criticism from environmentally oriented researchers, behavior geneticists are actively engaged in investigation of sources of environmental influences on cognitive abilities in adulthood. As Horowitz (1993) indicated, the efforts of both environmentally oriented researchers and behavioral geneticists would benefit from the development of better and more standardized measures of the family environment. We hope that behavioral geneticists and environmentally oriented researchers alike will perceive this chapter as a call for an increase in the level of effort directed toward our growing understanding of the long-term influence of environmental effects. The available data suggest that molecular measures of the environment (such as ATE) will play a more important role in identifying the sources of environmental influences on cognitive abilities in adulthood than global environmental measures (such SES).

REFERENCES

Bouchard, T. J., Jr. (1997). IQ similarity in twins reared apart: Findings and responses to critics. In R. J. Sternberg & E. Grigorenko (Eds.), *Intelligence, heredity, and environment* (pp. 126–160). Cambridge: Cambridge University Press.

Bouchard, T. J., Jr., Lykken, D. T., McGue, M., Segal, N. L., & Tellegen, A. (1990). Sources of human psychological differences: The Minnesota twin study of twins reared apart. *Science, 250,* 223–228.

Bronfenbrenner, U. (1986). Ecology of the family as a context for human development. *Developmental Psychology, 22,* 723–742.

Bronfenbrenner, U., & Ceci, S. J. (1993). Heredity, environment, and the question "How?"—A first approximation. In R. Plomin & G. E. McClearn (Eds.), *Nature, nurture and psychology* (pp. 313–324). Washington, DC: American Psychological Association.

Cardon, L. R., Smith, S. D., Fulker, D. W., & Kimberling, W. J. (1994). Quantitative trait locus for reading disability on chromosome 6. *Science, 266,* 276–279.

Cattell, R. B. (1957). *Personality and motivation structure and measurement.* New York: World Book.

Cherny, S. S., Fulker, D. W., & Hewitt, J. K. (1996). Cognitive development from infancy to middle childhood. In R. J. Sternberg & E. Grigorenko (Eds.), *Intelligence: Heredity and environment.* Cambridge: Cambridge University Press.

Coon, H., Fulker, D. W., DeFries, J. C., & Plomin, R. (1990). Home environment and cognitive ability of 7-year-old children in the Colorado adoption project: Genetic and environmental etiologies. *Developmental Psychology, 26,* 459–468.

Cooper, R. M., & Zubek, J. P. (1958). Effects of enriched and restricted early environment on the learning ability of bright and dull rats. *Canadian Journal of Psychology, 12,* 159–164.

DeFries, J. C., & Fulker, D. W. (1985). Multiple regression analysis of twin data. *Behavior Genetics, 15,* 467–473.

Falconer, D. S. (1960). *Introduction to quantitative genetics.* New York: Ronald Press.

Farber, S. L. (1981). *Identical twins reared apart: A reanalysis.* New York: Basic Books.

Finkel, D., & McGue, M. (1993). The origins of individual differences in memory among the elderly: A behavior genetic analysis. *Psychology and Aging, 8,* 527–537.

Finkel, D., Pedersen, N. L., McGue, M., & McClearn, G. E. (1995). Heritability of cognitive abilities in adult twins: Comparison of Minnesota and Swedish data. *Behavior Genetics, 25,* 421–431.

Fulker, D. W., Cherny, S. S., & Cardon, L. R. (1993). Continuity and change in cognitive development. In R. Plomin & G. E. McClearn (Eds.), *Nature, nurture and psychology* (pp. 77–97). Washington, DC: American Psychological Association.

Gatz, M., Pedersen, N. L., Berg, S., Johansson, B., Johansson, K., Mortimer, J. A., Posner, S. F., Viitanen, M., Winblad, B., & Ahlbom, A. (1997). Heritability for Alzheimer's Disease: The study of dementia in Swedish twins. *Journal of Gerontology: Medical Sciences, 52A,* M117–M125.

Goldsmith, H. H. (1993). Nature–nurture issues in the behavior genetics context: Overcoming barriers to communication. In R. Plomin & G. E. McClearn (Eds.), *Nature, nurture and psychology* (pp. 325–339). Washington, DC: American Psychological Corporation.

Hayakawa, K., Shimizu, T., Ohba, Y., & Tomioka, S. (1992). Risk factors for cognitive aging in adult twins. *Acta Geneticae Medicae Gemellologiae, 41,* 187–195.

Heath, A. C., Neale, M. C., Hewitt, J. K., Eaves, L. J., & Fulker, D. W. (1989). Testing structural equation models for twin data using LISREL. *Behavior Genetics, 19,* 9–36.

Hetherington, E. M., Reiss, D., & Plomin, R. (Eds.). (1994). *Separate social worlds of siblings: Impact of nonshared environment on development.* Hillsdale, NJ: Lawrence Erlbaum Associates.

Hoffman, L. (1991). The influences of the family environment on personality. *Psychological Bulletin, 110,* 187–203.

Horowitz, F. D. (1993). The need for a comprehensive new environmentalism. In R. Plomin & G. E. McClearn (Eds.), *Nature, nurture and psychology.* (pp. 341–353). Washington, DC: American Psychological Corporation.

Jarvik, L. F., Blum, J. E., & Varma, A. O. (1972). Genetic components and intellectual functioning during senescence: A 20-year study of aging twins. *Behavior Genetics, 2,* 159–171.

Jinks, J. L., & Fulker, D. W. (1970). Comparison of the biometrical genetical, MAVA, and classical approaches to the analysis of human behavior. *Psychological Bulletin, 73,* 311–349.

Kallmann, F. J., Feingold, L., & Bondy, E. (1951). Comparative, adaptational, social, and psychometric data of the life histories of senescent twin pairs. *American Journal of Human Genetics, 3,* 65–73.

Kasl-Godley, J. E., Pedersen, & N. L., Gatz, M. (1998). *Smoking and cognitive performance in non-demented older adults.* Manuscript submitted for publication.

Marjoribanks, K. (1977). Socioeconomic status and its relation to cognitive performance as mediated through the family environment. In A. Oliverio (Ed.), *Genetics, environment and intelligence.* Amsterdam: Elsevier.

Mascie-Taylor, C. G. N. (1993). How do social, biological, and genetic factors contribute to individual differences in cognitive abilities? In T. J. Bouchard, Jr. & P. Propping (Eds.), *Twins as a tool of behavioral genetics.* (pp. 53–65). New York: Wiley.

Martin, N., Boomsma, D., & Machin, G. (1997). A twin-proned attack on complex traits. *Nature Genetics, 17,* 387–391.

McCall, R. B. (1983). Environmental effects on intelligence: The forgotten realm of discontinuous nonshared within-family factors. *Child Development, 54,* 408–415.

McClearn, G. E., Johansson, B., Berg, S., Pedersen, N. L., Ahern, F., Petrill, S. A., & Plomin, R. (1997). Substantial genetic influence on cognitive abilities in twins 80 or more years old. *Science, 276,* 1560–1563.

Neale, M. C. (1996). Genetic analysis with Mx [Abstract]. *Behavior Genetics, 26,* 593.

Neale, M. C., & Cardon, L. R. (1992). *Methodology for genetic studies for twins and families.* London: Kluwer.

Pedersen, N. L., & Lichtenstein, P. (1997). Biometric analyses of human abilities. In C. Cooper & V. Varma (Eds.), *Processes of individual differences* (pp. 126–148). London: Routledge.

Pedersen, N. L, Lichtenstein, P., Plomin, R., & McClearn, G. E. (1996). Identification of specific factors responsible for shared environmental effects for cognitive abilities. *Institute for Environmental Medicine Report.* Karolinska Institute, Stockholm, Sweden.

Pedersen, N. L., McClearn, G. E., Plomin, R., & Nesselroade, J. R. (1992). Effects of early rearing environment on twin similarity in the last half of the life span. *British Journal of Developmental Psychology, 10,* 255–267.

Pedersen, N. L., Plomin, R., Nesselroade, J. R., & McClearn, G. E. (1992). A quantitative genetic analysis of cognitive abilities during the second half of the life span. *Psychological Science, 3,* 346–353.

Plassman, B. L., Welsh, K. A., Helms, M., Brandt, J., Page, W. F., & Breitner, J. C. S. (1995). Intelligence and education as predictors of cognitive state in late life: A 50-year follow-up. *Neurology, 45,* 1446–1450.

Plomin, R. (1994). *Genetics and experience.* Newbury Park, CA: Sage.

Plomin, R., & Bergeman, C. S. (1991). The nature of nurture: Genetic influences on "environmental" measures. *Behavioral and Brain Sciences, 14,* 373–427.

Plomin, R., & Daniels, D. (1987). Why are children in the same family so different from one another? *Behavioral and Brain Sciences, 10,* 1–16.

Plomin, R., McClearn, G. E., Pedersen, N. L., Nesselroade, J. R., & Bergeman, C. S. (1988). Genetic influences on childhood family environment perceived retrospectively from the last half of the lifespan. *Developmental Psychology, 24,* 738–745.

Posner, S. F., Pedersen, N. L., & Gatz, M. (1999). The application of life table analysis to the onset of dementia in a genetically informative design. *Neuropsychiatric Genetics, 88*(2), 207–210.

Reiss, D., Neiderhiser, J., Hetherington, E. M., & Plomin, R. (2000). *The relationship code: Deciphering genetic and social patterns in adolescent development.* Cambridge, MA: Harvard University Press.

Rowe, D. C. (1994). *The limits of family influence: Genes, experience, and behavior.* New York: Guilford.

Rowe, D. C., & Waldman, I. C. (1993). The question "how" reconsidered. In R. Plomin & G. E. McClearn (Eds.), *Nature, nurture and psychology* (pp. 355–374). Washington, DC: American Psychological Corporation.

Saudino, K. J., Plomin, R., Pedersen, N. L., & McClearn, G. E. (1994). The etiology of high and low cognitive ability during the second half of the life span. *Intelligence, 19*(3), 359–371.

Scarr, S., & Weinberg, R. A. (1978). The influence of "family background" on intellectual attainment. *American Sociological Review, 43,* 674–692.

Spuhler, K. P., & Vandenberg, S. G. (1978). Relationship between family environment and children's and parent's cognitive performance [Abstract]. *Behavior Genetics, 8,* 114–115.

Sundet, J. M., Eilertsen, D. E., Tambs, K., & Magnus, P. (1994). No differential heritability of intelligence test scores across ability levels in Norway. *Behavior Genetics, 24*(4), 337–339.

Swan, G. E., Carmelli, D., Reed, T., Harshfield, G. A., Fabsitz, R. R., & Eslinger, P. J. (1990). Heritability of cognitive performance in aging twins. *Archives of Neurology, 47,* 259–262.

Tambs, K., Sundet, J. M., & Magnus, P. (1984). Heritability analysis of the WAIS subtests: A study of twin. *Intelligence, 8,* 283–293.

Tambs, K., Sundet, J. M., & Magnus, P. (1986). Genetic and environmental contributions to the covariation between the Wechsler Adult Intelligence Scale (WAIS) subtests: A study of twins. *Behavior Genetics, 16,* 475–491.

Tambs, K., Sundet, J. M., Magnus, P., & Berg, K. (1989). Genetic and environmental contributions to the covariance between occupational status, educational attainment, and IQ: A twin study. *Behavior Genetics, 19,* 209–222.

Wachs, T. D. (1983). The use and abuse of environment in behavior genetic research. *Child Development, 54,* 396–407.

Wachs, T. D. (1993). *The nature of nurture.* Newbury Park, CA: Sage.

Wilson, R. S. (1985). Continuity and change in cognitive ability profile. *Behavior Genetics, 16,* 45–60.

Wolf, R. H. (1964). *The identification and measurement of environmental process variables that are related to intelligence.* Unpublished doctoral dissertation, Chicago, IL: University of Chicago.

9

Family Functioning and Intellectual Functioning in Later Life

Colleen L. Johnson
University of California, San Francisco

Even a cursory review of the literature leaves the impression that the relationship between family involvements and intellectual development at the beginning and end of life entail entirely different processes. In early life, the role of the family is critical in shaping the immediate environment and the developmental processes of a child. In contrast, the literature on the family as a potential enhancer of intellectual processes in old age is virtually nonexistent, a gap that suggests the family may play a less important role in the last stage of life than earlier. In fact, researchers have consistently found evidence that the family in later life is less important than friends in sustaining morale. An adage encountered in the aging literature is, "When you are old and in need of help, one good friend is worth a dozen grandchildren" (Wood & Robertson, 1978).

In a review of the aging literature on human development and the family, Ryff and Selzer (1995) concluded that only oblique links exist between the two, most likely because disciplinary boundaries make it conceptually difficult to bridge the gap between the study of the individual and the family. Because most changes in old age entail losses rather than gains, adapting to such changes potentially places demands on the family. Research is particularly needed to explain how families handle the major demands posed by the onset of cognitive declines, a risk that increases in advanced old age (Schaie, 1996). Among those 85 years of age and older, 16% have dementia (Regier et al., 1988), a proportion that increases to around 25% among those who survive into their 90s (Gatz, Kasl-Godley, & Karel, 1991). In fact, a Boston study reported the incidence as high as 47% (Evans et al., 1992). Because those 85 and older comprise the fastest growing age group, the effects of mental declines will have a major impact on needed supports from formal and informal networks.

In order to explore interactions between the family and intellectual development, I first focus on the structure and functioning of the contemporary American family as it affects the family status of older people. Then three potential functions to facilitate intellectual functioning the family can perform are explored. First, aging researchers generally agree that family members are a major source of social integration for older relatives. So, in the process, they may indirectly enhance intellectual development by enriching the social environment. Second, the family is the primary provider of the social supports needed by many older people who experience declines in physical and mental functioning. Third, the family can potentially minimize declines in intellectual functioning by providing a normative anchorage that reinforces social conventions and expectations about appropriate behavior. Family involvements may also provide a reality orientation that ameliorates increased eccentricity, forgetfulness, and mental confusion (Johnson & Johnson, 1983). In the process, family members are the primary agents who define and evaluate the cognitive status of their older relatives, as they must make decisions about what behaviors are considered normal and abnormal.

To illustrate such a process, I report my own research findings on family responses after an older member was discharged from the hospital with symptoms of mental confusion (Johnson & Johnson, 1983). As intermediaries between their relative and the health and social service bureaucracies, a family's definition of mental competence can either magnify or lessen the perceived severity of cognitive declines that may follow an illness or accident. When such an event leads to a hospitalization, family interventions can influence discharge planning and, in the process, lessen or increase the risk of institutionalization.

This chapter concludes with an analysis of how very old people develop their own psychological strategies to enhance their intellectual functioning (Johnson & Barer, 1997). These findings come from a 10-year study of 150 Whites and 122 Blacks, all 85 years of age and older at the beginning of the first interview. The objective was to explore the social and psychological aspects of adaptation as the very old deal with the predictable age-related declines in functioning. Although these findings consistently indicate how older individuals respond to emotional and cognitive demands in late life, they are less clear about the extent to which families turn these potentialities into an attempt to preserve intellectual functioning.

Although many older people retain their capacity to grow intellectually and absorb new experiences (Abeles & Riley, 1987; Schaie, 1996), researchers who study those in advanced old age observe inevitable declines in attention span, sensory acuity, and memory. Although the literature is noticeably devoid of information about how families can assist in compensatory measures, realistically, family members can provide informal socialization in the form of natural conversations that give orientation to time and place, reminders of recent activities, and even scolding to reinforce "normal" behaviors. To perform such a role, however, family members should be in frequent interaction with their older relative.

Such face-to-face involvements also depend on structural factors such as household composition and geographic mobility. In addition, these interactions are affected by how society structures social roles in old age, how compatible the roles are with individual capacities, and the extent to which the family facilitates the performance of social roles (Blanchard-Fields & Abeles, 1996; Sternberg & Berg, 1987). In recent years, there have been unprecedented changes in our age structure with the fastest growing group being those 85 years and older. Undoubtedly, their families must adjust to the increased needs of those family members who are living beyond the predictable life span (Abeles & Riley, 1987; Siegel, 1994). Consequently these "oblique" links between family processes and intellectual development occur in a dynamic context of family changes and individual changes during the aging process.

THE FAMILY AND THE STUDY
OF ADAPTATION IN LATER LIFE

Surprisingly, family variables are missing from most models of successful aging. Moreover, these models rarely treat intellectual development as an outcome variable, but instead focus on measures of mood, efficacy, or a sense of control. In this perspective on adaptation, personal attributes and actions are the major agents of adaptation, not external social and cultural processes (Baltes & Baltes, 1990). Most recently, for instance, Rowe and Kahn (1987) identified "engagement with life" as one of three dimensions related to successful aging, but they did not mention the family in their model except to report that marriage had positive effects on men. Rowe and Kahn also identified social isolation as a risk factor and the receipt of social support as positively associated with health. Schaie (1996) reported that an intact marriage and a well-educated spouse are associated with higher mental competence in later life. The literature on adaptation has provided strong empirical support on benefits of strong social networks and health (Berkman & Syme, 1979; Blazer, 1982; & House, Landis, & Umberson, 1988).

Other models proposed that successful aging entails limiting one's tasks and avoiding excessive demands. Baltes and Baltes (1990) used the concept of selection to refer to a self-imposed restriction in one's life to fewer domains of functioning as a means to adapt to age-related losses. They found that by concentrating on high-priority domains, individuals could optimize their general reserves. They could also compensate by devising new operational strategies. Although this process of compensation drew on social comparisons with reference persons, the family per se was not singled out as performing such functions (Baltes, 1993).

Clark and Anderson (1967) also identified the tasks necessary to adapt in old age. The individual must come to terms with his or her increasing limitations by contracting social space and seeking alternate sources of need satisfaction. Similarly Carstensen's (1992) theory of socioemotional selectivity involved shedding less important social relationships and concentrating on special relationships. Likewise, Neugarten (1977) described a process of increased interiority or introspection with aging. Older people may slough off bothersome social relationships with a sense of good riddance (Lowenthal & Robinson, 1976). In all, these conceptions suggested that successful aging comes through creating a smaller, less complex social world.

In contrast to conceptions that place the responsibility for successful aging on the individual, there is increased recognition that social forces diminish the structuring and content of social roles as individuals age. Most controversial, and largely rejected by gerontologists, is the theory of disengagement that stems from structural-functionalism and the social determinism of Talcott Parsons. Cumming and Henry (1961) posited a universal process of mutual withdrawal between the aging individual and society. They viewed this process as a positive force in which the individual was better able to meet the demands imposed by age-related losses by selectively withdrawing from active social participation. As a corollary to this idea, they suggested that society also benefits because younger members need to move into the positions abandoned by the disengaged.

Central to the theory of disengagement, but mostly ignored currently by aging researchers, is the proposition that as individuals age and disengage from social life, they withdraw from normative constraints that regulate social relationships. In a self-perpetuating process, decreased interactions lead to increased freedom from further normative controls. When social expectations are ignored, eccentric behaviors may increase, which further isolate the disengaged from the social regulation of their behavior. In his book, *Socialization to Old Age*, Rosow (1974) developed a similar theme: Adult socialization ceases in old age as one enters a roleless status without normative guidance.

More recently, Riley and Riley (1994) posited a theory of structural lag whereby changes in the age structure lag behind changes in lives. The extension of the life span occurs in the context of major ongoing social, technological, and value changes. These alterations occur in the context of life extension, but change in age structure is not accompanied by changes in status and role opportunities that reward people at later stages in their lives. Thus, they point to the need to extend and redistribute work, leisure, education, and family involvements over the life course to take advantage of the extra years of life people often experience today.

Haraven (1994) translated the concept of structural lag into her analysis of the uneasy relationship between family change and historical change. She maintained that this asynchrony affects the position of older people because the family of procreation has become increasingly separated from the family of orientation. Additionally, the nuclear family is becoming a more private unit that excludes kin and friends from daily family activities. These processes are changing the quality of kin relationships, but most importantly, they also have an isolating effect on older family members who are increasingly excluded from the day-to-day family life of their children. With the exception of immigrants and some working class families, moreover, kin relationships no longer include extensive instrumental exchanges. At the same time, a historic shift has occurred in the transfer of responsibility for the elderly from the family to the public domain. To compound these historical and family changes, Haraven concluded that a value shift is also evident in the increased emphasis on the individual and the adherence to personal priorities over family responsibilities.

Consequently, theories of successful aging tend to concentrate on the individual and his or her successes in meeting the challenges of physical and mental losses. Others point out that broad social changes do not invariably enrich the daily lives of older people. In adapting to social, physical, and often cognitive losses, the psychology of the aging individual is marked as much by change as by continuity (Lieberman & Tobin, 1983). In conceptualizing adaptation after age 85, we concluded that adapting to increased longevity entails a developmental reversal that rests on the antithesis of successful behaviors in younger years (Johnson & Barer, 1992, 1993, 1997). Namely, it is adaptive for older people to disengage from demanding and problematic social relationships, accept some measure of dependency on others over independence, withdraw from active concerns about the larger world, and moderate unrealistic attempts to exercise control over their lives. Disengagement may impose a risk, however, for increased incidence of cognitive declines (Abeles & Riley, 1987). Nonetheless, it is likely that some older people who disengage do so because the effects of their mental and physical declines prevent a continuation of active social involvements.

THE STRUCTURE AND FUNCTIONING
OF THE FAMILY IN LATER LIFE

The family is an omnibus term that can refer to one-parent households, conventional nuclear families, or large extended families. This linguistic blurring between various family structures is more exaggerated when referring to the family in later life, for these structures are rarely synonymous with households. With advancing age, fewer remain married. Following customary usage, thus, the term family refers to a system of relationships that include lineal relations between generations, collateral relationships linked through siblings and relatives of similar age, and the relatives by marriage. Unlike earlier stages in the family cycle, the residential independence of older people places limitations on any day-to-day interactions and social support among kin. Because nuclear families in most White nonethnic groups are only loosely linked to kin, few norms of responsibility extend beyond the marital dyad and the parent–adult child bond (Adams, 1971). Consequently, lineal or intergenerational bonds constitute the strongest and the preferred relationships in most kinship net-works (Bengtson, Rosenthal, & Burton, 1995). As one ages, siblings are more likely to be deceased or geographically dispersed, and relationships with nieces, nephews, and cousins are optional and most often relegated to the category of "wedding and funeral relatives." Fisher (1982a) concluded that kinship rela-tionships beyond generational links consist of voluntary and selective bonds. The contemporary kinship structure is limited in size, and its functions lie in their potentialities rather than ongoing activities.

New models are needed to understand the family in later life. For example, without shared households or even face-to-face interactions, some family ger-ontologists maintain that sentiments can also reinforce strong family alliances (Troll & Bengtson, 1992). Even in the provision of social supports, actual con-tact is not necessarily required because family members can extend support such as financial help from afar (Litwak & Kulis, 1989). Riley (1983) described the contemporary family in later life as "a latent web of continually shifting link-ages that provide the opportunity for activating and intensifying close family re-lationships" (p. 439). Such a model provides a useful framework for depicting the diversity and dynamics of families today.

Determinants of Family Structure

If family members function to maintain adequate mental functioning, they need to reinforce and stimulate memory and provide a temporal orientation and spatial location. Only in face-to-face interactions can they focus atten-tion, revive memory, and activate conversation. Consequently, structural variables such as household composition and geographic proximity are impor-tant indicators of family availability. Reviews of the literature on the demo-graphic factors that underlie diversity in family and kinship structures reported decidedly mixed findings most likely because no simple relationship exists between the major determinant variables (Kinsella, 1995; Uhlenberg, 1993). For example, the greatest consensus relates to gender. Family charac-teristics in later life vary by gender in major dimensions because of the greater longevity among women. [Thus, marital status after age 65 varies greatly with 75% of the men being married, but less than half of the women are. Even by age 75, 70% of the men are still married, but only 33% of the women are mar-ried.] By 85 years and older, only 18% of the women are married (U. S. Bureau of the Census, 1992).

As a direct result of gender differences, household composition is affected. Women are much more likely to live alone; 33% live alone from ages 65 to 74 in comparison to only 13% of men. After age 75, more than 50% of women and only 21% of the men live alone. However, women are twice as likely than men to live with a family member other than a spouse. Twenty percent of the women but only 11% of the men live with another family member, with most of these women living in two-generation households with their children (U.S. Bureau of the Census, 1992). Research findings also uniformly found that women are more involved with kin than men. They are known as the "kinkeepers," who plan and orchestrate kinship affairs (Adams, 1971; Hagestad, 1992; Rosenthal, 1985).

Geographic mobility results in the dispersion of kin and thus less contact among them (Fisher, 1982a, 1982b). Estimates of residential proximity of children range widely from 51% living in the vicinity (Mercier, Paulson, & Morris, 1989), to 72% (Frankel & DeWitt, 1989), to Shanas' findings of 84% (1979a). In contrast to the traditional extended family, in which kin are more likely to live nearby, contemporary families freely move away from kin to seek opportunities for occupational advancement (Litwak, 1960, 1965; Litwak & Kulis, 1989). Because those with a higher educational level are more geographically dispersed from kin (Fisher, 1982a), socioeconomic status (SES) interacts with geographic mobility. Members of the middle class generally give primacy to the nuclear family and are more distant from kin (Schneider & Smith, 1973), whereas working-class families live near kin and are actively involved with them (Bott, 1971; Fisher, 1982b; Reiss & Oliveri, 1983).

Ethnic and minority status are also sources of diversity. The assumption is that people of color and immigrant groups have closer extended families than the dominant White group (Bengtson, Rosenthal, & Burton, 1990). For example, Blacks, a group that has been studied more than most ethnic groups, are particularly noted for greater extended family solidarity. Unlike Whites, caregiving strain does not seem to result in a poorer quality parent–child relationship (Chatters, Taylor, & Neighbors, 1989; Connell & Gibson, 1997; Taylor & Chatters, 1991), perhaps because Black caregivers have a larger pool of extended kin available to share the burdens of caregiving (Deimling, (Smerglia, & Barresi, 1988).

Consequently, with the exception of some ethnic families, the capacities of family members to sustain frequent contacts with older kin are to some extent limited. If family members are to provide intellectual stimulation and discourage cognitive decline, they need to be in frequent interaction. In the Western family today, family relationships are described as "intimate at a distance," a label that applies to most White, nonethnic older people, both literally and physically (Rosenmayr & Krockeis, 1963).

Demographic Shifts and Family Resources

With recent demographic shifts, projected changes in family structure may lessen the future potential of families to compensate for the predictable social and mental losses of very old people. Declines in mortality results in more older members and declines in fertility results in fewer members in the younger generations (George & Gold, 1991). Family gerontologists speak of a new vertical family structure that is no longer a pyramid, but rather, it is becoming a top-heavy age structure (Burton & Sorenson, 1993).

Due to the strong emphasis in the U.S. family on lineal or intergenerational bonds, the family's role as a source of social integration and support may not extend to those truncated families without lineal kin. To most older widowed parents, children are their most important family members, so declines in birth rates may undermine future family resources. There is some evidence that social and emotional benefits accrue to older parents with each additional child (Uhlenberg & Cooney, 1990). Declines in birth rates also ultimately result in more childless people who predictably have fewer family members available to help them (Farkas & Hogan, 1995; Uhlenberg, 1993). Decreasing family size paired with increasing age also occurs through the death of spouses, siblings, and other age peers (Baldwin & Nord, 1984; Hagestad, 1992). By advanced old age, as many as 30% of the elderly will have experienced the death of a child (Johnson & Barer, 1995)

One may appropriately ask, do additional benefits stem from four- or five-generation families? Most evidence for such a family type is anecdotal because no surveys with representative samples have collected such information (Uhlenberg, 1993). Assumptions that older people have four or more generations in their families are misleading, for such situations apply to only a small portion of older people (Treas, 1995). For example, in the Boston study, Rossi & Rossi (1990) found that almost as many individuals had no direct lineal kin as had four generations families, a finding in agreement with Johnson and Troll's study of the oldest old (1996). In fact, what evidence we have accumulated indicates that the presence of grandchildren and great grandchildren is probably inconsequential in meeting the practical needs of older people, irrespective of the emotional benefits descendants provide.

The Timing Of Transitions. Given the emphasis on the marriage relationship and the privacy of the nuclear family, two transitions in late life change the status and roles of older people and the family functions that support them. First, older people and particularly women experience the end of their marriage and a transition to widowhood. Second, with of the loss of a spouse, people are likely to change from living with others to living alone (Johnson & Troll, l996). Such transitions often entail moving into more protected housing in age-segregated communities. We found that these changes are likely to occur in the mid-to-late 70s, some years before the onset of actual disability. In our study, we found that in their 70s, 82% to 97% of elderly adults were fully independent in their activities of daily living, but by their mid-80s, most older people needed some help from others.

The Parent–Adult Child Relationship

This key family relationship for most older people is well researched. Shanas's surveys (1979a, 1979b) reported that a large majority of older people lived within 40 minutes of at least one child, and 75% had at least weekly contact with a child, a finding that has remained stable in surveys between 1957 and 1977. In rejecting the idea that families abandon their elderly, Shanas also concluded that everyone had someone to help when needed, and that only 3% had no family relationships. She posited a principle of substitution: If children were not available, another relative would help. In contradiction, however, her own findings revealed that 25% of the housebound or bedfast elderly had no family member to help.

Likewise, my more recent research with the White oldest old found that 24% no longer maintained family relationships, mostly because they had outlived their children or were permanently childless. In sharp contrast, however, more Black oldest old were childless, but fewer were isolated from their family because nieces and nephews took on the helping roles that children ordinarily performed (Johnson & Barer, 1995). We attributed these ethnic differences to a strong collateral emphasis in Black families that resulted in higher sibling solidarity. With a sibling's death, this solidarity continued in older aunts' relationships with siblings' children, who became their helpers when they were needed.

Given the generational emphasis in White families and the high incidence of widowhood with advancing age, adult children are the primary family members who potentially facilitate intellectual acuity in old age. Intergenerational relationships are remarkably strong (Bengtson et al., 1995). Second only to a spouse, children are the most important source of emotional and instrumental support. In that role, family members can enrich the immediate environment of older parents. In the American kinship system, the parent–adult child dyad is regulated by the strongest norms of attachment and responsibility (Rossi & Rossi, 1990). The immense caregiving literature in gerontology also reveals that second to the marital bond, children are the most attentive to the needs of older people.

With increasing age, the parent–child relationship is likely to be closer and less conflictual than in earlier years (Bengtson et al., 1990; Blenkner, 1965). Children are also an effective source of social integration for older people (Rossi & Rossi, 1990; Umberson, 1992). Moreover, children are potentially the primary family members who assess age-related cognitive declines and mediate with professionals in deciding what to do about these declines (Johnson & Johnson, 1983).

Researchers who study the parent–child relationship in later life tend to use one of two paradigms. On one hand, they focus on a family solidarity thesis and stress the mutual supports inherent in the parent–child relationship and the potential benefits of more generations surviving concurrently. In fact, a theory of solidarity was applied to research on intergenerational relationships that has no negative dimensions (Roberts & Bengston, 1990). Thus, these studies are viewed mainly through a positive psychological lens, or what Sprey (1991) identified as "a search for inner forces." Love, solidarity, and attachment are viewed as the primary determinants of social interaction and support, rather than broader social and cultural forces.

Less optimistic views on the parent–child relationship come from the vast literature on caregiving that depicts an insidious tension activated by the emotional and physical burdens of care. Hess and Waring (1978) identified the constraints to affectual bonds between a parent and adult child that can lead to attenuated bonds, value conflicts, and numerous psychological barriers to intimacy. Although the strategic role of children as helpers of their older parents is unquestioned, their support is tempered by structural constraints. Children rarely live in the same household or even in the same vicinity, so they may have difficulty providing hands-on practical assistance (Johnson, 1983; Suiter, Pillemer, Keeton, & Robison, 1995). Today, daughters are much more likely to work or be less available due to divorce or the demands of their nuclear family (Johnson & Catalano, 1983).

Nevertheless, children of older parents have come to a time in life that they are expected to reciprocate the many benefits they have received from parents in the past (Zarit & Eggebeen, 1995). In those cases where this responsibility is accepted and welcome, children have reached a level of filial maturity (Blenkner, 1965). Some suggested, however, that a more accurate label of this situation is filial anxiety (Cicerelli, 1988), a situation where children adhere to norms of obligation, yet do so out of an uneasy fear that they may ultimately have to assume such responsibilities and be unable to meet escalating demands.

Nevertheless, where children are available, they more than adequately, but indirectly, facilitate their parents' social integration.

In summary, this review of the structure and functioning of the contemporary family in later life described its capacity to provide social integration of older members and in the process facilitate intellectual functioning. Certainly most people have families and the majority are active in family life. The key family relationship that potentially fulfills that role is the parent–adult child dyad. Children are likely to evaluate and oversee their older parents' mental functioning in the process of socializing and providing help.

THE FAMILY AS A SOURCE OF SUPPORT

The second indirect function of the family on intellectual status lies in the provision of social support. Unfortunately, this literature is more about stressed caregivers rather than older people in need of help. Because the sizable drop in mortality rates have not been accompanied by declines in morbidity (Suzman, Manton, & Willis, 1992; Verbrugge, 1984), more older people are living beyond their independent status and thus require help from others. Although public funds in the United States have relieved the family of much financial responsibility for their parents, family members are still the major providers of 60% to 80% of the long-term care needs of older people (Bengtson et al., 1995). Consequently, the potential resources of the family in the provision of social supports are a major policy concern.

Since the 1980s, research on the family's role in assisting older people changed from the study of a support process by a family unit to a focus on the study of an individual in a caregiving role. Encouraged by the National Institutes of Health's funding priorities, studies of caregiving have proliferated and include a repetitive and resounding theme about the stresses and burdens of care that dependent parents are imposing on their children. With caregiving officially designated as a social problem, self-help group organizers, counselors, and academic researchers on caregiving dominate professional meetings and journal contents (Pillager, 1996). A voluminous literature has accumulated, and within its narrow focus, much of the late-life family research lies. Ryff & Seltzer (1995) pointed out that the caregiving literature has centered primarily on three subjects: (a) social and demographic factors that influence who becomes a family caregiver; (b) the stresses, burdens of care, and depression that accompany such a role; and (c) interventions that can ease the role strains of caregiving. Surprisingly, researchers on caregiving rarely study the older recipient of care.

In their longitudinal study of caregivers of Alzheimer's patients, Aneshensel, Pearlin, Mullan, Zarit, and Whitlach (1995) reported that the caregiver is usually a spouse or a child. Although relationships before the onset of caregiving are reciprocal, the caregiver must now take care of someone who has been transformed by cognitive deterioration into one without the capacity for two-way social interactions. In this study, the average time of caregiving was eight years before either the death or institutionalization of the patient. Not only was the experience stressful, but after caregiving ended, they found that it was often followed by a period of bereavement.

The major conceptual framework in studies of caregiving come from stress and coping research, and the unit of study is the individual caregiver, not a family process. Despite such a concentration on the problematic aspects of caregiving, it seems that various studies found that only 25% of the older population had a caregiver (Kovar & Stone, 1992; Stone et al., 1987) and only one third of the caregivers reported stress (Kane & Penrod, 1995). Consequently, the major emphasis on stress insinuated negative valences on the family position of older people. A further problem with this research area lies in the propensity for researchers to study individuals from self-help groups or other opportunity samples. Understandably, these volunteers add negative overtones that may overemphasize the stresses and burdens of care.

Unfortunately, this research concentration has deflected research interests not only from other models and theories of family functioning in later life, but it also overshadows the study of older individuals who are experiencing cognitive declines and out of necessity become dependent recipients of care. When concentrating research efforts on easing the burdens of caregivers, there are few efforts to teach family members standard techniques of reality orientation commonly used in institutions. Thus, there is little discussion in the literature on what the family can actually do to lessen the effects of cognitive declines.

THE FAMILY AS ASSESSOR OF MENTAL STATUS

In the event that mental status deteriorates, family members are the primary mediators with health care professionals, and in that role, they evaluate what is normal and abnormal behavior. This role can be critical because those with symptoms of dementia are more likely to be placed in a nursing home. In our study of the oldest old, those who exhibited this confusion and who were hospitalized were also more likely to be institutionalized on discharge from the hospital (Johnson & Barer, 1997). Another project that studied family support to posthospitalized older people found that those with behavioral problems were viewed as more aberrant after they entered the hospital (Johnson & Johnson, 1983).

In a case study analysis of 30 patients with behavioral problems, we concluded that the outcomes were related to how the family defined the behavioral problem, who participated in the decision making after discharge from the hospital, and how the meanings of the behavioral problem underwent redefinition in the process (Johnson & Johnson, 1983). In interpreting this process, Emerson and Messenger's (1977) framework in the study of deviance was used. Titled "the micropolitics of trouble," their conceptual scheme depicted how behavioral problems are identified, reacted to, elaborated, and finally transformed into a specific form of deviance.

Families may initially tolerate eccentric behaviors or mild symptoms of mental decline, often treating the oldster like a wayward child. At some point, however, even subtle changes in behavior are noted in retrospect as significant and portentous. As the accounts emerged during the interviews, we heard such comments as, "She had been slipping for some time, but we were slow to recognize the problems." As the symptoms were reviewed and the complaints specified, the older relative became "a more difficult person," "more forgetful," "eccentric," or "more of a loner." Then they became more specific: "She leaves the burner on under empty pans," "He has let his apartment go to shambles." Worse yet was the recognition of deteriorating personal hygiene, when a slovenly appearance leads to further isolation. When behaviors formerly ignored were recounted and temporary solutions sought, expectations for the patient were lowered and additional surveillance was initiated to minimize the "trouble."

Initially these complaints are private and colloquially defined at home, but the need for a hospitalization for a physical problem turns a private family matter into a publicly observed form of deviance. Rather than being viewed as an eccentric, the patient is officially recognized as a psychiatric problem that must be more formally handled. Understandably, iatrogenic effects of hospitalization and new medications may intensify the symptoms of mental declines. Throughout this process, the symptoms are diagnostically interpreted and legitimized by professionals. As symptoms become clarified and specified, the hospital staff are the official trouble-shooters and often view the patient as a troublemaker. In this new status, the patient's ambiguous behaviors are crystallized through a process of formal charting, documentation, and psychiatric classification. When family members see the patient under stress in a foreign setting, the older person can also become depersonalized. "Mother is no longer the person we knew." This altered view of the person alleviates guilt and might break down family members resistance to institutionalization. "Since she doesn't know what's going on, a nursing home might be all right."

Emerson and Messenger (1977) identified "trouble" as a point when official troubleshooters, such as the doctors and nurses, enter the scene and impose a definition of the problem. At that point, a formal statement of complaints becomes the official record. During the course of the hospitalization, the family is given a respite from the burdens of care and might become resistant to reassuming responsibility on discharge. Discharge decisions are facilitated by an officially designated hospital discharge planner who is available to arrange for nursing home placement. Finally, the family is likely to come to the conclusion that the behavioral problems are irreversible.

In only one of the 30 cases analyzed, the patient received medical management of her symptoms of dementia that resulted in a reversal of her symptoms. When the woman's behavior rapidly deteriorated, she came to the attention of a university researcher on tropical diseases who diagnosed a rare but treatable form of meningitis. Because cures such as this example are rare, however, it is difficult to estimate how many cases could be reversed with a proper diagnosis and treatment.

FAMILY FUNCTIONING AND INTELLECTUAL FUNCTIONING OF WHITE OLDEST OLD

The Role of the Family

A more recent longitudinal study of the oldest old offered insights on how intellectual processes facilitate adaptation over time. In this study of adaptation, 150 Whites, 85 years and older, were interviewed five times over 6 years and 122 Blacks of the same age were interviewed three times over 4 years (Johnson & Barer, 1997). Because the analysis of data on Blacks is still in process, this section on adaptation deals only with White oldest old.

Using mostly open-ended interviews with individuals 85 years of age and older, this research addressed a simple, straightforward question about adaptation: What competencies are needed to survive and continue community living during a period of rising disabilities? We went on to explore the objective and subjective experiences of daily life. We also tracked those capacities needed to manage both the physical and social environment and to sustain a sense of well-being. Early in the interviews, we were impressed with how respondents dealt with their losses by developing patterns of thinking that made sense out of their situation. Logically, coping with pain, disability, and deaths of family and friends should have made them lonely and anxious. Yet most were managing their lives competently and in good spirits. More importantly, they discussed the experiential dimensions of their lives candidly and with a profound grasp of both the practical and existential dimensions of their long-term survivorship.

What role did the family have in this impressive adaptation? Over time, family variables did not change nor did family variables correlate meaningfully with physical and psychological variables. In their family relationships, 68% had a surviving child, 55% had a child living in proximity, and 44% were in weekly or more frequent contact. These proximal children were frequent visitors and potential supporters. From our observations, family members, particularly children, were attentive to a parent's physical and mental status and responded rapidly when changes occurred. Children were a major source of social integration because those that were in frequent contact with children saw more people than those who were not. This occurred when children linked their parents to their grandchildren, great grandchildren, and their relatives by marriage.

Weekly or more contacts with other relatives were minimal, however, ranging from 4% in contact with siblings to 19% with grandchildren (Johnson & Troll, 1992). In a range of family types, 25% were immersed in strong, multifunctional families who were in frequent contact and available to help when needed (Johnson, 1993). In contrast, 25% of the sample had attenuated families and maintained no functioning relationships beyond intermittent phone calls and letters. The remaining 50% had families who stood by as potential helpers and comforters to respond only when needed. Others expressed strong sentiments about their families but had few family involvements.

In examining the cases where mental functioning declined over the course of the study, there was little evidence to suggest that the family intervened in stemming cognitive losses, even though the supportive families continued to be supportive and the distant ones continued their aloofness. After ruling out family dimensions as a source of explaining the impressive adaptation of most oldest old, four individual-centered adaptive strategies were identified: (a) daily problem solving, (b) redefinitions of one's self-concept, (c) a reorientation of the meaning of time, and (d) a self-regulation of their emotional life (Johnson & Barer, 1997).

Aging as an Individual Affair

Daily Problem Solving.   To gain a sense of control over their lives, many of these very old people take methodical practical steps to manage their environment (Willis, 1996). They must continually handle essential activities of daily living, usually made more difficult by increased disabilities. Who will change a light bulb for them or help them shop for clothes when they can no longer read price labels? Even ordinary expenditures are called into question, such as the dilemma one woman raised, "Is it worthwhile to buy a new vacuum cleaner when I'm 90 and won't be around much longer to use it."

To cope with their physical losses, most respondents simplified their physical environment in order to make it more manageable. In doing so they retained essential activities and objects but stripped their homes of nonessential objects or those that were difficult to maintain. These respondents also established daily regimens that carefully regulated time so that one had neither too much nor too little time to accomplish daily tasks. Health, diet, and personal hygiene often dominated these activities. These mundane but necessary activities to maintain independence were also ritualized and time-regulated to endow them with greater significance. As one woman proudly concluded after a detailed description of her daily activities, "I'm still alive, I have all my marbles, I can get out of bed each morning, and I can take care of myself."

Redefinition Of Self.   In charting the interior world of the oldest old, open-ended interviewing was particularly appropriate. The spontaneous responses of the interviews concerned, not only objective experiences about surviving day to day, but also descriptions of cognitive and emotional processes that were central to interpreting their experiences. Most had to deal with pain and disability, losses of vision and hearing, loss of contemporaries, and for 30%, the experience of outliving a child. They realistically described a sense of aloneness or a status in social limbo. In their discourses with us, it was apparent that existentially, they had to alter the meanings of their self-concept, their physical status, and their status as survivors.

Intellectual functioning is most prominent in the strategies that emerged from the discussions. To adapt to the losses of advanced old age, at some point the self-concept is usually redefined. This can occur after the death of one's last contemporary or the last person who knew them as a young person, or who knew their parents, or it can occur after recovery from a life-threatening illness. Some respondents also described a realization that they are very old, even though they may feel young and independent, that they have outlived their contemporaries, and they have the special status as a survivor. Some concluded with relief that they have outlived worries, even about their children, and now only think about themselves.

Although they come to terms with their age, they usually resisted the notion that others might define them as old and decrepit. They described various techniques they used to challenge such assumptions. For example, some did not look in the mirror any more, so they did not see evidence of an advanced aging process. Others defied notions that they were becoming forgetful by solving crossword puzzles, memorizing sections of the Bible, or watching serious television programs. One woman told us, "My daughter thinks I'm forgetful. I'll show her I'm not. Every night when I go to bed, I memorize all fifty states backwards."

Second, most respondents reported that they were in good health considering their age. Using positive comparisons, they could always find someone who was worse off. One woman concluded that she was healthier than others because she could still breathe lying down. Some also defined themselves as healthy because they retained a sense of control over their bodies.

A third discourse described themselves as a detached self, one who has disengaged from bothersome or demanding roles and relationships and retreated into an interior world. Interiority, one of the few personality changes associated with aging (Neugarten, 1977; Schulz, 1985), was described as a conscious choice. This change was usually described as an advantage: "I have reached a peaceful age of quietude." In the process, they also redefined their social needs and gave a positive slant to their shrinking social world. By redefining their social expectations, they came to terms with and even welcomed being alone. Some said it helped them prepare for their imminent death.

Reorientation Of Time. At a practical level, memory problems were prominent, so time was frequently confused on a neuropsychological basis. Even among those who had no symptoms of serious declines associated with dementia, there was a progressive loss of the facility to recall with accuracy the chronology of their lives. It is even possible that time may be segmented differently among the very old, "I've lived so long, I tend to think in decades, not years." Or a long-time widow referred to her marriage as having been so long ago, it seemed like another life. Some respondents refused to answer any questions that required a date such as the year they married or the ages of their children.

Despite confusions about time, conceptions about time were frequently included in their explanatory schemes. Contrary to popular beliefs, these very old people did not dwell on reminiscences about their past, nor did they refer in detail to the future. They lived in the present and concentrated on coping with daily activities. As one man concluded, "My past is so long ago, I've forgotten it, and I have no future. I live one day at a time." Any memories about the past are selective, "I've whitewashed my past," or "I only remember pleasant things." Having no future is also seen as an advantage, "I don't worry anymore. Worry has a future—I don't." As an age group without a future, they described their relationship to time as: "I'm just marking time," "living on borrowed time," "beyond time," or "accidents of time." This discussion of time, on occasion, led to a conclusion that they no longer feared death.

The Regulation Of Emotions.   Cognitive strategies were particularly evident in the regulation of their emotional life. Over 6 years, the survivors experienced rising disabilities yet they continued to express contentment with their lives and their scores on the Bradburn Affect Balance Scale actually improved with time. Consequently in terms of their emotional life, most survivors were content, and they consciously minimized the emotional effects of pain and disability. To explore possible explanations, we analyzed their comments as they responded to open-ended questioning about their mood or items of the Affect Balance Scale.

The intensity of their emotions declined significantly over time on most items of the Affect Balance Scale. Negative emotions were rationalized by attributing them to a natural part of the aging process or outside social forces such as the state of the country. When asked about anger, for example, either they said they had outlived anger or they identified this emotion as useful, "Getting angry keeps depression at bay," or "It keeps me on my toes." Lethargy was usually accepted with resignation as a normal part of the aging process. When asked about depression, they spoke of how they moderated its effects. "I cry and then get over it." "I get depressed at night, but then I know daytime is just around the corner," "I accept sadness because at 90, I know I have to suffer." Likewise boredom was deemphasized. "Boredom is my middle name, but what can you expect at my age?" "When I get bored, I look out the window and watch the birds fly by." Being uneasy or lonely brought negative responses, but they were followed by such comments as, "I know it will go away tomorrow," or "I call my daughter."

When asked about how happy they were, only 30% reported they were unhappy. Some respondents explained that they had reached a plateau and their emotions had evened out. Their muted emotions were sometimes traced to living in an environment devoid of the stimuli that had formerly triggered irritations. Others traced their happiness or contentment to a lifelong personality trait, still others to love of family. A blurring between positive and negative mood states also occurred. "I'm not exactly happy but I'm not sad either." In other words, these resourceful individuals were active agents in moderating the effects of negative emotions and enhancing a positive emotional status. They also used positive comparisons with those much worse off, or they used their the past life as a reference point. Having been through the best and the worst of life, there is nothing more to react to.

In summary, adaptation in advanced old age appears to rest, not so much on family actions, but instead on those cognitive processes that entail both daily problem solving and discourses that explore the meanings of their long-term survivorship. Balance is also achieved through practical actions that simplify the environment and regulate their activities of daily living. Logically, the process of assigning positive interpretations to the experiences of living so long helps to buffer depression and loneliness that may accelerate cognitive declines.

COMPARISONS OF BLACK AND WHITE OLDEST OLD

Early in my own research on the oldest old, I concluded that data from Black and White respondents needed to be analyzed separately, for comparisons by race were invidious to both groups. Not only did their families function quite differently, but their world views, and hence their systems of meanings and emotional processes, were markedly different. On one hand, among Whites, adapting to life in their 80s and 90s was taken quite seriously as a personal responsibility. Theories of self-efficacy and a sense of control seem to be tailor-made for their approach to life and perhaps culturally most appropriate to that group. In their responses to open-ended questioning, they made sense of their long-term survivorship and combined systematic actions and existential reasoning that sought meanings regarding their lives. Unlike Blacks, discussions with Whites dealt most with secular matters; rarely were their religious beliefs associated with the positive aspects of their adaptation.

The Black oldest old displayed stronger survivor effects in their recognition of their special status. The fact that they had experienced difficult lives, and they had survived was usually attributed to a supernatural power. In the Black church, they also had an accessible belief system that made their lives meaningful in understanding the prejudice and discrimination they had faced. At the social level, their religiosity also played a large role. The church was the focal point for socializing. The study of the scriptures and memorizing hymns that filled their days were intellectual exercises that strengthened memory and reasoning. In other words, this adaptation was not the sole responsibility of the individual as it was among Whites. Instead, one's fate was intimately bound up with social and religious institutions.

Family functioning also varied between groups. Blacks were more deeply embedded in a family group that included relationships with more distant relatives and fictive kin. They were also active in community networks, particularly in their church. In contrast, White families were supportive, but that support came primarily from children and only rarely from other relatives.

Although competencies in adapting to the disabilities of advanced old age were observed in both groups, an analysis of differences between the Black and White oldest old suggested processes by which their intellectual development could be maintained. In psychological variables, there were no racial differences in the incidence of cognitive declines after 4 years in the study, but Blacks and Whites differed significantly in mood, with Blacks having a significantly higher sense of well-being. The fact that Blacks adapted to advanced old age by being socially embedded in an extended family and community life may account for their high morale. They were also cognitively immersed in their religious beliefs that provided meaning and explanations about their experiences and attitudes about life and death.

CONCLUSIONS

The preparation of this chapter on the family's role in maintaining intellectual functioning in later life was hampered by large gaps in the literature that bore directly on this topic. Although social variables were considered in models of successful aging and theories of social change, the family as a social unit is not usually singled out as a facilitator in maintaining mental functioning or in lessening mental declines. Consequently, indirect links between the individual and the family were described here. Such conclusions refer primarily to White families, for this chapter has barely covered the great variation in families on the basis of ethnicity.

Findings from my 10-year research project on the oldest old suggested that the potential functions of the family in enhancing the intellectual functioning and stemming mental declines of older members principally center on facilitating social integration. Approximately half of the older parents with children nearby benefit in this respect. Their children are in frequent contact, and most importantly, they link a parent to other relatives. They are able to monitor a parent who is experiencing mental declines by enriching the environment, offering reminders when memory fails, correcting eccentric behaviors, and providing diversions.

Likewise, the family's functioning in providing social support depends on geographic proximity. If the literature on caregiving is an accurate indicator, it would seem that families, if nearby, are active in providing care, but in the process, caregivers are subject to stresses and burdens in filling that role. The important point in evaluating research on social support functions is the fact that the recipient of care is rarely even interviewed. Moreover, there have been few attempts to track how families respond to declining mental functions. It also appears that only a minority of families function as actual "hands on" caregivers to older people, and only a minority of caregivers report being stressed. Thus, much of the research on the family in later life has been redirected to cover only a narrow area of family functioning. Since the caregiver literature is also dominated by care of Alzheimer patients, there is a heavier emphasis on irreversible mental declines rather than the enhancement of intellectual functioning.

The family potentially has the important function of acting as a normative anchorage for older members as they evaluate conventional versus eccentric behaviors and establish the dimensions of normality. They also must determine when to intervene as unconventional behaviors are observed. In such situations as a hospitalization of an older person, mental declines may be accentuated and behaviors formerly tolerated in the privacy of the family are made public. When professionals are called in and the diagnosis is made, the mental declines become medicalized and designated as a disease. At the point of discharge from the hospital, the family and professionals generally work together in making decisions about institutionalizing the elderly patient. At that point, the patient faces a high-risk situation because their recent symptoms may be exaggerated due to the illness and hospitalization. Once institutionalized, that elderly person is unlikely to return to the community.

Data from my longitudinal study of the oldest old indicate that the extent families fulfill these functions depends on structural and cultural factors. Although the family functions in caregiving and in mediating with the health care bureaucracy in the event of an illness, there is little evidence that the family intervenes directly to enhance mental functioning or to prevent declines. Nevertheless, our research on the oldest old gives impressive evidence that the individual person not only takes practical actions to simplify their environment so as to make it more manageable, but also develops cognitive discourses on the meanings of their long-term survivorship. The outcome is a realistic strategy to deal with the losses of advanced old age.

White, nonethnic families also maintain a private nuclear unit that shields their lives from outsiders. This propensity may have an isolating effect on older people. Other than the marital bond, which is less frequently encountered with advancing age, the parent–adult child relationship is the key family relationship in old age. Consequently, the family's role in maintaining intellectual functioning of older members usually devolves on adult children. Social and geographic mobility, however, may dilute the importance of this relationship, for intellectual stimulation requires face-to-face contact. Because the dominant family configuration emphasizes generational bonds, the childless elderly may be particularly isolated from family life. Nonetheless, any projections about the family status of older people is made at a time when the conventional nuclear family is no longer the statistically dominant family form. The rising numbers of alternate family forms may respond differently to the needs of older people.

Perhaps more direct links between family functioning and mental functioning in later life could be more clearly identified by introducing the variable of ethnicity into the analysis. The strong emphasis on the individual is found in most models of successful aging and, in fact, the family is rarely mentioned as contributing to the process. Concepts of control and efficacy linked to better health and adaptation in later life is directly correlated to individual actions. These theories may be culture-bound, geared mostly to the dominant group in which individualism and personal freedom are particularly endorsed. Such values are less applicable to the culturally diverse groups in which the family is central to everyday life, and family values have priority over personal values. For instance, such individualistic maneuvers were rarely observed among Blacks, whom identify happiness as related to the family, and life itself is often attributed to a gift from the supernatural.

In conclusion, the family is the pivotal institution that sustains the comfort and security of older people. There is little in the research literature that contradicts this assumption. Among parents, few are abandoned by their families, and most are strongly supported by family members. Presumably, the benefits families potentially provide include the facilitation of intellectual functioning. Perhaps the absence of direct links between family functioning and intellectual functioning stems, not from the absence of such connections, but from the fact that they are simply not studied.

REFERENCES

Abeles, R. P., & Riley, M. N. (1987). Longevity, social structure, and cognitive aging. In C. Schooler & K. W. Schaie (Eds.), *Cognitive aging and social structure over the life course* (pp. 142–157. Norwood, NJ: Ablex.

Adams, B. (1971). Isolation, function, and beyond: American kinship in the 1960s. *Journal of Marriage and the Family: Decade Review*. Minneapolis, MN: National Council of Family Relations.

Aneshensel, C. S., Pearlin, L. I., Mullan, J. T., Zarit, S. H., & Whitlach, C. J. (1995). *Profiles in caregiving: The unexpected career*. New York: Academic Press.

Baldwin, W. H., & Nord, C. W. (1984). Delayed childbearing in the U.S.:Facts and fictions. *Population Bulletin, 39*, 1–42.

Baltes, P. B. (1993). The aging mind: Potentials and limits. *The Gerontologist, 33*, 580–594.

Baltes, P., & Baltes, M. M. (1990). Psychological perspectives on successful aging: The model of selective optimization with compensation. In P. Baltes, & M. M. Baltes (Eds.), *Successful aging: Perspectives from the behavioral sciences* (pp. 1–34). New York: Cambridge University Press.

Bengtson, V. L., Rosenthal, C., & Burton, L. (1990). Families and aging: Diversity and heterogeneity. In R. Binstock & L. George (Eds.), *Handbook of aging and the social sciences*. New York: Academic Press

Bengtson, V. L., Rosenthal, C., & Burton, L. (1995). The paradox of families and aging. In R. Binstock & L. George (Eds.), *Handbook of aging and the social sciences*. New York: Academic Press.

Berkman, L. F., & Syme, L. S. (1979). Social networks, host resistance, and mortality: A nine year follow-up study of Alameda County Residents. *American Journal of Epidemiology, 109,* 186–204.

Blanchard-Fields, F., & Abeles, R. P. (1996). Social cognition and aging. In J. Birren & K. Warner Schaie (Eds.), *Handbook of psychology of aging* (pp. 150–161). New York: Academic Press.

Blazer, D. (1982). Social support and mortality in the elderly population. *American Journal of Epidemiology, 115,* 684–694.

Blenkner, M. (1965). Social work and family relationships in late life with some thoughts on filial maturity. In E. Shanas & G. Streib (Eds.), *Social structure and intergenerational relation* (3rd. ed., pp. 263–287). New York: Academic Press.

Bott, E. (1971). *Family and social network*. New York: The Free Press.

Burton, L. M., & Sorensen, S. (1993). Temporal context and the caregiver role: Perspectives from ethnographic studies of multigeneration African American families. In S. H. Zarit, L. I. Pearlin, & K. W. Schaie (Eds.), *Caregiving systems: Formal and informal helpers* (pp. 47–66). Hillsdale, NJ: Lawrence Erlbaum Associates.

Carstensen, L. L. (1992). Social and emotional patterns in adulthood: Support for socioemotional selectivity theory. *Psychology and Aging, 7,* 331–338.

Chatters, L., Taylor, R. J., & Neighbors, H. W. (1989). Size of informal helper network mobilized during a serious problems among Black Americans. *Journal of Marriage and the Family, 51,* 667–676.

Cicirelli, V. G. (1988). A measure of filial anxiety regarding anticipated care of elderly parents. *The Gerontologist, 28,* 478–482.

Clark, M. M., & Anderson, B. G. (1967). *Culture and aging*. Springfield, IL: Thomas.

Connell, C. M., & Gibson, G. D. (1997). Racial, ethnic, and cultural differences in dementia caregiving. *The Gerontologist, 37,* 355–364.

Cumming, E., & Henry, W. (1961). *Growing old*. New York: Basic Books.

Deimling, G. T., Smerglia, V. L., & Barresi, C. M. (1990). Health care professionals and family involvement in care-related decisions concerning older patients. *Journal of Aging & Health, 2*(3). 310–325.

Emerson, R. M., & Messenger, S. L. (1977). The micropolitics of trouble. *Social Problems, 5,* 121–134.

Evans, D. A., Scherr, P. A., Cook, N. R., Albert, M. S., Funkenstein, H. H., Beckett, L. A., Hebert, L. E., Wetle, T. T., Branch, L. G., Chown, M. J., Hennekens, C. H., & Taylor, J. O. (1992). The impact of Alzheimer's disease in the United States population. In R. M. Suzman, K. G. Manton, & D. P. Willis (Eds.), *The oldest old* (pp. 283–299). New York: Oxford University Press.

Farkas, J. L., & Hogan, D. P. (1995). Demography of changing intergenerational relationships. In V. L. Bengtson, K. W. Schaie, & L. M. Burton (Eds.), *Adult intergenerational relationships*. New York: Springer.

Fisher, C. (1982a). The dispersion of kin in modern society: Contemporary data and historical speculation. *Journal of Family History, 7,* 353–375.

Fisher, C. (1982b). *To dwell among friends: Personal networks in town and country*. Chicago: University of Chicago.

Frankel, B. G., & DeWitt, D. (1989). Geographic distance and intergenerational contact: An empirical examination of the relationship. *Journal of aging studies, 3,* 139–162.

Gatz, M., Kasl-Godley, J. E., & Karel, M. J. (1996). Aging and mental disorders. In J. E. Birren & K. W. Schaie (Eds.), *Handbook of the psychology of aging* (pp. 365–382). New York: The Free Press.

George, L. K., & Gold, D. T. (1991). Life course perspectives on intergenerational and generational connections. In S. P. Pfeifer & M. Sussman (Eds.), *Families: Intergenerational and generational connections* (pp. 67–88). New York: Haworth.

Hagestad, G. O. (1992). Family networks in an ageing society: Some reflections and explorations. In W. J. A. van den Heuvel, R. Illsley, A. Jamieson, & C. P. M. Knipscheer (Eds.), *Opportunities and challenges in an aging society* (pp. 44–52). Amsterdam: North Holland.

Haravan, T. K. (1994). Family change and historical changes: An uneasy relationship. In M. W. Riley, R. L. Kahn, & A. Foner (Eds.), *Age and structural lag.* New York: Wiley.

Hess, B., & Waring, J. (1978). Parent and child in late life: Rethinking the relationships. In G. Spanier (Ed.), *Child influences in marital and family interaction.* New York: Academic Press.

House, J. S. Landes, K. R., & Umberson, D. (1988). Social relationships and health, *Science, 241,* 540–544.

Johnson, C. L. (1983). Dyadic family relations and social supports. *The Gerontologist, 23,* 377–383.

Johnson, C. L. (1993). The prolongation of life and the extension of family relationships: The families of the oldest old. In P. A. Cowan, D. Field, D. A. Hansen, A. Skolnick, & G. E. Swanson (Eds.), *Family, self, and society* (pp. 317–330). Hillsdale, NJ: Lawrence Erlbaum Associates.

Johnson, C. L., & Barer, B. M. (1992). Patterns of engagement and disengagement among the oldest old. *Journal of Aging Studies, 6,* 351–364.

Johnson, C. L., & Barer, B. M. (1993). Coping and a sense of control among the oldest-old. *Journal of Aging Studies, 7,* 67–80.

Johnson, C. L., & Barer, B. M. (1995). Childlessness in late life: Comparisons by race. *Journal of Cross Cultural Gerontology, 9,* 289–306.

Johnson, C. L., & Barer, B. M. (1997). *Life beyond 85 years: The aura of survivorship.* New York: Springer.

Johnson, C. L., & Catalano, D. J. (1983). A longitudinal study of family supports to impaired elderly. *The Gerontologist, 23,* 612–618.

Johnson, C. L., & Johnson, F. A. (1983). A microanalysis of senility: Responses of the family and the health care professional. *Culture, Medicine, and Psychiatry, 7,* 77–96.

Johnson, C. L., & Troll, L. (1996). Family transitions from 70 to 103 years of age. *Journal of Marriage and the Family, 58,* 178–187.

Kane, R. A., & Penrod, J. D. (1995). *Family caregiving in an aging society.* Thousand Oaks, CA: Sage.

Kinsella, K. (1995). Aging and the family: Present and future demographic issues. In R. Blieszner & V. Bedford (Eds.), *Handbook of aging and the family.* Westport, CT: Greenwood.

Kovar, M. G., & Stone, R. (1992). The social environment of the oldest old. In R. M. Suzman, D. P. Willis, & K. G. Manton (Eds.), *The oldest old* (pp. 303–320). New York: Oxford University Press.

Lieberman, M. A., & Tobin, S. S. (1983). *The experience of old age: Stress, coping, and survival.* New York: Basic Books.

Litwak, R. (1960). Geographic mobility and extended family cohesion. *American Sociological Review, 25,* 9–21.

Litwak, E., & Kulis, S. (1989). Technology, proximity, & measures of kin support. *Journal of Marriage and the Family, 49,* 649–662.

Lowenthal, M. F., & Robinson, B. (1976). Social networks and isolation. In R. H. Binstodk & E. Shanas, E. (Eds.), *Handbook of aging and the social sciences.* New York: Van Nostrand Reinhold.

Mercier, J. M., Paulson, L., & Morrris, E. W. (1989). Proximity as a mediating influence on perceived aging parent–adult child relationship. *The Gerontologist, 26,* 785–791.

Neugarten, B. L. (1977). Personality and aging. In J. E. Birren, & K. W. Schaie (Eds.), *Handbook of the psychology of aging* (pp. 626–649). New York: Van Nostrand Reinhold.

Pillemer, K. (1996). Family caregiving. What would a Martian think? *The Gerontologist, 36,* 269–271.

Regier, D. A., Boyd, J. H., Burke, J. D., Rae, D. S., Myers, J. K., Kraemer, M., Robins, L. N., George, L. K., Karno, M., & Locke, B. Z. (1988). One-month prevalence of mental disorders in the United States. *Archives of General Psychiatry, 45,* 977–986.

Reiss, D., & Oliveri, M. E. (1983). The family's construction of social reality and its close ties to its kin network. *Journal of Marriage and the Family, 45,* 81–91.

Riley, M. (1983). The family in an aging society: A matrix of latent relationships. *Journal of Family Issues, 4,* 439–454.

Riley, M., & Riley, J. W. (1994). Structural lag: Past and future. In M. W. Riley, R. L. Kahn, & A. Foner (Eds.), *Age and structural lag.* New York: Wiley.

Roberts, R. E., & Bengston, V. L. (1990). Is intergenerational solidarity a unidimensional construct? A second test of a formal model. *Journals of Gerontology, 45*(1), S12–S20.

Rosenmayr, L., & Krockeis, E. (1963). Propositions for a sociological theory of aging and the family. *International Social Science nal, 15,* 410–426.

Rosenthal, C. (1985). Kinkeeping in the family division of labor: Parent–child relationships across the life course. *Journal of Marriage and the Family, 45,* 509–521.

Rosow, I. (1974). *Socialization to old age.* Berkeley: University of California Press.

Rossi, A. S., & Rossi, P. H. (1990). *Of human bonding: Parent–child relations across the life course.* New York: de Gruyter.

Rowe, J. W., & Kahn, R. L. (1987). Human aging: Usual and successful. *Science, 237,* 143–149.

Ryff, C. D., & Seltzer, M. M. (1995). Family relations and individual development in adulthood and aging. In R. Blieszner & V. H. Bedford (Eds.), *Handbook of aging and the family* (pp. 95–113). Westport, CT: Greenwood Press.

Schaie, K. W. (1996). Intellectual development in adulthood. In J. E. Birren & K. W. Schaie (Eds.), *Handbook of psychology and aging* (pp. 266–286). New York: The Free Press.

Schneider, D., & Smith, R. (1973). *Class differences and sex roles in American kinship and family structure.* Englewood Cliffs, NJ: Prentice Hall.

Schultz, R. (1985). Emotions and affect. In J. E. Birren & K. W. Schaie (Eds.), *Handbook of the psychology of aging* (pp. 531–543). New York: Van Nostrand Reinhold.

Shanas, E. (1979a). The family as a social support system in old age. *The Gerontologist, 19,* 169–174.

Shanas, E. (1979b). Social myth as hypothesis: The case of family relationships of old people. *The Gerontologist, 19,* 3–9.

Siegel, J. S. (1994). Plotting the course: Individual aging and population aging in the West. *The Gerontologist, 34,* 420–426.

Sprey, J. (1991). Studying adult children and parents. *Families: Intergenerational and generational connections, pt. 2. Marriage and Family Review, 16,* 221–236.

Sternberg, R. J., & Berg, C. A. (1987). What are the theories of adult development theories of? In C. Schooler & K. W. Schaie (Eds.), *Cognitive functioning and social structure over the live course* (pp. 3–23). Norwood, NJ: Ablex.

Stone, R., Cafferata, G. L., & Sangl, J. (1987). Caregivers of the frail elderly: A national profile. *The Gerontologist, 27,* 616–626.

Suiter, J. J., Pillemer, K., Keeton, S., & Robison, J. (1995). Aged parents and aging children: Determinants of relationship quality. In R. Bleiszner & R. Bedford (Eds.), *Handbook of aging and the family* (pp. 223–242). Westport, CT: Greenwood.

Suzman, M., Manton, K. G., & Willis, D. P. (Eds.). (1992). *The oldest old.* New York: Oxford University Press.

Taylor, R., & Chatters, L. M. (1991). Extended family networks of older Black adults. *Journal of Gerontology, 25,* 488–495.

Treas, J. (1995). Beanpole or beanstalk? Comments on the demography of changing intergenerational relations. In V. L. Bengtson, K. W. Schaie, & L. M. Burton (Eds.), Adult Interpersonal Relationships. New York: Springer.

Troll, L., & Bengtson, V. (1992). The oldest old in families: An intergenerational perspective. Symbolic and intergenerational links. *Generations, 17*(3 Summer), 39–44.

Uhlenberg, P. (1993). Demographic change and kin relationships in later life. In G. L. Maddox, & M. Powell (Eds.), *Annual review of gerontology and geriatrics, Vol. 13, Focus on kinship, aging, and social change* (pp. 219–238). New York: Springer.

Uhlenberg, P. & Cooney, T. M. (1990). Family size and mother–child relations in laterlife. *The Gerontologist, 30,* 318–325.

Umberson, D. 1992. Relations between adult children and their parents: Psychological consequences for both generations. *Journal of Marriage and the Family, 51,* 664–674.

U.S. Bureau of the Census. (1992). *Household and family characteristics: March, 1991. Current Population Reports, Series P. 20, No 458.* Washington DC: U.S. Bureau of the Census.

Verbrugge, L. (1984). Longer life but worsening health: Trends in health and mortality of middle aged and older persons. *Milbank Memorial Fund Quarterly, 62*(2), 475–519.

Willis, S. L. (1996). Everyday problem solving. In J. E. Birren & K. W. Schaie (Eds.), *Handbook of psychology and aging* (pp. 287–307). New York: The Free Press.

Wood, V., & Robertson, J. (1978). Friendship and kinship interaction: Differential effects on the morale of the elderly. *Journal of Marriage and the Family, 40,* 367–375.

Zarit, S. H., & Eggebeen, D. J. (1995). Parent–child relationships in adulthood and old age. In M. H. Bornstein (Ed.), *Handbook of parenting,* (Vol. 1, pp. 119–40). Mahwah, NJ: Lawrence Erlbaum Associates.

10

Grandchildren as Moderator Variables in the Family, Social, Physiological, and Intellectual Development of Grandparents Who Are Raising Them

Glenda M. Ehrle
Texas Woman's University

Most people who become grandparents do so during their middle and late adulthood stages of life span development. Considerable observation and research has described, from a variety of perspectives, the expected physiological, social, and cognitive changes associated with middle and late adulthood. Moreover, there are also predictable shifts in family relationships. Becoming a grandparent in either middle or late adulthood is generally associated with a time when one's own adult children have left home to become independently functioning adults with children of their own to raise. In general, grandparents expect their adult children to be primary caretakers of their grandchildren. They, not the grandparents, would be responsible for providing a relatively consistent environment of physical and psychological support and guidance necessary for a child to develop into a productive adult. Grandparents expect to form relationships with grandchildren free of the responsibility of being the primary caretakers.

It is not always the case that parents are fully functioning parents. A variety of factors including illness, death, economics, and dysfunctional behaviors may interfere with effective parenting. In January 1990, the report of the U.S. House Select Committee on Children, Youth, and Families reported to the 101st Congress that approximately 500,000 children were formally placed in out-of-home care such as foster homes, shelters, and institutions. Furthermore, the House Select Committee's report estimated that by the mid-1990s the number of children placed in out-of-home care would increase to approximately 875,000, with drug and alcohol abuse of the parents of such children as a substantial contributing factor to the need for placement. Approximately 375,000 drug-exposed babies were born in 1988. Large inner city populations such as those in California, Florida, New York, and Washington, DC have significantly increased the case loads of Child Protective Services. It is important to note that the report of the House Select Committee on Children, Youth and Families focused only on the children formally processed through various state protective agencies and the courts. The children formally processed through protective agencies may be only a small portion of children actually affected by parental incapacity and in need of alternative care.

Increases in the foster child population along with decreases in available foster families has increased the use of relatives as foster parents whenever they are available (Everett, 1995). Grandparents often become surrogate parents on a part-time or full-time basis (Minkler & Roe, 1996). The 1990 Census Report estimated that approximately 3.2 million children lived with relatives, including grandparents, other than their biological parents with or without becoming involved in formal custody procedures. Of the 3.2 million children reported to be

The author would like to offer a special thank you to Dr. H.D. Day of Texas Woman's University for his guidance and patience in helping me with all of my research and writing.

living with extended kin, it was estimated that 1.8 million are living with grandparents (Carlson, 1993). Marx and Solomon (1993) reported that African-American and Hispanic children who live with grandparents are over represented among guardian grandparent families. Cultural factors may contribute to the larger proportion among minority groups. However, the largest rate of increase is among White families (The Menninger Letter, 1995). It seems reasonable that grandparents would have significant adjustments to make in order to resume parenting roles at a time in life when they expect to be free of primary responsibility for growing children.

Despite reasonably apparent adjustments and the large numbers of grandchildren who are being raised by grandparents, few studies have attempted to examine the impact of on either grandchildren or grandparents. It stands to reason that raising one's grandchildren would have significant impact on the expected family processes and roles. Moreover, it seems likely that assuming responsibility for rearing grandchildren could have consequences affecting the physiological, cognitive, and social functioning of grandparents. In order to begin to understand what happens when grandparents raise grandchildren, it is important to consider the relatively small body of research that specifically addresses guardian grandparent families. It could be useful to attempt to put it in the context of literature describing nonguardian grandparent roles and expectation as well as literature describing expected physiological, cognitive, and social expectations of middle adulthood and late adulthood.

RESEARCH-IDENTIFIED GRANDPARENT–GRANDCHILD RELATIONSHIPS

Current literature indicates a growing interest in the grandparent–grandchild relationship and roles. Early studies regarding grandparents were discussed by Kivnick (1982) in *The Meaning of Grandparenthood*. Qualitative and quantitative data was used to derive and affirm five dimensions of grandparenthood: centrality, valued elder, immortality through clan, reinvolvement with personal past, and indulgence. Kivnick concluded that grandparenthood was an important source of delight, enrichment, and vitality for aging adults. She also suggested that disappointment in any of the five dimensions could result in the need for some therapeutic intervention. When grandparents are compelled to assume parenting responsibilities, it stands to reason that the indulgence dimension, and possibly the valued elder and reinvolvement with personal past, may be compromised. If the middle generation is hostile to them, grandparents may feel more embattled than valued, and the recent personal past may be quite painful. In addition, the responsibility for guiding and disciplining grandchildren may interfere with the pleasure indul-gence. Nevertheless, grandparents often feel that the most important thing that they can do for a grandchild is to assume parenting responsibilities, often at great personal cost. A review of current grandparent and grandchild studies may reveal the reasons for these attitudes.

In 1991, Kivett noted that the grandparent and grandchild connection is second only, in biological linkages to the parent and child dyad. She also dis-cusses the "vertical expansion" of the family that results from increases in the number of older adults and now having more living grandparents and great-grandparents is increasing. In reviews of recent literature on grandparenting, grandparents, parents, and grandchildren have formed a vari-ety of "multigenerational" families (Dressel, 1996; Giarrusso, Silverstein, & Bengston, 1996; Gratton & Haber, 1996; Longino & Earle, 1996; Pruchno & Johnson, 1996). These same studies also indicated that, because there is no le-gally defined responsibility for grandparents, a wide range of age for grandpar-ents, significant variations in geographic proximity to grandchildren, and ethnic and family differences in role expectations, there is no homogeneous family form, particularly in multigenerational families. Giarrusso et al. (1996) suggested that the tendency for earlier researchers to refer to the grandparent role as tenuous or without clear prescriptions regarding the rights and duties of grandparents may be confusing a rich variety in styles of grandparenting with lack of role definition. They suggested that a typology that classified and de-scribed different styles of grandparenting might be more useful than trying to develop a normative description of grandparenting roles.

Gratton and Haber (1996) suggested that United States American grand-parents have evolved over the years from being an authority figure in the family to being a burden on the family, and finally, to being an autonomous and valu-able companion to grandchildren. Grandparents, in a variety of cultures, play important roles in identity development of grandchildren by storytelling and passing on the family history (Barusch & Steen, 1996; Hodgson, 1992; Ken-nedy, 1992; McAdoo & McWright, 1994; Nussbaum & Bettini, 1994). Adult grandchildren perceive their grandparents as influential in their lives (Roberto & Stroes, 1992), providing for them family heritage and stability. Adolescents who lived with a stepparent reported closer relationships with grandparents than did those who lived in either intact or single-parent families (Kennedy & Kennedy, 1993). Some small age and gender effects were found to influence re-ported supportive relationships with grandparents. Younger children perceived grandparents as more supportive than older grandchildren and paternal grand-fathers were less supportive than the other three grandparents (Creasey &

Kaliher, 1994). In a study of teen mothers and infants, nurturing grandfathers demonstrated a strong impulse to care for, and exerted significant influence on, the grandchild (Oyserman, Radin, & Benn, 1993).

Grandparenting relationships are shaped by cultural forces and change with geographic mobility, maturation of the grandchildren, aging of the grandparent, and family crisis (Longino & Earle, 1996). Frequency of contact and grandparent health influenced grandparent and grandchild relationships (Creasy & Kaliher, 1994). Especially in times of crisis, grandparents tended to give both time and economic support to younger family members (Bass & Caro, 1996). Several researchers noted a relationship between poverty and multigenerational families where grandparents often assume parenting responsibilities (Bass & Caro, 1996; Giarrusso et al., 1996; Minkler & Roe, 1996; Roe, Minkler, & Barnwell, 1994).

Carlson (1993) suggested that both economics and ethnicity affects the role of a grandmother in the lives of her grandchildren. She posited that changes in family structure, the general economy, and the lack of affordable and adequate daycare has brought about a trend toward grandmothers at least sharing primary child-care roles for the children of their working or adolescent daughters. Carlson reported that a 1988 study by Raphael demonstrated that the Hispanic immigrant grandmother's role as a babysitter is culturally valued. In addition, Carlson cited a 1987 study by Flaherty and reported that African-American grandmothers assumed the primary casemaking roles for their grandchildren born to adolescent daughters. In this study, Flaherty asserted the notion that African-American grandmothers were more likely than their Anglo counterparts to assume managing, casemaking, coaching, assessing, nurturing, assigning, and patrolling roles as part of their involvement with grandchildren. Single grandmothers, African-Americans, and low-income grandparents were found to be approximately twice as likely to become guardian grandparents, although guardian grandparents cross gender, class, and ethnic lines (Fuller-Thomson, Minkler, & Driver, 1997). Their roles as surrogate parents to their grandchildren appear to range from total responsibility to minimal back-up support. Saluter (1992) noted that, although there were more Anglo than African-American children who lived with grandparents, the proportion of African-American children living with grandparents was three times as large. African-American grandparents and grandchildren, more often than their counterparts, rated their relationships as successful.

It is clear that there is considerable variability in the quantity and quality of relationships that may be shared by grandparents and grandchildren. Age, gender, ethnicity, geographic proximity, and frequency of contact are all important factors in shaping the relationships. It makes sense that the same factors would influence the adjustment of the family formed when grandparents parent grandchildren. At risk for these grandparents may be some of the pleasure and vitality associated with Kivnick's five dimensions of grandparenthood (Kivnick, 1982). A better understanding of the source and importance of such a risk might be gleaned from family development models.

FAMILY DEVELOPMENT

Family Development Theory

In the recent past, the popular image of traditional family values in our culture meant child-centered families with proscribed gender roles. The father was cast in the role of the breadwinner whose self-efficacy was often measured by the amount of financial security he could provide his family. A mother's self-worth often was grounded in her unflinching self-sacrifice to see to the physical and emotional needs of her husband and children. In fact, fathers were often so immersed in earning money to support the family that they become alienated. Mothers focused on meeting the day to day physical and emotional needs of her husband and children had little time to develop interests and goals outside the home. It was in a similar environment that Erikson (1963) suggested a crisis of generativity versus stagnation would emerge in middle adulthood. Rethought in terms of traditional gender roles, it could be said that much of each parent's motivation leaves home with the children. In addition, the marital dyad may have been pulled in different directions by rigid gender roles that resulted in a loss of some degree of relationship. In this case, generativity for each parent, and the marital dyad, may be undermined by a feeling of stagnation and loss of purpose, popularly referred to as the "empty nest syndrome."

The notion of midlife crisis was reinvented by Levinson et al. (1978) for individuals, with an emphasis on men. Gilligan (1982) responded to his theory of male midlife crisis with a theory of female development in which she suggested that women undergo a transition from being cared for to caring for others. Based on more current research, Levinson (1996) insisted that both men and women who experience a midlife crisis brought about by reviewing past accomplishments are recognizing that they will not likely accomplish all of their youthful dreams. Both Levinson and Gilligan reflected our culture's image of traditional family gender roles. More recent rhythms in the family life cycle such that the chances of a child studies described the passage from early adulthood during middle adulthood as a transition rather than crisis.

Sheehy (1995) proposed a notion of "second adulthood" in which new opportunities for fulfillment emerge in mid-life, particularly for women. Sheehy presented an optimistic theory in which she described mid-life as an "age of mastery." With changing cultural attitudes about gender-appropriate roles, many women reported more confidence, assertiveness, achievement, and influence at work and in politics in midlife (Reinke, Holmes, & Harris, 1985). Furthermore, there appears to be some role reversal for both women and men when children leave home (Wink & Helson, 1993). Women become more confident and competent outside the home, whereas men become more nurturing and emotionally oriented in the context of their families. The "empty nest" may be a time for setting new goals, creating new opportunities, and transition to a different measure of self-worth and efficacy for both men and women. In this more optimistic view of midlife, it may also be an opportunity for a renewal of the marital dyad. In 1971, Duvall proposed a structural eight-stage theory of family development, five of which are predicated on parenting tasks from welcoming the first child into the family to releasing the youngest child into adulthood. When all of the children have been successfully launched into adulthood, the parenting dyad shifts from a focus on parenting tasks to recreating the marital relationship. Other research demonstrates that marital satisfaction seems to decline during the child-rearing years and tends to rebound during the postparental years. (Bradburn & Caplovita, 1966; Burr, 1970; Johnson, 1968; Reinke, et al. 1985; Rollins & Feldman, 1978), The increase in marital satisfaction during postparental years may be a result of more leisure time together (Deutscher, 1964) and less role strain (Rollins & Cannon, 1974). In other words, parenting children alters the marital relationship to some degree.

UNIQUE PROBLEMS REPORTED BY GRANDPARENTS WHO ARE RAISING GRANDCHILDREN

Ehrle and Day (1994) compared a group of 23 grandparents who were raising grandchildren with a control group of 27 grandparents who were not raising grandchildren using the Dyadic Adjustment Scale and the Family Assessment Scale. Discriminant function analysis of the data indicated that grandparents who were raising grandchildren reported less dyadic satisfaction and dyadic consensus than grandparents who were not raising grandchildren. Grandparents not raising grandchildren demonstrated lower dyadic cohesion than grandparents raising grandchildren. The results of this study appear to support the theory that the parenting roles strain the marital relationship. On the other hand, the cohesiveness score suggests that the rearing of grandchildren may in-

fluence grandparents to act together as a parenting dyad until they are successfully launched into adulthood.

The results of a second study reported by Ehrle & Day (1994) used structured interviews to reveal how grandmothers who were primary caretakers of at
least one grandchild perceive themselves in relationship to their grandchildren.
Despite concerns about aging, they expressed confidence in their ability to provide adequate care for grandchildren and reported receiving much pleasure
from the close bonds with their grandchildren. Many of them expressed the belief that they had been give a second chance to be successful parents. A second
chance at successful parenting seemed especially important since most grandparents who parent their grandchildren are doing so in the context of a family
trauma centered around the middle generation of the family. Illness or death of
an adult child may compel some grandparents to assume guardianship of grandchildren, but much of the research suggests that substance abuse and related
physical abuse or neglect of grandchildren by the middle generation are the
overwhelming factors in compelling grandparents assume parental roles for
their grandchildren Especially in instances of abuse and neglect, grandparents
may be caring for grandchildren with special physical and emotional needs for
which their own children are responsible. In the context of family conflict and
confusion, grandparents often report feeling angry, frustrated, guilty, and fear of
failing as effective parents to there grandchildren (Ehrle & Day, 1994, Jendrick,
1994; Kennedy & Kenney, 1988; Minkler et al., 1992; O'Reilly & Morrison,
1992; Smetana et al., 1991).

The results of a team research study of grandparent families in therapy were reported in a symposium at the November, 1990 meeting of the Texas Psychological
Association (Day et al., 1990). Among the characteristics demonstrated by the
small clinical sample were child-centered families with minimal spousal interaction, rigid gender roles, and overly strong, sacrificial, work ethic. Communication in
the clinical sample demonstrated weak verbal skills, low rates of positive verbaliza-
tion, high rates of negative verbalizations, poor attentiveness to others, and incon-
gruence between verbalizations and affect. Bartram (1996) suggested that poor
family subsystem boundaries threaten guardian grandparents' ability to nurture,
control, and maintain appropriate peer relationships. Such characteristics seem to
isolate each member of the nuclear family from one another and often spill over
into broader social system. Although there are no quantitative studies addressing
the effects of raising grandchildren on individual development of grandparents, anecdotal reports in studies and informal interviews with guardian grandparent families do suggest that grandchildren may very well moderate the expected social tasks,
physiological well-being, and intellectual development of grandparents.

IMPLICATIONS FOR SOCIAL DEVELOPMENT

Social Isolation

Social isolation is a perception consistently expressed by grandparents in inter-views conducted in person and on the Internet. Grandparents often reported feeling alienated from some of their own family members. They reported that they often faced criticism of their parenting skills with the middle generation from their own parents and siblings. Sibling rivalry between their adult children may be projected into the family system when grandparents have more than one adult child with children but are parenting the child or children of only one adult child. One or more of their adult children may express jealousy on behalf of his or her children because of the time and money that grandparents spend in parenting a sibling's child. In these families, grandparents reported frustrating and tiring conflict that often led to alienation from one or more of their adult children as well as the grandchildren of those children.

Working grandparents find themselves in the same situation with grandchil-dren as they experience raising their children; that is, they sometimes must choose between work and a child's needs. Obtaining child care, coping with sick children, and being involved with school-related activities often interfere with work schedules and leaves grandparents tired and frustrated. Moreover, the initial interviews with grandparents raising grandchildren revealed that their employers expressed negative attitudes toward their situation and insur-ance benefits provided for parents raising their own children, or even unadopted stepchildren was not made available to grandparents for their grand-children.

Grandparents reported that friends cultivated over the years may drift away as a result of guardian grandparent's bringing children into their social situa-tions. Grandparents who were raising grandchildren often reported feeling compelled to decline invitations because of having to find and pay for child care or take grandchildren with them in social situations where they feel that chil-dren are not welcome; they also reported a decline in the number of invitations to social events.

The parents of the playmates and friends of the grandchildren are generally of a different generation with few interests in common with grandparents. Grandparents reported feeling out of place at school functions such as Par-ent–Teacher Association meetings and other organizational events for children such as sports or scouting activities. Grandparents reported feeling that they were viewed negatively by parents and teachers of the peers of the grandchil-dren they were raising. Grandparents who are raising grandchildren often reported feeling as if they were the only ones in this situation and had no understanding or support from either family or friends.

Social Perceptions Experienced in Institutional Situations

The loss of personal social support is only one dimension of the social isolation grandparents reported; social judgement of them as parents also was perceived to be negative. Many grandparents find themselves in courtrooms trying to secure temporary or permanent custody of grandchildren. Very often, grandparents believe that family court judges and attorneys are very biased against them. One family court judge, in an address to an assembly of guardian grandparents, said that grandparents were the very last choice for custody in his court because they were too old to be raising children and they had obviously done a poor job with their own children as evidenced by their irresponsible behavior.

Wilson and DeShane (1982) reported that grandparents rarely obtained legal rights to make welfare decisions for grandchildren when a biological parent resisted giving up parental rights. Grandparents indicated in interviews that they were reluctant to go to court to attempt to publically declare that their on child is unfit to parent and they do not want to give up the belief that their children will overcome their problems and regain the ability to be adequate parents.

Legal guardianship of grandchildren is important to many of the functions of parenting. Physicians and Dentists are sometimes reluctant to treat children with only the grandparents' consent as treating children without a parent's consent could create legal problems. Even when physicians and dentists are willing to treat grandchildren with grandparent consent alone, insurance may not be available to make the treatment affordable.

Grandparents have reported feeling that school teachers and counselors assume that the grandchildren must have serious learning and emotional difficulties because of the family situation. Just as grandparents generally blamed themselves and their parenting skills for the problems exhibited by the middle generation, they believed that teachers and counselors also blamed them. Insensitive questions and comments not only occur in the contact that grandparents have with professionals in the course of taking care of grandchildren; they also occur in ordinary daily circumstances. One grandmother even reported that a checkout clerk in a grocery store asked what she had done to raise a daughter so irresponsible that she would abandon her own child. Grandparents often reported being told by family, professionals, and even strangers that they should make their children take responsibility for their children.

Implications for Psychosocial Development for Guardian Grandparents

At a stage of development that is supposed to be a time for a transition from parenting duties to freedom to explore personal interests and opportunities, guardian grandparents take a step back to child rearing. Both work and leisure activities are vulnerable to the demands of parenting grandchildren. Family difficulties and perceived negativity suggested by social systems insensitive to the grandparents needs undermines' more than expected social developmental tasks. Researchers have reported that they also undermine confidence, stability, and satisfaction (Reinke et al., 1985) Emick and Hayslip (1996) noted that a review of the literature regarding guardian grandparents suggests that psychosocial development may be compromised to the point of needing mental health services, especially when caring for grandchildren with problems. With so much negativity and so little social support, it is not surprising that many grandparents report feeling frustrated and stressed.

PHYSIOLOGICAL DEVELOPMENT

Serious stress during the mid-life years can result in creating or exacerbating health problems. Mid-life is associated with a gradual decline in physical abilities and acuity. The loss of estrogen and progesterone brings about menopause and results in some loss of soft tissue, skin elasticity, and bone density in women. Arthritis, heart disease, high blood pressure, and a variety of other maladies are more commonly diagnosed in mid-life than in early adulthood. Stress is a significant contributor to these health problems (Smith, Small, & Placek, 1990) and may be an important variable in guardian grandparent families.

Kennedy and Keeney (1988) reported that guardian grandparents suppressed personal needs, experienced guilt and anger regarding the middle generation, faced intergenerational value conflicts and ongoing family disputes, and had considerable concerns regarding the grandchild's welfare. Assumption of parenting responsibilities for grandchildren is often sudden and the result of serious family trauma (Ehrle & Day, 1994; Jendrek, 1994). The absence of the middle generation, legal problems, economic problems, work-related problems, and family conflict are among stress-generating problems for guardian grandparents (Burton, 1992; Ehrle & Day, 1994; Kennedy & Kenney, 1988; Minkler & Roe, 1996; Morrow-Kondos et al. 1997; Smetana et al. 1991).

Chalfie (1994) reported that approximately 27% of the grandparent families live below the poverty level. Financial assistance, health insurance, housing, and obtaining legal rights to make decisions regarding the welfare of grandchildren are among problems that distress guardian grandparents (Burton, 1992; Chalfie, 1994; Ehrle & Day, 1994; Mullen, 1996; Nersessian, 1996; Shore & Hayslip, 1994). Pinson-Millburn et al. (1996) found that the significant stressors for their research sample included age, low income, absence of a time limit for care giving, and abusive, ill, and/or incarcerated parents of the grandchildren. Raising grandchildren with neurological, physical, emotional, or behavioral problems increases the level of distress, reduces role satisfaction and meaning, and threatens the grandparent and grandchild relationship even more than raising grandchildren without problems (Hayslip, Shore, Henderson, & Lambert, 1998). A perceived lack of choice, referred to as an "impulse to care," (Jendrek, 1993) may also contribute to experienced stress. The result of stressful problems is increased health problems (Burton, 1992; Edwards, 1998; Minkler & Roe, 1996; Minkler, Roe, & Price, 1992; Roe et al., 1994; Roe et al., 1996).

On the other hand, grandparents insist that they are physically able to care for grandchildren. Despite acknowledging physical problems, many grandparents perceive themselves to be in fair to excellent health (Ehrle, 1997; Ehrle & Day, 1994; Roe, Minkler, Saunders, & Thomson, 1996). Grandparents reported that being needed and the love and joy of having their grandchildren with them helps them cope with stress and the physical problems. Some said that their grandchildren keep them feeling "on their toes" and young (Ehrle, 1997; Ehrle & Day, 1994). Emick and Hayslip (1996) found that raising grandchildren may result in developing strengths and feeling rewarded later in life. Jendrek's (1994) "impulse to care" might be associated with Kivnick's (1982) dimensions of grandparenthood. Centrality, valued elder, immortality through clan, reinvolvement with personal past, and indulgence can be reasonably proposed as possible factors for an "impulse to care" for the children of one's own children.

As stressful and health endangering as it seems to be to parent grandchildren, the actual presence of the grandchild may modify the grandparents' perception of their physical ability to do the job. That perception may be part of a cognitive restructuring by which a grandparent may increase his or her ability to solve problems and cope with whatever physical and emotional demands they encounter in rearing grandchildren. Although there is no definitive research demonstrating it, increases in problem solving and developing new coping skills suggest an impact on the intellectual development of grandparents who are raising grandchildren.

INTELLECTUAL DEVELOPMENT

In cognitive restructuring, one must use what Cattell (1987) referred to as "fluid intelligence." That is, one must process perceptual information through reason and remembering. Reason suggests that guardian grandparents must cognitively restructure their expectations and perceptions of the family structure and their relationship with their adult children and grandchildren. Cognitive restructuring is not the only form of intelligence that would be necessary for grandparents to be able to successfully parent grandchildren. Their years of experience, information, skill, and strategies for problem solving, what Cattell called "crystallized intelligence," must also be exercised to solve new unexpected problems encountered in raising grandchildren different from those encountered raising their own children. Historically, fluid intelligence was presumed to decline in later adulthood; however, Schaie (1993) suggested that the decline in intelligence as demonstrated on traditional IQ tests was more reflective of a slowing of physical performance of reaction time. Schaie (1993) further proposed that crystallized intelligence may actually improve with age. Certainly, rearing grandchildren is likely to call for vigorous exercise of both general types of intelligence described by Cattell and described by Schaie.

A practical view of intelligence based on information processing and adaptation to an environment is represented in the Triarchic Model of Intelligence proposed by Sternberg (1985, 1997). The three aspects of the triarchic model are componential, experiential, and contextual intelligence. With componential intelligence, a person breaks information into components to encode, combine, and compare fragments of information in order to solve a problem. That would certainly account for a grandparent's ability to cognitively restructure his or her perception of a situation. Experiential intelligence represents the ability to become effective at adapting to new circumstances by relating new situations to familiar ones in order to solve problems. Parenting experiences, experience dealing with a variety of social circumstances, and experience with health issues might be useful to grandparents who resume parenting activities during midlife with little social support. The third type of intelligence, contextual, would be of the utmost importance to a grandparents' successful adaptation to raising grandchildren. They must be able to either manipulate the environment to facilitate their needs as guardian grandparents, or find alternative environments that are more suitable for their needs.

Guardian grandparents have often demonstrated componential, experiential, and contextual intelligence in regard to their raising grandchildren. The formation of support groups is a good example of how they use practical intelligence. One grandmother who was interviewed (Ehrle & Day, 1994) reported feeling very isolated socially. She recognized that her isolation was twofold, a lack of general understanding of her situation and a lack of contact with others in her situation. With a variety of experiences including Parent–Teacher Association organization and garage sale advertising in local news media, she generated a solution to her isolation problem. She placed ads in local newspapers and cable stations to search for other grandparents raising grandchildren. She then approached a local church and secured a meeting place for those who responded to her ads. She was aware that grandparents might have difficulty obtaining childcare and that grandchildren should not be present while family problems were being discussed, so she arranged for child care at the meeting location. She then arranged the meeting room so that everyone would be sitting in a circle in order to make face-to-face contact during discussions. She even prepared light refreshments to help create a socially comforting atmosphere. In this context, a network of support groups formed and influenced family court judges, attorneys, and legislators to help solve legal problems in obtaining custody of grandchildren, obtaining adequate medical and dental care and the insurance to pay for it, and change the perceptions of their families held by the general public. Support groups also became rich sources of information for grandparents who found themselves returning to parenthood and to professionals who work with guardian grandparent families.

Kivnick's (1982) work related the dimensions of grandparenthood to mental health of grandparents. She professes a "profound" connection between grandparenthood and mental health. She believes that grandparents can make the most of their existing strengths and rework existing weaknesses through their relationships with grandchildren in health-enhancing activities. She advocates frequent contact between grandparents and grandchildren in a variety of shared activities as a source of mental, and physical, vitality for grandparents.

Kivnick did not address the type of contact guardian grandparents experience, but it could be hypothesized that, although emotionally and physically stressed, guardian grandparents maintain a form of centrality, valued elder, immortality through clan, reinvolvement with personal past, and indulgence with their grandchildren. They define themselves as grandparents who are able to rise to the occasion of protecting their link with immortality and personal past by indulging their grandchildren's needs for care and stability. Motivation to provide the best possible care for grandchildren despite a plethora of problems enhances the practical intelligence required to solve those problems. In other words, grandchildren may be a motivation moderator variable that keeps grandparents vigorously exercising practical intelligence as long as the grandparents are responsible for their care and well-being.

Forming support groups, seeking professional help, informing helping professions and the general public, and creating resources for other grandparents are evidence that guardian grandparents can successfully solve problems. The Grandfamily School Support Network was proposed as a useful resource in helping grandparents cope with the difficulties of raising grandchildren. A small group intervention directed by a social worker has also been useful in increased confidence in grandparents' ability to solve the unique problems of rearing grandchildren, social support systems, a and knowledge of grandparent-related social services (Burnette, 1998).

This kind of problem solving is compatible with Cattell's theory of fluid and crystallized intelligence as well as Sternberg's Triarchic Model of Intelligence. Perhaps the best indicator of the successful problem solving capabilities of guardian grandparents to date is the results of a study that compared the adjustment of guardian grandchildren to children in both intact and divorced families. In general the adjustment of guardian grandchildren was not as desirable as the adjustment of children in intact families, but it was better than that of children who experience parental divorce and remarriage (Ehrle, 1997). Grandparents may not be able to provide as stable an environment as biological parents who raise their children together, but they apparently offer more benefits than nonrelated surrogate parents.

CONCLUSIONS

The overwhelming conclusion that must be addressed is that there is still too little research to examine what happens to a family, to grandparents, and to grandchildren when grandparents are pressed into service as parents. From both family and individual life-span development perspectives, there are obvious indications that the presence of grandchildren and the demands of parenting them will modify the grandparents' development, apparently in family development and all three general forms of individual development: social, physiological, and intellectual. At this point, one can only speculate as to how and how much the grandparents' development is affected.

The issues are made more complicated by the probability that guardian grandparent families are as heterogenous as more traditional grandparent–grandchild relationships. Factors like age, gender, ethnicity, marital status, and geographical proximity and frequency of contact before the assumption of guardianship will likely require a variety of adjustment strategies by grandparents and grandchildren alike. Much more research is needed to understand all of the factors and processes involved in grandparents and grandchildren to adapt to and restructure their relationship amid what must be considerable confusion and difficulty Nevertheless, reason suggests that it is likely that assuming parenting responsibilities for grandchildren does act as a moderator variable for social, physical, and intellectual states for grandparents. Moreover, based on self-reports in informal and structured interviews with grandparents, raising a grandchild may influence intelligence in a positive way by requiring grandparents to restructure their expectations and perceptions of their family structure , restructuring their relationships with their adult children and with their grandchildren, and solving the unique social problems they encounter. In her own words in an informal interview with the author, one grandmother said that raising her grandchildren made her feel younger and "kept her on her toes."

REFERENCES

Bartram, M. H. (1996). Clarifying subsystem boundaries in grandparent families. *Contemporary Family Therapy, 18*(2), 267–277.

Barusch, A. S., & Steen, P. (1996). Keepers of community in a changing world. *Generations, Spring,* 49–55.

Bass, S. A., & Caro, F. G. (1996). The economic value of grandparent assistance. *Generations, Spring,* 29–32.

Bradburn, N. M., & Caplovita, D. (1966). *Reports on unhappiness.* Chicago: Aldine.

Burnette, D. (1998). Grandparents rearing grandchildren: A school-based small group intervention. *Research on Social Work Practice, 8*(1), 10–27.

Burr, W. R. (1970). Satisfaction with various aspects of marriage over the life cycle: A random middle class sample. *Journal of Marriage and the Family, 32*(1), 29–37.

Burton, L. M. (1992). Black grandparents rearing children of drug-addicted parents: Stressors, outcomes and social service needs. *The Gerontologists, 32*(6), 744–751.

Carlson, G. E. (1993). When grandmothers take care of grandchildren. *Maternal and Child Nursing, 18,* 206–207.

Cattell, J. B. (1987). *Intelligence: Its structure, growth, and action.* Amsterdam: North-Holland.

Chalfie, D. (1994). *Going it alone: A closer look at grandparents parenting grandchildren.* Washington, DC: AARP Women's Initiative.

Creasey, G. L., & Kaliher, G. (1994). Age differences in grandchildren's perceptions of relations with grandparents. *Journal of Adolescence, 17*(5), 411–426.

Day, H. D., Amos, I., Ehrle, G. M., Noah, N., Neal, V. (1990). *Counseling issues for guardian grandparent families.* A symposium presented at the meeting of the Dallas Psychological Association. Dallas.

Deutscher, I. (1964). The quality of postparental life: Definitions of the situation, *Journal of Marriage and the Family, 26,* 52–59.

Dressel, P. (1996). A deep social consciousness. *Generations, Spring,* 4.

Duvall, E. M. (1971). *Family development.* Philadelphia: J. B. Lippincott.

Edwards, O. W. (1998). Helping grandkin–grandchildren raised by grandparents: Expanding psychology in the schools. *Psychology in the Schools, 35*(2), 173–181.

Ehrle, G. M. (1987) *Dyadic adjustment and family functioning in guardian and nonguardian grandparent families*, Unpublished master's thesis, Texas Woman's University: Denton.

Ehrle, G. M. (1997) *Adjustment in children being reared by grandparents because of substance abuse of their parents: A comparison of children from intact families, divorced families, and guardian grandparent families*. Unpublished doctoral dissertation: Texas Woman's University. Denton.

Ehrle, G. M., & Day, H. D. (1994). Adjustment and family functioning of grandmothers who are rearing their grandchildren. *Contemporary Family Therapy: An International Journal, April, 34*(2), 206–216

Emick, M. A., & Hayslip, B. (1996). Custodial grandparenting: New roles for middle-aged and older adults. *International Journal of Aging & Human Development, 43*(2), 135–154.

Erikson, E. H. (1963) *Childhood and society*. New York: W. W. Norton.

Everett, J. E. (1995). Relative foster care: An emerging trend in foster care placement and practice. *Smith College Studies in Social Work, 65*(3), 239–254.

Fuller-Thomson, E., Minkler, M., & Driver, D. (1997) A profile of grandparents raising grandchildren in the United States. *Gerontologist, 37*(3), 406–411.

Giarrusso, R., Silverstein, M., & Bengtson, V. L. (1996, Spring). Family complexity and the grandparent role. *Generations,* 17–23.

Gilligan, C. (1982) *In a Different Voice*. Cambridge, MA: Harvard University Press.

Gratton, B., & Haber, C. (1996). Three phases in history of American grandparents. *Generations, Spring,* 7–12.

Hayslip, B. J., Shore, J., Henderson, C. E., & Lambert, P. L. (1998). Custodial grandparenting and the impact of grandchildren with problems on role satisfaction and role meaning. *Journal of Gerontology: Series B. Psychological Sciences and Social Sciences, 53B*(3), S164–S173

Hodgson, L. G. (1992) Adult grandchildren and their grandparents: The enduring bond. *International Journal of Aging and Human Development, 34*(3), 209–225.

Jendrek, M. P. (1993). Grandparents who parent their grandchildren: Effects on Lifestyle. Report to AARP Andrus Foundation.

Jendrek, M. P. (1994). Grandparents who parent their grandchildren: Circumstances and Decisions. *Gerontologist, 34*(2), 206–216.

Johnson, R. E. Jr. (1968). Marital patterns during the middle years, Unpublished doctoral dissertation, University of Minnesota, Minneapolis.

Kennedy, G. F. (1992). Quality in grandparent/grandchild relationships. *International Journal of Aging and Human Development, 35*(2), 83–98.

Kennedy, G. F., & Kennedy, C. E. (1993). The stepfamily puzzle: Intergenerational influences. *Journal of Divorce and Remarriage, 19*(3–4), 40–68

Kennedy, J. F., & Keeney, V. T. (1988). The extended family revisited: Grandparents rearing grandchildren. *Child Psychiatry and Human Development, 19,* 26–35.

Kivett, V. R. (1991). The grandparent–grandchild connection. *Marriage and Family Review, 16,* 167–190.

Kivnik, H. Q. (1982). *The meaning of grandparenthood* Ann Arbor, MI: UMI Research Press: University Microfilms International.

Levinson, D. J. (1996). *The seasons of a woman's life*. New York: Knopf

Levinson, D. J., Darrow, C. N., Klein, E. B., Levinson, M. H., & McKee, B. (1978). *The seasons of a man's life*. New York: Knopf.

Longino, C. E., & Earle, J. R., (1996). Who are the grandparents at century's end? *Generations, Spring,* 13–16.

Marx, J., & Solomon, J. (1993). Healths and school adjustment of children raised by grand-parents. *Sociological Focus, 26*(1), 81–86.

McAdoo, H. P., & McWright, L. A. (1994). The roles of grandparents: The use of proverbs in value transmissions. Special issue: Aging families and use of proverbs for value enrich-ment. *Activities, Adaptation, and Aging, 19*(2), 27–38.

Menninger Letter (1995). January issue.

Minkler, M., Driver, D., Roe, K. M., & Bedeian, K. (1993). Community interventions to sup-port grandparent caregivers. *Gerontologist, 33*(6), 807–811.

Minkler, M., & Roe, K. M. (1996). Grandparents as surrogate parents. *Generations, Spring,* 34–38.

Minkler, M., Roe, K. M., & Price, M. (1992). The physical and emotional health of grand-mothers raising grandchildren in the crack cocaine epidemic. *The Gerontologist, 32*(6), 752–76.

Morrow-Kondos, D., Weber, J. A., Cooper, K., & Hesser, J. L. (1997). Becoming parents again: Grandparents raising grandchildren. *Journal of Gerontological Social Work, 28*(1–2), 35–46.

Mullen, F. (1996, Spring). Public benefits: Grandparents, grandchildren, and welfare reform. *Generations,* 61–64.

Nussbaum, J. F., & Bettini, L. M. (1994). Shared stories of the grandparent–grandchild rela-tionship. Special issue: *Intergenerational Communication, 39*(1), 67–80.

O'Reilly, E., & Morrison, M. L. (1992). Grandparent-headed families: New therapeutic challenges. *Child Psychiatry and Human Development, 23*(3), 147–160.

Oyserman, D., Radin, N., & Benn, R. (1993). Dynamics in a three-generational family: Teens, grandparents, and babies. *Developmental Psychology, 29*(3), 564–572.

Pinson-Millburn, N. M., Fabian, E. S., Schlossberg, N. K., & Pyle, M. (1996). Grandparents raising grandchildren. *Journal of Counseling and Development, 74*(6), 549–554.

Pruchno, R. A., & Johnson, K. W., (1996, Spring). Research on grandparenting: Review of current studies and future needs. *Generations,* 65–70.

Reinke, B. J., Holmes, D. S., & Harris, R. L. (1985). The timing of psychosocial changes in women's lives. *Journal of Personality and Social Psychology, 48,* 1353–1364.

Report by the Select Committee on Children, Youth, and Families. (1990). *No place to call home: Discarded children in America.* U.S. House, 101st Congress, 2nd session, January, 12, 1990, Washington, DC, 227.

Rollins, B. C. & Cannon, K. L., (1974). Marital satisfaction over the family life cycle: A re-evaluation. *Journal of marriage and the family, 36*(2), 271–282.

Rollins, B. C. & Feldman, H. (1978). Marital satisfaction over the family life cycle. *Journal of marriage and the family, 32*(1), 20–28.

Roberto, L. A., & Stroes, J. (1992). Grandchildren and grandparents: Roles, influences, and relationships. *International Journal of Aging and Human Development, 34*(3), 227–238.

Roe, K. M., Minkler, M., & Barnwell, R. S. (1994). The assumption of care giving: Grand-mothers raising the children lot the crack cocaine epidemic. *Qualitative Health Research,* 4(3), 281–303.

Roe, K. M., Minkler, M., Saunders, F., & Thomson, G. E. (1996). Health of grandmothers raising children of the crack cocaine epidemic. *Medical Care, 34*(11), 1072–1084.

Saluter, A. (1992). *Marital status and living arrangements,* Washington DC: U.S. Department of Commerce, Bureau of the Census.

Schaie, K. W. (1991). Developmental designs revisited. In S. H. Cohen & H. W. Reese (Eds.), *Lifespan Developmental Psychology: Methodological innovations.* Hillsdale, NJ: Lawrence Erlbaum Associates.

Schaie, K. W. (1993). The Seattle longitudinal studies of adult intelligence. *Current Directions in Psychological Science, 2,* 171–173.

Sheehy, G. (1995) *New passages: Mapping your life across time.* New York: Random House.

Shore, R. J., & Hayslip, B., Jr. (1994). Custodial grandparenting: Implications for children's development. In A. W. Gottfried & A. E. Gottfried (Eds.), *Redefining Families: Implications for Children's Development.* New York: Plenum Press.

Smetana, J. G., Yau, J., Restrepo, A., & Braeges, J. L. (1991). Adolescent–parent conflict in married and divorced families. *Developmental Psychology, 27*(6), 93–104.

Smith, R. L., Small, F. L., & Placek, J. T. (1990). Conjunctive moderator variables in vulnerability and resiliency research. *Journal of Personality and Social Psychology, 58,* 360–370.

Spanier, G. B. (1976). Measuring dyadic adjustment: New scales for assessing the duality of marriage dyads. *Journal of marriage and the family, 17*(4), 339–341.

Sternberg, R. J. (1985). *Beyond IQ: A triarchic theory of human intelligence.* New York: Cambridge University Press.

Sternberg, R. J. (1997). The concept of intelligence and its role in lifelong learning and success. *American Psychologist, 52,* 1030–1037.

U.S. Bureau of the Census. (1990). *Statistical Abstract of the United States: The 115th edition,* Washington, DC, The Bureau, 377.

Wilson, K. B., & DeShane, M. R. (1982). The legal rights of grandparents: Preliminary discussion. *The Gerontologist, 22,* 67–71.

Wink, P., & Helson, R. (1993). Personality changes in women and their partners. *Journal of Personality and Social Psychology, 65,* 597–606.

11

Degree of Embeddedness of Ecological Systems as a Measure of Ease of Adaptation to the Environment

Robert J. Sternberg
Yale University

Elena L. Grigorenko
Yale University
Moscow State University

Various cultural and subcultural groups adapt differentially to a given cultural environment. The differences have been shown in many respects, both in this volume and in its companion volume (Sternberg & Grigorenko, 2001). The differences in adaptation can be measured in many ways: health, nutrition, school grades, cognitive test scores, achievement test scores, income, wealth, and so forth. In this volume and elsewhere, behavioral researchers have been trying to figure out the cause of the groups' differential adaptation.

THE EMBEDDEDNESS OF THE LEVELS
OF THE ECOLOGICAL THEORY

One route to understanding this differential adaptation is through Bronfenbrenner's (1986, 1995; also see Carter, this volume) ecological systems theory of the relations among the multiple levels that occur in the environment. According to this theory, there exists a series of nested systems in which everybody operates:

1. the *microsystem*, which consists of the immediate contexts that an individual experiences
2. the *mesosystem*, which consists of the interconnections (links) among the microsystems
3. the *exosystem*, which consists of settings that are not experienced directly but that may nevertheless affect an individual's development (e.g., the parental workplace)
4. the *macrosystem*, which consists of the cultural context in which the other systems are embedded
5. the *chronosystem*, which consists of the patterns of events and transitions between events that occur over the lifespan of an individual

This theory has had a tremendous impact on the study of human development, both in its original form, as described here, and in its more recently described bioecological form (Bronfenbrenner, 1995; Bronfenbrenner & Ceci, 1994; Bronfenbrenner & Morris, 1998). The theory generated a number of hypotheses about the nature of environmental action, among which is the hypothesis of the primary salience of proximal processes of the microsystem (Bronfenbrenner & Ceci, 1994; Greenberger & Chen, 1996; Taylor, 1996) and the hypothesis of the impact of higher order environmental systems on caregiver beliefs and practices (Brody, Stoneman, & Flor, 1996; Cotterell, 1986; Larson, Richards, Moneta, Holmbeck, & Duckett, 1996; Wachs, 1992). The usefulness of the theory extends to helping us understand the role of the family in development because the influence of the family so much permeates an individual's life that, in one way or another, it affects all these systemic levels.

We believe that the theory is in need of modification and extension in one crucial respect, and that this aspect helps explain why it is that some groups and even individuals find adaptation to a given sociocultural environment far easier than other groups and individuals. The modification and extension is with respect to an assumption we believe to be only partially correct, namely, that the different levels in the system are nested or embedded within each other.

An alternative perspective is that the systems are, on rare occasions, fully embedded, but much more often, only partially embedded so that they correspond to each other only to certain degrees. The more embedded the systems, the easier the individual is likely to find adaptation to the environment. But the less embedded the systems, the more difficult adaptation is likely to be.

ETHNOGRAPHIC CHALLENGES TO THE NOTION OF EMBEDDEDNESS

An extreme example of what we are discussing can be found in the case of street children. Consider, for example, the case of street children in Caracas, as discussed by Márquez (1999). "Young children on the streets of Caracas are compelled to develop a complex body of knowledge very different from that of privileged young people in the city. They have to learn how to get food, where to find shelter, how to avoid falling into the hands of the authorities, and how to decide with whom to share their profits" (p. 3).

These children do not fit into the existing notions of how families or society should operate. Aptekar (1988a, 1988b, 1989, 1991), who worked with Colombian street children, argued that such children represent a threat to the patriarchal family and social order. Although many institutions may express sympathy toward these children, the children are nevertheless viewed as a threat, which they are, because although they engage in some legal activities such as shoe shining, rag collecting, and food selling (Muñoz & Palacios, 1980), they also engage in illegal activities such as thievery, drug consumption and sales, and prostitution (Márquez, 1999), as well as more serious forms of crime. Although it might seem as though such children are simply rebellious, in fact, many are not. The society and the police, in particular, distinguish between middle-class children in rebellion and the more commonplace children of the lowest social classes whose parents or stepparents have encouraged the children to go out onto the streets, either so that the family would no longer be responsible for them or so that they would provide income from the streets to the family (Márquez, 1999). The microsystem and the macrosystem in which these children live, far from being embedded, are at odds with each other. The macrosystem rejects the microsystem yet at the same time tolerates it, because the society does not quite know what to do with the street children. In the case of Latin America, there are roughly 40 million of them (Tacon, 1981, 1983).

These kinds of findings are not limited to developing countries. Similar findings emerged from the work of Heath (1983). Heath studied children in three settings in North Carolina: Gateway, a largely middle-class White community; Roadville, a largely lower socioeconomic status (SES) White community; and Trackton, a largely lower-class SES Black community. Heath found that the microsystem of the home community in Gateway was an excellent match to the microsystem of the school. In other words, the mesosystem that linked the two provided a good fit. But the microsystem of the home community in Trackton was a poor match to the microsystem of the school. In other words, the mesosystem that linked the two provided a poor fit. In terms of the larger society, or macrosystem, the Gateway environment was well embedded: It fit what the society expected of a microsystem. The macrosystem of the Trackton environment, however, was not well embedded at all: It did not fit society's expectations.

There were many examples of the relatively greater fit of the Gateway than of the Trackton microsystems but perhaps the best was in the relative uses of verbal versus nonverbal communication. Almost from the day the children were born, the Trackton environment emphasized the importance of nonverbal communication, and much of the children's socialization taught them the subtleties of nonverbal communication. Nonverbal communication included skills such as decoding the meaning of posture, tone of voice, gestures, and other aspects of body language. The Gateway environment, in contrast, emphasized much more verbal rather than nonverbal communication. Of course, schools emphasized much more verbal than nonverbal communication, so the children from Gateway were better prepared to adapt to the school environment. The same difference applied to street children. Interpreting nonverbal cues can be, for this group of children, a matter of life or death: If they cannot distinguish a genuinely threatening gesture from a fake-out, it can cost them their life.

Whether children live in homes or on the streets, if their environments are sufficiently nonmainstream, their chances of crossing over into the mainstream may be practically nil. For example, Venezuelan children who grow up in ranchos (illegally constructed squatter-type very low-cost housing that are built on unoccupied land) are rarely able to cross over into the mainstream of society. In India, children who grow up in the slums are so disadvantaged in terms of caste, health, nutrition, and education that their chances of crossing over also are close to nil (Sternberg & Grigorenko, 1999). In other words, the microsystems in which they live and the mesosystems that connect them practically guarantee that they will be excluded from the mainstream macrosystem. In effect, their lifelong chronosystem is determined by their early environment without hope of crossing over. There are few or no "Horatio Algers" in these kinds of environments.

EXPERIMENTAL CHALLENGES TO THE NOTION OF EMBEDDEDNESS

Studies With Children

Experimental studies reveal that the skills these children develop may be useful in their own lives but are not credited by the institutions that give "credit" to young children, namely, schools. Carraher, Carraher, and Schliemann (1985) studied Brazilian children who, for economic reasons, often worked as street vendors (see also Nuñes, 1994; Nuñes, Schliemann, & Carraher, 1993). Most of these children had little formal schooling. Carraher et al. compared the performance of these children on mathematical problems that were embedded in a real-life situation (i.e., vending) to problems presented in an academic context (e.g., $2 + 4 = ?$). The children correctly solved significantly more questions that related to vending than math problems that were academic in nature. When the academic problems were presented as word problems (e.g., If an orange costs 76 cruzeiros and a passion fruit cost 50, how much do the two cost together?), the rate of correct responses was substantially better, but still not as high as when the problems were presented in the context of vending. In other words, the children were able to do the mathematics they needed to do on the street, but not the mathematics they needed to do well in school, even when the operations were essentially the same.

How would middle-class children do on the streets? Roazzi (1987) compared street-vendor children to middle-class school children. He compared the performance of children on a class-inclusion task. To assess the performance of the street-vendor children, the researcher posed as a customer and asked questions about the items to find out if the children understood the relationship among classes and subclasses of food (e.g., mint and strawberry chewing gum as part of the class "chewing gum"). At a later time the same children were given a formal test with the same logical structure, but that was irrelevant to their street-vending jobs. The middle-class children were given the same two tests. Street-vendor children performed significantly better on the class-inclusion task in the natural than in the formal context, whereas middle-class children were more successful on the formal version of the task.

Lack of transfer is common when it comes to cognitive skills (see Gick & Holyoak, 1983). For example, Perret-Clermont (1980) found that many school children had no problem solving paper-and-pencil arithmetic questions, but could not solve the same type of problem in a different context (e.g., counting bunches of flowers). That is, school children may fail to transfer the academic knowledge to everyday problems.

Sometimes, there even appears to be negative transfer. In a rural village in Kenya, Sternberg et al. (in press) found that children who learned how to apply natural herbal medicines to their various ailments were viewed as adaptive and intelligent; in fact, both adult and children in this community stressed, in their interviews, the value of such knowledge. But this knowledge of natural herbal medicines was negatively correlated both with school achievement and with scores on conventional tests of crystallized abilities, which suggested that those who display higher levels of intelligence relevant to a particular contextualized situation actually may do worse on standardized measures of intelligence.

Related findings of a separation between the academic and the practical can be found across time as well as across cultural groups. Cohen (1994) studied the mathematically oriented activity of 3- and 4-year olds and found that, when mathematical operations were embedded in the broader context of a "play-store" setting, children were able to solve problems that exceeded an age-appropriate level of difficulty. In addition, the children satisfied the demands of the task in using a variety of solution strategies.

Studies With Adults

People often develop the skills that matter for their microsystem, whether or not these skills translate into behaviors valued by the society. Scribner (1984, 1986), for example, studied the strategies used by milk processing plant workers, who would be considered relatively lower in SES, to fill orders. Workers who assemble orders for cases of various quantities (e.g., gallons, quarts, or pints) and products (e.g., whole milk, two percent milk, or buttermilk) are called assemblers. Rather than employing typical mathematical algorithms learned in the classroom, Scribner found that experienced assemblers used complex strategies for combining partially filled cases in a manner that minimized the number of moves required to complete an order. Although the assemblers were the least educated workers in the plant, they were able to calculate in their heads quantities expressed in different base number systems, and they routinely outperformed the more highly educated white-collar workers who substituted when assemblers were absent. Scribner found that the order-filling performance of the assemblers was unrelated to measures of school performance, which included intelligence test scores, arithmetic test scores, and grades. Thus, in terms of the credentials that lead to certificated "success" in the macrosystem, the workers would look inept. In terms of the requirements of their jobs, they are quite skilled.

Another series of studies of everyday mathematics involved women shoppers in California grocery stores who sought to buy at the cheapest cost when the same products were available in different-sized containers (Lave, Murtaugh, & de la Roche, 1984; Murtaugh, 1985. These studies were performed before cost per unit quantity information was routinely posted.). For example, oatmeal may come in two sizes, 10 ounces for 98 cents or 24 ounces for $2.29. One might adopt the strategy of always buying the largest size and assume that the larger size is always the most economical. However, the researchers (and savvy shoppers) learned that the larger size did not represent the least cost per unit quantity for about one third of the items purchased. The findings of these studies were that effective shoppers used mental shortcuts to calculate an easily obtained answer, accurate enough to determine which size to buy. A common strategy, for example, was mentally to change the size and price of an item to make it more comparable with the other size available. For example, one might mentally double the smaller size, thereby comparing 20 ounces at $1.96 versus 24 ounces at $2.29. The difference of 4 ounces for about 35 cents, or about 9 cents per ounce, seems to favor the 24-ounce size, given that the smaller size of 10 ounces for 98 cents is about 10 cents per ounce. These mathematical shortcuts yield approximations that are as useful as the actual values of 9.80 and 9.33 cents per ounce for the smaller and larger sizes, respectively, and are much more easily computed in the absence of a calculator. When the shoppers were given a mental-arithmetic test, no relation was found between test performance and accuracy in picking the best values.

Ceci and colleagues (Ceci & Liker, 1986, 1988; also see Ceci & Ruiz, 1991) studied expert racetrack handicappers who were at the top of their microsystem but who were marginalized by society. Ceci and Liker (1986) found that expert handicappers used a highly complex algorithm for predicting post time odds that involved interactions among seven kinds of information. By applying the complex algorithm, handicappers adjusted times posted for each quarter mile on a previous outing by factors such as whether the horse attempted to pass other horses, and if so, the speed of the other horses passed and where the attempted passes took place. By adjusting posted times for these factors, a better measure of a horse's speed is obtained. It could be argued that the use of complex interactions to predict a horse's speed would require considerable cognitive ability (at least as it is traditionally measured). However, Ceci and Liker reported that the successful use of these interactions by handicappers was unrelated to their IQ.

A subsequent study attempted to relate performance at the racetrack to making stock market predictions in which the same algorithm was involved. Ceci and Ruiz (1993) asked racetrack handicappers to solve a stock market-prediction task that was structured similarly to the racetrack problem. After 611 trials on the stock market task, the handicappers performed no better than chance, and there was no difference in performance as a function of IQ. Ceci and Roazzi (1994) attributed this lack of transfer to the low correlation between performance on problems and their isomorphs. *Problem isomorphs* refer to two or more problems that involve the same cognitive processes but that use different terminology or take place in different contexts.

Measures of conventional abilities are variable predictors of work performance, and not only at the race track. Although there is no doubt that they provide good prediction in many situations (Schmidt & Hunter, 1993, 1998), their prediction may be positive or negative. Fiedler (1995), for example, found that IQ was positively correlated with leadership success under conditions of low stress, but that it was negatively correlated with success under conditions of high stress. Furthermore, he found that the relationship between experience and leadership performance was greater under conditions of high stress than of low stress. As Fiedler (1995) also pointed out, "it is very difficult to believe that intellectual abilities fail to contribute to such critical leadership functions as decision-making and coordinating and organizing work processes, or that leaders cannot learn from past events" (p. 6).

Additional research has shown that the use of complex reasoning strategies does not necessarily correlate with IQ. Dörner and colleagues (Dörner & Kreuzig, 1983; Dörner, Kreuzig, Reither, & Staudel, 1983) studied individuals who were asked to play the role of city managers for the computer-simulated city of Lohhausen. A variety of problems were presented to these individuals, such as how best to raise revenue to build roads. The simulation involved more than 1,000 variables. Performance was quantified in terms of a hierarchy of strategies, ranging from the simplest (trial and error) to the most complex (hypothesis testing with multiple feedback loops). No relation was found between IQ and complexity of strategies used. A second problem was created to cross-validate these results. This problem, called the Sahara problem, required participants to determine the number of camels that could be kept alive by a small oasis. Once again, no relation was found between IQ and complexity of strategies employed.

Sternberg and his colleagues (Sternberg et al., 2000; Sternberg & Wagner, 1993; Sternberg, Wagner, & Okagaki, 1993; Sternberg, Wagner, Williams, & Horvath, 1995; Wagner, 1987; Wagner & Sternberg, 1985) completed related work using a similar approach. They developed measures of tacit knowledge, or what one needs to know to succeed in a given environment that one is not explicitly taught and that usually is not even verbalized. For street children, such knowledge includes knowing whom to trust and whom not to, how to evade the police, how to forage for food, and so forth. For managers, such knowledge would include how to supervise difficult employees, how to get along with a boss with whom one is philosophically incompatible, and so forth. The tests consist of scenarios depicting real-world problem situations that the test-taker must resolve. For example, a manager might face a situation of dealing with an unruly employee.

Several major findings have consistently emerged from this work. First, experience on the job—passage through the chronosystem—affects performance on these tests. However, it turns out that what seems to matter most is not experience, per se, but rather, how well one utilizes the experience one has. Some people, given the opportunity to learn from experience, learn a lot. Others learn little. Second, scores on tacit-knowledge tests are not predicted by scores on conventional measures of intelligence. In other words, the kinds of measures used to determine who will be given opportunities in U.S. society are not good predictive of how well people will avail themselves of these opportunities. But third, scores on tacit-knowledge tests predict job performance as well as, and often better than, conventional measures of analytical abilities.

Some work has examined deductive reasoning whereby the same problem is presented in more abstract or more concrete contexts. For example, different kinds of cognitive performances vary across contexts. In one series of studies by Wason, Johnson-Laird, and colleagues (Wason, 1966; Wason & Johnson-Laird, 1972; Johnson-Laird, Legrenzi, & Legrenzi, 1972), the ability of individuals to solve conditional reasoning tasks varied across contexts. The task used involved asking participants to decide whether or not a particular rule is true (e.g., "If a card has a vowel on one side, then it has an even number on the other side"). According to formal logic, the appropriate response is to search for examples that could falsify the rule (e.g., in the series E, M, 2, and 5, a correct response would be to check E and 5). But some participants seek to verify the rule. Johnson-Laird and colleagues found that the use of verification or falsification strategies to solve to conditional reasoning tasks varied depending on the context. For example, Johnson-Laird et al. presented the task in the context of mail sorting in which the rule was "If a letter is sealed, then it has a 50-lire stamp on it." They found that even though participants were instructed to verify the rule, they selected cards that would falsify the rule. The participants' choice of strategy was attributed to their implicit understanding that overpayment is less of a concern to postal workers than underpayment. Therefore, practical concerns may influence the type of strategy (falsify or verify) that is considered appropriate. Abstract reasoning tasks do not provide such a context.

These findings again suggest that the people who grow up with the greatest mesh between their microsystem and the societal macrosystem are not necessarily those who ultimately will have the most to contribute to the macrosystem. Yet they are given the opportunity to do so, regardless.

IMPLICATIONS

The irony in the work cited so far is transparent. Children who may have the greatest potential to succeed in everyday real-world environments may not be recognized as "smart," and therefore as capable of attaining the credentials that will enable them to achieve this success. Children who have lesser potential may nevertheless do well on the kinds of academic tasks that lead them to attain the credentials they need to be labeled as successful in the society.

This is precisely the position that has been taken by Sternberg (1988, 1997, 1999; Sternberg et al., 2000). He argued that children who excel in creative and practical abilities, the kinds of abilities often most useful in life, are not valued by schools because these abilities play a small role in success in assessments of abilities or achievement. Yet creative and especially practical abilities can be at least as predictive of success in life as are analytical abilities, and arguably, more so.

One reason is that the kinds of problems people encounter in everyday life are different in many respects from the kinds of problems people encounter in school. Everyone encounters problems in which solutions are neither readily available nor readily derivable from acquired knowledge. This type of problem solving, frequently experienced in daily life, is referred to as *practical problem solving*. Such problems can be experienced at the work place, or in school, the household, stores, movie theaters, or anywhere. There is no consensus on how to define practical problems encountered in life, but building on a distinction made by Neisser (1976), Sternberg and his colleagues (Sternberg, 1985, 1997; Wagner & Sternberg, 1985) classified problems as academic or practical in nature. Academic problems tend to be (a) formulated by others, (b) well-defined, (c) complete in the information they provide, (d) characterized by having only one correct answer, (e) characterized by having only one method of obtaining the correct answer, (f) disembedded from ordinary experience, and (g) of little or no intrinsic interest.

Practical problems, in contrast to academic problems, tend to be (a) unformulated or in need of reformulation, (b) of personal interest, (c) lacking in information necessary for solution, (d) related to everyday experience, (e) poorly defined, (f) characterized by multiple "correct" solutions, each with liabilities as well as assets, and (g) characterized by multiple methods for picking a problem solution. Given the differences in the nature of academic and practical problems, it is no surprise that people who are adept at solving one kind of problem may not be adept at solving problems of the other kind.

This lack of concordance between who gets opportunities and who is best able to avail him or herself of such opportunities is in no way limited to societies that use tests to determine for whom the doors to opportunity will open and for whom they will close. On the contrary, the tests were created in order better to determine for whom the doors should open. The problem is that the tests measure an incomplete range of skills. Societies use a variety of means to determine for whom the doors should open in addition to test scores—height, interpersonal attractiveness, caste, religion, ethnic group, and so forth—and presumably many and indeed most of these means are considerably worse than the tests currently being used in the United States. At the same time, indications are that the United States could do better. When children are tested for the range not only of analytical, but also of creative and practical abilities, and then are taught in a way that values the pattern of abilities they have, their school achievement increases (Sternberg, Ferrari, Clinkenbeard, & Grigorenko, 1996; Sternberg, Grigorenko, Ferrari, & Clinkenbeard, 1999). If children are simply taught in all three ways, regardless of abilities pattern, their achievement also increases, even if achievement is measured only through straightforward memory assessments (Sternberg, Torff, & Grigorenko, 1998). How well children do in school therefore may depend on the kind of context for learning that the school provides.

Academic and practical abilities may have different developmental trajectories (see Berg & Klaczynski, 1996, for a review). Denney and Palmer (1981) were one of the first research teams to demonstrate this discrepancy. They compared the performance of adults (ages 20 through 79) on traditional analytical reasoning problems (e.g., a "20 questions" task) and a problem-solving task that involved real-life situations (e.g., "If you were traveling by car and got stranded out on an interstate highway during a blizzard, what would you do?"). One of the many interesting results obtained in this study was a difference in the shape of the developmental function for performance on the two types of problems. Performance on the traditional problem-solving task or cognitive measure declined almost linearly from age 20, onward. Performance on the practical problem-solving task increased to a peak in the 40- and 50-year-old groups and declined thereafter. Expanding on this line of research, Smith and colleagues (Smith, Staudinger, & Baltes, 1994) compared responses to life-planning dilemmas in a group of younger (mean age 32) and older (mean age 70) adults. Unlike the results of studies of aging and academic abilities, which demonstrated the superior performance of younger adults over the elderly, in this study, young and older adults did not differ. In addition, each age-cohort group received the highest ratings when responding to a dilemma matched to their own life phase.

There is virtually unanimous agreement on the centrality of context for understanding practical problem solving. This view, which holds that practical problem solving cannot be separated from the context in which it unfolds, is referred to as the *contextual perspective* (e.g., Dixon, 1994; Wertsch & Kanner, 1994). In general, the metaphor used to describe the contextual approach is that of trying to follow forever changing events (i.e., the chronosystem of life is represented as being a series of changing events, activities, and contexts). When applied to studies of practical problem solving, this perspective assumes that (a) the demands posed by these contexts vary across development, (b) strategies accomplishing adaptation differ across contexts, (c) these strategies also differ across individuals, and, (d) the effectiveness of everyday problem solving is determined by the interaction of individual and context (Berg & Calderone, 1994). Several studies have found that the context in which the problem occurs (e.g., family, work, or school) impacts everyday problem solving in all its components (content, goal, and strategy).

Consider the following examples. Ceci and Bronfenbrenner (1985; Ceci, 1990) employed a dual context paradigm and conducted a series of studies that concerned the impact of physical and social contexts on cognition. The dual context paradigm proposes that children be made to perform the same task in two or more contexts. The assumption here is that some settings elicit more effective forms of cognition than others by stimulating or activating different strategies. The Ceci–Bronfenbrenner view is that a task perceived in a modified form might recruit a set of strategies acquired previously but not elicited by the original, unmodified task. (For example, a video game task, which is a modification of a simple task that requires a participant to follow the movements of dots, might recruit strategies that the dot task alone would not.)

One of the most interesting developments in studies on context and practical problem solving concerns the effect of compensation: the phenomenon in which gains in (mostly) practical intelligence balance out age-related decrements in others. Researchers argue that compensation—considered in terms of the dynamic relationship between the individual's changing cognitive skills and expectations of performance, on the one hand, and shifting contextual demands, on the other hand—should be viewed as central to cognitive aging (e.g., Dixon, 1994). One example of practical intelligence compensating for declines in g-based intellectual performance is older adults' effective use of external aids. One common source of external cognitive aid is other people. For example, Dixon and his colleagues (Dixon, 1994) explored the extent to which older and younger adults use same-age collaborators to solve memory problems and found that older adults used previously unknown collaborators to boost their performance levels to a much greater extent than younger adults.

STUDIES OF IMPLICIT THEORIES AND THEIR IMPLICATIONS FOR EMBEDDEDNESS

Research on implicit theories of intelligence further suggests that the measures society uses to apportion opportunities may not correspond well to what people mean by intelligence or adaptive behavior. In implicit theorizing about intelligence, one asks people what they believe intelligence to be, in order to discover an "ordinary-language" definition. This approach was suggested by Neisser (1979), and was implemented by Sternberg, Conway, Ketron, and Bernstein (1981). They asked samples of laypeople in a supermarket, a library, and a train station, as well as samples of academic researchers who study intelligence, to provide and rate the importance and frequency of characteristics of intelligent individuals. Factor analyses of the frequency ratings showed three major aspects of people's conceptions of intelligence: the ability to solve practical problems (e.g., balancing a checkbook), verbal ability (e.g., writing and speaking well), and social competence (e.g., getting along with other people).

There are limitations, however, with this ordinary-language view of intelligence. One is with respect to age. Siegler and Richards (1982) asked adult subjects to characterize intelligence as it applies to people of different ages. They found that adults tended to view intelligence as increasingly less perceptual–motor and as increasingly more cognitive with advanced age. Thus, coordination of hand and eye was seen as more important to the intelligence of an infant, whereas reason ability was more important to the intelligence of an adult. When children are asked to characterize intelligence, their answers differ from those of adults. Yussen and Kane (1985) asked children at roughly 6 to 7, 8 to 9, and 11 to 12 years of age what their conceptions of intelligence were. They found that older children's conceptions of intelligence included more aspects than younger children's and that older children were less likely than younger children to think that certain kinds of overt behavior signal intelligence.

Another limitation of implicit theories of intelligence is with respect to culture. Different cultures perceive intelligence in different ways, and a view held in one culture may be diametrically opposed to that held in another culture. Western notions of intelligence, for example, differ in many ways from those of other cultures. In contrast to Sternberg et al.'s (1981) findings, Yang and Sternberg (1997) found that Taiwanese Chinese conceptions of intelligence included five factors: (a) a general cognitive factor, (b) interpersonal intelligence, (c) intrapersonal intelligence, (d) intellectual self-assertion, and (e) intellectual self-effacement. Chen (1994) found three factors that underlie Chinese concepts of intelligence: nonverbal reasoning ability, verbal reasoning ability, and rote memory. Chen's methodology was different from and perhaps less sensitive than Yang and Sternberg's, which may account for the difference in results. In addition, Gill and Keats (1980) noted differences between Australian University students, who viewed academic skills and the ability to adapt to new events as intelligence, and Malay students, who considered practical skills, speed, and creativity to be indicators of intelligence.

Studies conducted in Africa also provide a useful contrast to Western societies. Serpell (1982) found that Chewa adults in Zambia emphasize social responsibility, cooperativeness, and obedience. Kenyan parents view responsible participation in family and social life as important aspects of intelligence (Super & Harkness, 1982). In Zimbabwe, the word for intelligence, *ngware*, means to be prudent and cautious (Dasen, 1984).

Grigorenko et al. (in press) examined the organization of conceptions of intelligence among the Luo people in rural Kenya. The Luo conception of intelligence is primarily expressed in the DhoLuo vocabulary by four concepts (*rieko, luoro, paro,* and *winjo*), which appear to form two latent structures, *social-emotional competence* and *cognitive competence*. Indicators of only one of these concepts (*rieko*) and only one latent structure (*cognitive competence*) correlate with scores on conventional Western cognitive-ability tests and with school achievement in English and mathematics. Thus, the emphasis on social aspects of intelligence seems to be a part of both Asian and African cultures, much more so than is emphasized by the conventional Western view, although there is variability in conceptions of intelligence within it.

Of particular relevance here is a study by Okagaki and Sternberg (1993). These investigators asked parents of three different ethnic groups—Anglos, Asians, and Latinos—what they meant when they talked about an "intelligent child." The investigators also asked teachers in the children's schools what they meant by the same term. It became clear that the teachers, as well as the Anglo and Asian parents, largely emphasized cognitive abilities. The Latino parents, however, largely emphasized social abilities. More importantly, however, the closer the parents' conception of intelligence to the teachers' conception of intelligence, the better children of a given group did in school, on average. In other words, teachers value children whose parents socialize them in ways that match the teachers' conception of what it means to be intelligent, much the same situation that would be found by comparing children in Trackton with those in Gateway in the work of Heath (1983).

CONCLUSION

The conclusion we draw from these various lines of research is that Bronfenbrenner's useful ecological theory may best be seen in a somewhat different perspective from that in which it has been presented. Bronfenbrenner conceived of the various systems in which people live as being nested or embedded. We believe that complete embeddedness is probably rare, and even that high levels of embeddedness may be relatively rare. Children grow up in a variety of circumstances, and the more children live at the margins of society or the more they grow up in circumstances that depart from the mainstream, the less embedded their various systems are likely to be. At the extremes, they live in microsystems that are largely disembedded from the macrosystems of their society, and that are likely to end them up as delinquent or even incarcerated.

The children viewed as delinquent may not have committed any crime. Police distinguish between different social groups of children who perform the same acts. Children of the middle class may be ignored or let off with a warning, whereas those of the street or of the lower class or even of the wrong race or ethnic group may find themselves in serious legal jeopardy. The criminal justice system may not view itself as discriminating against the marginalized children, per se. Rather it may "correctly" view them as a greater threat. The greater threat is not always, however, a legal one. It may be, rather, to the values the society holds dear. The middle-class children on the street have their middle-class home and future to which they can return; the marginalized children do not. To the people on the streets, conventional homes are an exosystem in which they are not taking part and probably never will. To the people who make the rules, these conventional homes are part of the daily microsystem in which they live.

The problem is not one that applies only to children, of course. Cities periodically crack down on their homeless, as New York City did in late 1999. The Mayor argued that those who did not go to shelters should be jailed. Until societies learn how to better deal with individuals whose microsystems and mesosystems are not well embedded in their macrosystems, problems of marginalization, unfairness, and loss of talent to society will inevitably continue.

ACKNOWLEDGMENTS

Preparation of this chapter was supported by Grant REC-9979843 from the National Science Foundation and by a grant under the Javits Act Program (Grant No. R206R950001) as administered by the Office of Educational Research and Improvement, U.S. Department of Education. Grantees undertaking such projects are encouraged to express freely their professional judgment. This article, therefore, does not necessarily represent the position or policies of the National Science Foundation, Office of Educational Research and Improvement or the U.S. Department of Education, and no official endorsement should be inferred.

REFERENCES

Aptekar, L. (1988a). Colombian street children: Their mental health and how they can be served. *International Journal of Mental Health, 88*, 81–104.

Aptekar, L. (1988b). Street children of Colombia. *Journal of Early Adolescence, 8*, 225–241.

Aptekar, L. (1989). Colombian street children: Gamines and chupagruesos. *Adolescence, 24*, 783–794.

Aptekar, L. (1991). Are Colombian street children neglected? The contributions of ethnographic and ethnohistorical approaches to the study of children. *Anthropology & Education Quarterly, 22*, 326–349.

Berg, C. A., & Calderone, K. (1994). The role of problem interpretations in understanding the development of everyday problem solving. In R. J. Sternberg & R. K. Wagner (Eds.), *Mind in context* (pp. 105–132). New York: Cambridge University Press.

Berg, C. A., & Klaczynski, P. (1996). Practical intelligence and problem solving: Searching for perspective. In F. Blanchard-Fields & T. M. Hess (Eds.), *Perspectives on Cognitive Change in Adulthood and Aging* (pp. 323–357). New York: McGraw-Hill.

Brody, G. H., Stoneman, Z., & Flor, D. (1996). Parental religiosity, family processes, and youth competence in rural, two-parent African-American families. *Developmental Psychology, 32*, 696–706.

Bronfenbrenner, U. (1986). Ecology of the family as a context for human development: Research perspectives. *Developmental Psychology, 22*, 723–742.

Bronfenbrenner, U. (1995). The bioecological model from a life course perspective: Reflections of a participant observer. In P. Moen & G. H. Elder Jr. (Eds), *Examining lives in context: Perspectives on the ecology of human development* (pp. 599–618). Washington, DC: American Psychological Association.

Bronfenbrenner, U., & Ceci, S. J. (1994). Nature–nurture reconceptualized in developmental perspective: A bioecological model. *Psychological Review, 101*, 568–586.

Bronfenbrenner, U., & Morris, P. A. (1998). The ecology of developmental processes. In R. M. Lerner (Ed.), *Handbook of Child Psychology* (5th ed., Vol. 1, pp. 993–1028): *Theory*. New York: Wiley.

Carraher, T. N., Carraher, D., & Schliemann, A. D. (1985). Mathematics in the streets and in schools. *British Journal of Developmental Psychology, 3*, 21–29.

Ceci, S. J. (1990). *On intelligence … more or less: A bio-ecological treatise on intellectual development*. Englewood Cliffs, NJ: Prentice-Hall.

Ceci, S.J., & Brofenbrenner, U. (1985). Don't forget to take the cupcakes out of the oven: Strategic time-monitoring, prospective memory and context. *Child Development, 56,* 175–190.

Ceci, S. J., & Liker, J. (1986). Academic and nonacademic intelligence: An experimental separation. In R. J. Sternberg & R. K. Wagner (Eds.), *Practical intelligence: Nature and origins of competence in the everyday world* (pp. 119–142). New York: Cambridge University Press.

Ceci, S. J., & Liker, J. (1988). Stalking the IQ-expertise relationship: When the critics go fishing. *Journal of Experimental Psychology: General, 117,* 96–100.

Ceci, S. J., & Roazzi, A. (1994). The effects of context on cognition: Postcards from Brazil. In R. J. Sternberg & R. K. Wagner (Eds.), *Mind in context: Interactionist perspectives on human intelligence* (pp. 74–101). New York: Cambridge University Press.

Ceci, S.J., & Ruiz, A. (1991). Cognitive complexity and generality: A case study. In R. Hoffman (Ed.), *The psychology of expertise.* New York: Springer-Verlag.

Ceci, S. J., & Ruiz, A. (1993). Transfer, abstractness, and intelligence. In D. K. Detterman & Sternberg, R. J. (Eds.), *Transfer on trial: Intelligence, cognition, and instruction.* (pp. 168–191). Norwood, NJ: Ablex.

Chen, M. J. (1994). Chinese and Australian concepts of intelligence. *Psychology and Developing Societies, 6,* 101–117.

Cohen, A. D. (1994). The language used to perform cognitive operations during full-immersion math tasks. *Language Testing, 11,* 171–195.

Cotterell, J. (1986). Work and community influences and the quality of child rearing. *Child Development, 57,* 363–347.

Dasen, P. (1984). The cross-cultural study of intelligence: Piaget and the Baoule. *International Journal of Psychology, 19,* 407–434.

Denney, N. W., & Palmer, A. M. (1981). Adult age differences on traditional and practical problem-solving measures. *Journal of Gerontology, 36,* 323–328.

Dixon, R. A. (1994). Contextual approaches to adult intellectual development. In R. J. Sternberg & C. A. Berg (Eds.), *Intellectual development* (pp. 350–380). New York: Cambridge University Press.

Dörner, D., & Kreuzig, H. (1983). Problem solving and intelligence. *Psychologische Rundschaus, 34,* 185–192.

Dörner, D., Kreuzig, H., Reither, F., & Staudel, T. (1983). *Lohhausen: Vom Umgang mit Unbestimmtheir und Komplexitat.* Bern, Switzerland: Huber.

Fiedler, F. E. (1995). Cognitive resources and leadership performance. *Applied psychology: An International Review, 44,* 5–28.

Gick, M. L., & Holyoak, K. J. (1983). Schema induction and analogical transfer. *Cognitive Psychology, 15,* 1–38.

Gill, R., & Keats, D. M. (1980). Elements of intellectual competence: Judgments by Australian and Malay university students. *Journal of Cross-Cultural Psychology, 11,* 233–243.

Greenberger, E., & Chen, C. (1996). Perceived family relationships and depressed mood in early and late adolescence: A comparison of European and Asian Americans. *Developmental Psychology, 32,* 707–716.

Grigorenko, E. L., Geissler, P. W., Prince, R., Okatcha, F., Nokes, C., Kenny, D. A., Bundy, D. A., & Sternberg, R. J. (in press). The organization of Luo conceptions of intelligence: A study of implicit theories in a Kenyan village. *International Journal of Behavioral Development.*

Heath, S. B. (1983). *Ways with words.* New York: Cambridge University Press.

Johnson-Laird, P.N., Legrenzi, R., & Legrenzi, M. S. (1972). Reasoning and a sense of reality. *British Journal of Psychology, 63,* 395–400.

Larson, R. W., Richards, M. H., Moneta, G., Hombeck, G., & Duckett, E. (1996). Changes in adolescents' daily interactions with their families from ages 10 to 18: Disengagement and transformation. *Developmental Psychology, 32,* 744–754.

Lave, J., Murtaugh, M., & de la Roche, O. (1984). The dialectic of arithmetic in grocery shopping. In B. Rogoff & J. Lave (Eds.), *Everyday cognition: Its development in social context* (pp. 67–94). Cambridge, MA: Harvard University Press.

Marquez, P. C. (1999). *The street is my home: Youth and violence in Caracas.* Stanford, CA: Stanford University Press.

Muñoz, C., & Palacios, M. (1980). *Street children: Testimonies.* Bogotá: Carols Valencia Editores.

Murtaugh, M. (1985). The practice of arithmetic by American grocery shoppers. *Anthropology and Education Quarterly, 16,* 186–192.

Neisser, U. (1976). Cognition and reality: *Principles and implications of cognitive psychology.* San Francisco: Freeman.

Neisser, U. (1979). The concept of intelligence. In R. J. Sternberg & D. K. Detterman (Eds.). *Human intelligence: Perspectives on its theory and measurement* (pp. 179–89). Norwood, NJ: Ablex.

Nuñes, T. (1994). Street intelligence. In R. J. Sternberg (Ed.), *Encyclopedia of human intelligence* (Vol. 2, pp. 1045–1049). New York: Macmillan.

Nuñes, T., Schliemann, A. D., & Carraher, D. W. (1993). *Street mathematics and school mathematics.* New York: Cambridge University Press.

Okagaki, L., & Sternberg, R. J. (1993). Parental beliefs and children's school performance. *Child Development, 64*(1), 36–56.

Perret-Clermont, A.N. (1980). *Social interaction and cognitive development in children.* London: Academic Press.

Roazzi, A. (1987). Effects of context on cognitive development. In P. Light & G. Butterworth (Eds.), *Psicologia e Educao: Investigacao e intervencao.* (pp. 91–115). Porto: Associacao dos Piscologos Portugueses.

Schmidt, F. L., & Hunter, J. E. (1993). Tacit knowledge, practical intelligence, general mental ability, and job knowledge, *Current Directions in Psychological Science, 1,* 8–9.

Schmidt, F. L., & Hunter, J. E. (1998). The validity and utility of selection methods in personnel psychology: Practical and theoretical implications of 85 years of research findings. *Psychological Bulletin, 124,* 262–274.

Scribner, S. (1984). Studying working intelligence. In B. Rogoff & J. Lave (Eds.), *Everyday cognition: Its development in social context* (pp. 9–40). Cambridge, MA: Harvard University Press.

Scribner, S. (1986). Thinking in action: Some characteristics of practical thought. In R. J. Sternberg & R. K. Wagner (Eds.), *Practical intelligence: Nature and origins of competence in the everyday world* (pp. 13–30). New York: Cambridge University Press.

Serpell, R. (1982). Measures of perception, skills, and intelligence. In W. W. Hartup (Ed.), *Review of child development research* (Vol. 6, pp. 392–440). Chicago: University of Chicago Press.

Siegler, R. S., & Richards, D. D. (1982). The development of intelligence. In R. J. Sternberg (Ed.), *Handbook of human intelligence* (pp. 897–971). New York: Cambridge University Press.

Smith, J., Staudinger, U. M., & Baltes, P. B. (1994). Occupational settings facilitating wisdom-related knowledge: The sample case of clinical psychologists. *Journal of Consulting and Clinical Psychology, 66,* 989–999.

Sternberg, R. J. (1985). *Beyond IQ: A triarchic theory of human intelligence.* New York: Cambridge University Press.

Sternberg, R.J. (1988). *The triarchic mind: A theory of human intelligence.* New York: Viking.

Sternberg, R. J. (1997). *Successful intelligence.* New York: Plume.

Sternberg, R. J. (1999). The theory of successful intelligence. *Review of General Psychology, 3,* 292–316.

Sternberg, R. J., Conway, B. E., Ketron, J. L., & Bernstein, M. (1981). People's conceptions of intelligence. *Journal of Personality and Social Psychology, 41,* 37–55.

Sternberg, R. J., Ferrari, M., Clinkenbeard, P. R., & Grigorenko, E. L. (1996). Identification, instruction, and assessment of gifted children: A construct validation of a triarchic model. *Gifted Child Quarterly, 40,* 129–137.

Sternberg, R. J., Forsythe, G. B., Hedlund, J., Horvath, J., Snook, S., Williams, W. M., Wagner, R. K., & Grigorenko, E. L. (2000). *Practical intelligence.* New York: Cambridge University Press.

Sternberg, R. J., & Grigorenko, E. L. (1999). A smelly 113° in the shade, or, why we do field research. *APS Observer, 12,* 1, 10–11, & 20–21.

Sternberg, R. J., & Grigorenko, E. L. (Eds.). (2001). *Environmental effects on intellectual functioning.* Mahwah, NJ: Lawrence Erlbaum Associates.

Sternberg, R. J., Grigorenko, E. L., Ferrari, M., & Clinkenbeard, P. (1999). A triarchic analysis of an aptitude-treatment interaction. *European Journal of Psychological Assessment, 15,* 1–11.

Sternberg, R. J., Nokes, K., Geissler, P. W., Prince, R., Okatcha, F., Bundy, D. A., & Grigorenko, E. L. (in press). The relationship between academic and practical intelligence: A case study in Kenya. *Intelligence.*

Sternberg, R. J., Torff, B., & Grigorenko, E. L. (1998). Teaching triarchically improves school achievement. *Journal of Educational Psychology, 90*(3), 1–11.

Sternberg, R. J., & Wagner, R. K. (1993). The g-ocentric view of intelligence and job performance is wrong. *Current Directions in Psychological Science, 2,* 1–4.

Sternberg, R. J., Wagner, R. K., & Okagaki, L. (1993). Practical intelligence: The nature and role of tacit knowledge in work and at school. In H. Reese & J. Puckett (Eds.), *Advances in life-span development* (pp. 205–227). Hillsdale, NJ: Lawrence Erlbaum Associates.

Sternberg, R. J., Wagner, R. K., Williams, W. M., & Horvath, J. A. (1995). Testing common sense. *American Psychologist, 50,* 912–927.

Super C. M., & Harkness, S. (1982). The development of affect in infancy and early childhood. In D. Wagner & H. Stevenson (Eds.), *Cultural perspectives on child development* (pp. 1–19). San Francisco: W. H. Freeman.

Tacon, P. (1981). *My child now: An action on behalf of children without families.* New York: UNICEF.

Tacon, P. (1983). *Regional program for Latin America and the Caribbean,* New York: UNICEF.

Taylor, R. D. (1996). Adolescents' perceptions of kinship support and family management practices: Association with adolescent adjustment in African American families. *Developmental Psychology, 32,* 687–695.

Wagner, R. K. (1987). Tacit knowledge in everyday intelligent behavior. *Journal of Personality and Social Psychology, 52,* 1236–1247.

Wagner, R. K., & Sternberg, R. J. (1985). Practical intelligence in real-world pursuits: The role of tacit knowledge. *Journal of Personality and Social Psychology, 49,* 436–458.

Wachs, T. (1992). *The nature of nurture.* Newbury Park, CA: Sage.

Wason, P. C. (1966). Reasoning. In B. Foss (Ed.), *New horizons in psychology* (pp. 135–151). Harmondsworth, England: Penguin Books.

Wason, P. C., & Johnson-Laird, P. N. (1972). *Psychology of reasoning: Structure and content.* London: B. T. Batsford.

Wertsch, J., & Kanner, B. G. (1994). A sociocultural approach to intellectual development. In R. J. Sternberg & C. A. Berg (Eds.), *Intellectual development* (pp. 328–349). New York: Cambridge University Press.

Yang, S., & Sternberg, R. J. (1997). Taiwanese Chinese people's conceptions of intelligence. *Intelligence, 25*, 21–36.

Yussen, S. R., & Kane, P. (1985). Children's concept of intelligence. In S. R. Yussen (Ed.), *The growth of reflective thinking in children* (pp. 207–241). New York: Academic Press.

Author Index

Subject Index

www.ingramcontent.com/pod-product-compliance
Ingram Content Group UK Ltd.
Pitfield, Milton Keynes, MK11 3LW, UK
UKHW020433010325
455677UK00029B/1133

9 780415 647748